ADMISSION &

Admission to neonatal unit (NNU) 13
Death and extremely ill babies 57
Discharge 59
Follow up of infants discharged fr(................. 74
Labour ward calls 128
Transport and referral.. 198

CARDIOVASCULAR

Cardiac murmurs 32
Congenital cyanotic heart disease - the blue baby 54
Congenital heart disease - heart failure 83
Hypoplastic left heart syndrome and other duct-dependent lesions
(antenatally diagnosed).. 100
Hypotension 102
Patent ductus arteriosus (PDA) 159
Pericardiocentesis 161

CRITICAL CARE

Extreme prematurity 72
Hypothermia 104
Pain and stress... 156
Preterm care ('golden hour') 166
Resuscitation 176

ENDOCRINE/METABOLISM

Hyperglycaemia 94
Hyperkalaemia 95
Hypoglycaemia 97
Hypothyroidism 106
IV Fluid therapy 119
Metabolic disorders [inborn errors of metabolism (IEM)]................ 136

GASTROENTEROLOGY

Breastfeeding 27
Breast milk handling and storage 29
Gastro-oesophageal reflux (GOR)... 76
Gastroschisis 78
Jaundice 126
Liver dysfunction in preterm infants 129
Necrotizing enterocolitis (NEC) 145
Nutrition 149
Total parenteral nutrition (TPN) 192

CONTENTS • 2/3

HAEMATOLOGY

Blood group incompatibilities (including Rhesus disease) 24
Coagulopathy 39
Polycythaemia 162
Thrombocytopenia 187
Transfusion of red blood cells 196
Vitamin K 220

INFECTION

BCG immunisation 22
CMV.. 37
Conjunctivitis 41
Group B Streptococcus disease 79
Hepatitis B 86
Hepatitis C 88
Human Immunodeficiency Virus (HIV) 92
Immunisations 113
Infection 116
Syphilis 186
Varicella... 209

NEUROLOGY

Abstinence syndrome 10
Brachial plexus injury 26
Hypoxic Ischaemic Encephalopathy (HIE) 109
Seizures 180

PRACTICAL PROCEDURES

Arterial line insertion 18
Arterial line sampling 20
Cannulation 31
Chest drain insertion 33
Consent 43
Exchange transfusion 67
Extravasation injuries 70
Long lines (peripherally sited) 133
Nasogastric tube insertion 141
Skin biopsy 182
Umbilical artery catheterisation 203
Umbilical artery catheter removal.. 205
Umbilical venous catheterisation 206
Umbilical venous catheter removal 208
Venepuncture 212

Issue 02
Issued: October 2007
Expires: September 2009

CONTENTS • 3/3

RENAL

Renal abnormalities on antenatal scan 170
Renal failure 172

RESPIRATORY

Apnoea and bradycardia 16
Chronic lung disease 35
CPAP (Continuous Positive Airway Pressure) and Bubble CPAP 46
High Frequency Oscillatory Ventilation (HFOV) 89
Intubation 124
Nitric oxide 148
Oxygen on discharge 154
Persistent Pulmonary Hypertension of the Newborn (PPHN) 164
Pulmonary haemorrhage 168
Surfactant replacement therapy 184
Ventilation modes 213
Ventilation (basic principles) 215

SCREENING

Antenatal ultrasound abnormalities 15
Cranial ultrasound scans 51
Disorders of sexual development 61
Examination of the newborn 63
Hearing screening 81
Retinopathy of prematurity (ROP) screening 179

Issue 02
Issued: October 2007
Expires: September 2009

ACKNOWLEDGEMENTS • 1/1

We would like to thank the following for their assistance in producing this edition of the Neonatal Guidelines on behalf of the Bedside Clinical Guidelines Partnership and Staffordshire, Shropshire and Black Country Newborn Network

Contributors

Jacquie Angell
Damien Armstrong
Sue Bell
David Brookfield
Julia Brooks
Fiona Chambers
Sanjeev Deshpande
Maggie Doodson
Ian Freeman
Lyndola Greig
Jo Hacking
Chrisantha Halahakoon
Helen Haley
Jackie Harrison
Gina Hartwell
Jane Henley
Zala Ibrahim
Liz Jones
Babu Kumaratne
Tony Lander
Pek-Wan Lee
Subramanian Mahadevan
Pat McKiernan
Paddy McMaster
Ruth Moore
Kate Palmer
Tilly Pillay
Gill Platt
Mary Anne Preece
David Roden
Martin Samuels
Trisha Smith
Andy Spencer
Alyson Skinner
Oliver Stumper
Mahadevan Subramanian

Maxine Taplin
Arumugavelu Thirumurugan
Wendy Tyler
Rajneesh Walia
Julie Webster
Mike Williams

Neonatal Editors

Paddy McMaster
Alyson Skinner
Andy Spencer

Bedside Clinical Guidelines Partnership

Marian Kerr
Paddy McMaster
John Mucklow
Charles Pantin
David Rogers
Kay Hall

Staffordshire, Shropshire and Black Country Newborn Network

Sarah Carnwell
Ruth Moore
Andy Spencer

The editors would like thank the following people/organisations for allowing us to use/adapt their guidelines:

Birmingham Children's Hospital – Skin Biopsy guideline

Dr Carl Kuschel
Auckland District Health Board
Auckland, New Zealand – Ventilation guideline

Birmingham Women's Hospital Neonatal Unit – Extravasation injuries guideline

ACTH	Adrenocorticotropic hormone	HIV	Human immunodeficiency virus
AMH	Anti-Mullerian hormone	HLHS	Hypoplastic left heart syndrome
APTT	Activated partial thromboplastin time	IUGR	Intrauterine growth retardation
AVSD	Atrioventricular septal defect	IUT	In-utero blood transfusion or in-utero transfer
BAPM	British Association of Perinatal Medicine	IVH	Intraventricular haemorrhage
BCG	Bacille Calmette-Guerin	LHRH	Luteinizing hormone releasing hormone
BLISS	Baby Life Support Systems	LVOT	Left ventricular outflow tract
BPD	Bronchopulmonary dysplasia	NAIT	Neonatal allo-immune thrombocytopenia
CAIS	Complete androgen insensitivity syndrome	NGT	Naso gastric Tube
CAMT	Congenital amegakaryocytic thrombocytopenia	NHSP	Newborn Hearing Screening Programme
CDH	Congenital dislocation of hips or congenital diaphragmatic hernia!	NICU	Neonatal intensive care unit
		NNU	Neonatal unit
CH	Congenital hypothyroidism	OI	Oxygenation Index
CHD	Congenital heart disease	PCR	Polymerase chain reaction
CLD	Chronic lung disease	PEEP	Positive end respiratory pressure
CMV	Cytomegalovirus	PIH	Pregnancy-induced hypertension
CPAP	Continuous positive airway pressure	PKU	Phenylketonuria
DCT	Direct Coombs' test	PIP	Positive Inspiratory Pressure
DHEA	Dihydroepiandrostenedione	PPHN	Persistent pulmonary hypertension of the newborn
dHT	dihydrotestosterone	PT	Prothrombin time
DIC	Disseminating Intravascular Coagulation	PUV	Posterior Urethral Valve
DSD	Disorders of sexual development	RDS	Respiratory distress syndrome
EBM	Expressed Breast Milk	ROP	Retinopathy of prematurity
ETT	Endotracheal tubes	SIDS	Sudden Infant Death Syndrome
EUT	Extrauterine transfer	SPA	Supra-pubic aspiration
FFP	Fresh frozen plasma	TAR	Thrombocytopenia absent radii
GBS	Group B streptococcus	THAM	Trometamol
GIT	Gastro-intestinal tract	TPN	Total parenteral nutrition
GOR	Gastro-oesophageal reflux	UAC	Umbilical artery catheter
HCG	Human chorionic gonadotropin	UVC	Umbilical vein catheter
HCV	Hepatitis C virus	VSD	Ventricular septal defect
HFOV	High frequency oscillatory ventilation	VZV	Varicella-zoster virus
HIE	Hypoxic ischaemic encephalopathy		

This book has been compiled as an aide-memoire for all staff concerned with the management of neonates, towards a more uniform standard of care across the Staffordshire, Shropshire and Black Country Newborn Network hospitals. Further copies are available from Newborn Network www.newbornnetworks.org.uk/staffs

These guidelines have been drafted with reference to published medical literature and amended after extensive consultation. Wherever possible, the recommendations made are evidence based. Where no clear evidence has been identified from published literature the advice given represents a consensus of the expert authors and their peers and is based on their practical experience.

No guideline will apply to every patient, even where the diagnosis is clear-cut; there will always be exceptions. These guidelines are not intended as a substitute for logical thought and must be tempered by clinical judgement in the individual patient and advice from senior colleagues.

> ### The guidelines are advisory, NOT mandatory

Prescribing regimens and nomograms

The administration of certain drugs, especially those given intravenously, requires great care if hazardous errors are to be avoided. These guidelines do not include comprehensive guidance on the indications, contraindications, dosage and administration for all drugs. Please refer to the **Northern Neonatal Formulary Fifth edition 2007.**

Practical procedures

DO NOT attempt to carry out any of these procedures unless you have been trained to do so and have demonstrated your competence.

Legal advice

How to keep out of court:

- Write the patient's name and unit number on the top of each side of paper
- Time and date each entry.
- Sign and write your name legibly after every entry
- Document acknowledgement of results of all investigations (including radiology)
- Document all interactions including discussions with parents (and who was present)

Where possible the guidelines are based on evidence from the published literature. It is intended that the evidence relating to statements made in the guidelines and its quality will be made explicit.

Supporting information

Where supporting evidence has been identified it is graded I to V according to standard criteria of validity and methodological quality as detailed in the table below. A summary of the evidence supporting each statement is available, with the original sources referenced (ward-based copies only). The evidence summaries are being developed on a rolling programme which will be updated as the guideline is reviewed.

Issue 02
Issued: October 2007
Expires: September 2009

Level of evidence	Strength of evidence
I	Strong evidence from at least one systematic review of multiple well-designed randomized controlled trials
II	Strong evidence from at least one properly designed randomized controlled trial of appropriate size
III	Evidence from well-designed trials without randomization, single group pre-post, cohort, time series or matched case-control studies
IV	Evidence from well-designed non-experimental studies from more than one centre or research group
V	Opinions of respected authorities, based on clinical evidence, descriptive studies or reports of expert committees

JA Muir-Gray from Evidence Based Healthcare, Churchill Livingstone London 1997

Evaluation of the evidence-base of these guidelines involves review of existing literature then periodical review of anything else that has been published since last review. The editors encourage you to challenge the evidence provided in this document. If you know of evidence that contradicts, or additional evidence in support of, the advice given in these guidelines please forward it to the Clinical Guidelines Co-ordinator/Developer, Respiratory Medicine Department, University Hospital of North Staffordshire Stoke-on-Trent, ST4 6QG (Telephone 01782 552300) or Dr Paddy McMaster (paddy.mcmaster@uhns.nhs.uk).

Evidence-based developments for which funding is being sought

As new treatments prove themselves more effective than existing ones, the onus falls upon those practising evidence-based healthcare to adopt best practice. New treatments are usually, but not always, more expensive. Within the finite resources of each Trust and of the NHS as a whole adoption of these treatments has to be justified in terms of the improvements they will bring to the quality or cost-effectiveness of care. The priorities for funding new areas of treatment and patient care will be determined at Trust level.

Feedback and new guidelines

The Bedside Clinical Guidelines Partnership and the Staffordshire, Shropshire and Black Country Newborn Network have provided the logistical, financial and editorial expertise to produce the guidelines. These guidelines have been developed by clinicians for practice based on best available evidence and opinion. Any deviation in practice should be recorded in the patient's notes with reasons for deviation. The editors acknowledge the time and trouble taken by numerous colleagues in the drafting and amending of the text. The accuracy of the detailed advice given has been subject to exhaustive checks. However, any errors or omissions that become apparent should be drawn to the notice of the editors, via the Clinical Guidelines Co-ordinator/Developer (Telephone 01782 552300 or e-mail bedsideclinicalguidelines@uhns.nhs.uk) or Dr Paddy McMaster (paddy.mcmaster@uhns.nhs.uk), so that these can be amended in the next review, or, if necessary, be brought to the urgent attention of users. Constructive comments or suggestions would also be welcome. There are still many areas of neonatal care which are not included: please submit new guidelines as soon as possible for editorial comment. The deadline for suggestions for revisions or new guidelines to be included will be 1st March 2009 for printing by Autumn 2009.

For brevity, where the word 'parent(s)' is read, this means mothers, fathers, guardians or others with parental care responsibilities for babies.

Issue 02
Issued: October 2007
Expires: September 2009

RECOGNITION AND ASSESSMENT

Definition

Neonatal withdrawal/abstinence syndrome
● Symptoms evident in infants born to opiate-dependent mothers (generally milder with other drugs)

Timescale of withdrawal

● Withdrawal from opiates (misused drugs, such as heroin) can occur <24 hr after birth
● Withdrawal from opioids (prescribed drugs, such as methadone) can occur 3-4 days after birth, occasionally up to 2 wk after birth
● Multiple drug use can delay or confuse withdrawal signs

Minor signs

● Tremors when disturbed
● Tachypnoea (>60/min)
● Pyrexia
● Sweating
● Yawning
● Sneezing
● Nasal stuffiness
● Poor feeding
● Regurgitation
● Loose stools
● Sleeping less than 3 hr after feed (NB: usual among breastfed babies)

Major signs

● Convulsions
● Profuse vomiting or diarrhoea
● Inability to coordinate sucking, necessitating introduction of tube feeding
● Infant inconsolable after 2 consecutive feeds

AIMS

● To identify withdrawal symptoms following birth
● To keep baby as comfortable as possible
● To give effective medical treatment where necessary
● To promote bonding and facilitate good parenting skills
● To end physical dependence on drugs

Antenatal issues

● Where possible, check maternal hepatitis B, hepatitis C and HIV status and decide on management plan for baby

Management of labour

● Make sure you know:
  ● type and amount of drug(s) exposure
  ● route of administration
  ● when last dose was taken
● The paediatrician is not required to be present at delivery unless clinical situation dictates

IMMEDIATE TREATMENT

Delivery

● **Do not give naloxone** as this can exacerbate the withdrawal symptoms
● Care of baby should be as for any other baby, including encouragement of skin-to-skin contact and initiation of early breastfeeding, if this is mother's choice [see **Breastfeeding preterm infants (advocacy and contraindications)** guideline]

After delivery

● Transfer to postnatal ward as usual and commence normal care
● Admit to neonatal unit only if there are clinical indications

Issue 02
Issued: October 2007
Expires: September 2009

- Keep babies who are not withdrawing, feeding well and have no child protection issues with their mothers in the postnatal wards
- Babies who are symptomatic enough to require pharmacological treatment may not require admission to the neonatal unit (treatment can be started on the postnatal ward) – assess each case on an individual basis and refer to local procedures
- Start case notes
- Take a detailed history, including:
- social history, to facilitate discharge planning
- maternal hepatitis B & C & HIV status
- Postnatal baby check and daily review by paediatrician

> *Check maternal notes for case conference recommendations and discuss care plan for discharge with drug liaison midwife*
>
> *As symptoms of withdrawal can be delayed, keep baby in hospital for at least 4 days*

SUBSEQUENT MANAGEMENT

- The aims of managing an infant at risk of neonatal drug withdrawal are to:
- maintain normal temperature
- reduce hyperactivity
- reduce excessive crying
- reduce motor instability
- ensure adequate weight gain and sleep pattern

Comfort, not sedation

- Ensure baby reviewed daily by paediatric staff
- Avoid giving pharmacological treatment to babies with minor signs
- Start treatment (after other causes excluded) if there is:
- recurrent vomiting

- profuse watery diarrhoea
- requirement for tube feeds
- inconsolability after 2 consecutive feeds
- convulsions
- The assessment chart (see below) aims to reduce subjectivity associated with scoring systems
- When mother has been using an opiate or opioid, a morphine derivative is most effective way to relieve symptoms
- When there has been multiple drug usage, phenobarbital may be more effective
- Use chloral hydrate as required for distress

Opioids

- Start morphine 40 micrograms/kg orally 4 hrly – increasing the dose by 20 micrograms/kg increments if authorised by senior paediatrician
- If baby feeding well and settling between feeds, double dose interval, then reduce dosage by 10% every 24 hr – see assessment chart below
- If major signs continue, discuss with senior paediatrician
- Consider need for other medication (e.g. chloral hydrate)

Phenobarbital

- For treatment of convulsions give 20 mg/kg IV loading dose over 20 min, then maintenance 4 mg/kg orally daily

Chloral hydrate

- Give 30 mg/kg orally, up to 6 hrly as required

Chlorpromazine

- For babies of mothers who use benzodiazepines, give 1 mg/kg orally 8 hrly
- If control has not been achieved with morphine, give 0.5–1 mg/kg orally 8 hrly as general sedative
- remember that chlorpromazine can reduce seizure threshold

Breastfeeding

- Unless other contraindications co-exist or baby going for adoption, recommend breastfeeding strongly – see **Breastfeeding preterm infants (advocacy and contraindications)** guideline
- Support mother in her choice of feeding method
- Give mother all information she needs to make an informed choice about breastfeeding
- Drugs of misuse in general do not pass into breast milk in sufficient quantities to have a major effect in the newborn baby
- Breastfeeding will certainly support mother in feeling that she is positively comforting her baby, should he/she be harder to settle

Infections

- Follow relevant guidelines for specific situations, such as HIV or Hepatitis B positive mothers
- Give BCG immunization where indicated

ASSESSMENT CHART

- Aim of treatment is to reduce distress and control potentially dangerous signs
- Minor signs (e.g. jitters, sweating, yawning) do **not** require treatment
- Consider treatment (after other causes excluded) if there is:
- profuse vomiting
- profuse watery diarrhoea
- requirement for tube feeds
- infant inconsolable after two consecutive feeds (see below)

MONITORING

Has baby been inconsolable with standard comfort measures (cuddling, swaddling, or use of dummy) since the last feed?

Place a tick in the yes or no box (do not indicate any other signs in the boxes)

Date						
Time	4:00	8:00	12:00	16:00	20:00	24:00
Yes						
No						

- Record other symptoms, such as vomiting, diarrhoea

DISCHARGE POLICY

Babies who required treatment

- Ensure discharge planning involving:
- social worker
- health visitor
- community neonatal team if treated at home after discharge
- drug rehabilitation team
- If seizures or abnormal cranial ultrasound, arrange follow-up in the named consultant's developmental clinic

Babies who did not require treatment

- If no signs of withdrawal, discharge by 4-5 days
- Arrange follow-up by GP and health visitor, advise referral to hospital if there are concerns

Issue 02
Issued: October 2007
Expires: September 2009

- There should be good clinical reasons for admission to NNU
- Avoid unnecessary separation of mother and baby as it affects maternal bonding

CRITERIA FOR ADMISSION FROM LABOUR WARD OR POSTNATAL WARD

Discuss need for admission with senior medical staff

- Clinical condition requiring constant monitoring <34 wk or birth weight <1800 g (follow local guidelines for gestation and birth weight limits)
- Respiratory distress or cyanosis
- Apnoeic or cyanotic attacks
- Grade 2 and 3 hypoxic ischaemic encephalopathy (HIE)
- Jaundice needing intensive phototherapy or exchange transfusion
- Major congenital abnormality likely to threaten immediate survival
- Seizures
- Unable to tolerate enteral feeds with vomiting and/or abdominal distension and/or hypoglycaemia (blood glucose <2.6 mmol/L)
- Suspicion of sepsis
- Small for gestational age (BW <2nd centile) and hypoglycaemic or unable to tolerate feeds
- Mother in ITU

Procedure

- Deal with any immediate life-threatening clinical problems (e.g. airway, breathing circulation and seizures)
- Explain to parents reason for admission to NNU
- Inform NNU nursing staff that you wish to admit a baby and reason for admission

- Inform middle grade medical staff/consultant
- Ensure baby name labels present
- Document relevant history and examination
- Complete problem sheets and investigation charts (follow local guidelines)
- Measure and plot birth weight, head circumference and length on growth chart
- Measure admitting temperature
- If preterm <32 weeks or unwell, check blood glucose
- Measure blood pressure using non-invasive cuff
- Institute appropriate monitoring and treatment in conjunction with nursing and senior medical colleagues

Investigations

Choice depends on initial assessment and suspected clinical problem

Baby <28 weeks/1000g weight

- FBC
- Blood culture
- Blood glucose
- Blood gases

Unwell babies

- FBC
- Blood culture
- Blood glucose
- Blood gases
- CRP
- If suspicion of sepsis – lumbar puncture and urine suprapubic aspirate (SPA)

IMMEDIATE MANAGEMENT

- Evaluation of infant, including full clinical examination
- Define appropriate management plan and procedures and perform as efficiently as possible to ensure baby is not disturbed unnecessarily

Respiratory support

- If required, takes priority over other procedures
- includes incubator oxygen, CPAP or ventilatory support

Intravenous access

- If required, IV cannulation and/or UVC

MONITORING

Use minimal handling

- Cardio-respiratory monitoring through skin electrodes
- Pulse oximetry. Try to maintain saturation around 88-92% (follow local guidelines)
- Transcutaneous probe for $TcPO_2/TcPCO_2$ if available
- Temperature
- Blood glucose
- If ventilated, invasive monitoring for blood gases and blood pressure UAC/peripheral arterial line

Issue 02
Issued: October 2007
Expires: September 2009

DEFINITION

- Any lesion identified antenatally in the fetus (e.g. renal pelvic dilatation, hypoplastic left heart)
- Any maternal factor identified antenatally that could affect the baby after delivery (e.g. anhydramnios from preterm prolonged rupture of membranes)

COUNSELLING BEFORE DELIVERY

- Cleft lip and/or palate
- obstetric team to refer to regional multidisciplinary cleft palate team, who counsel parents, communicate plans for delivery and provide post-natal support for baby
- Hypoplastic left heart syndrome or other presumed duct-dependent lesions
- obstetric team to refer to regional cardiac team, who counsel parents and, where appropriate, confirm diagnosis
- All affected pregnancies will have detailed individualized plans for management of baby by consultant neonatologist, including place of delivery
- As some lesions are progressive (e.g. hypoplastic left heart syndrome, gastroschisis), the situation can change and information from the obstetric team can alter over time, discuss all affected pregnancies at the combined fetomaternal meeting until delivery
- Offer neonatal counselling to all women whose pregnancy has been affected by major lesions, to discuss the impact of the identified lesion on quality of life, including possible disabilities, investigations and surgery, and the plan for post delivery

MANAGEMENT AFTER DELIVERY

- For minor lesions, such as renal pelvic dilatation, follow appropriate guideline and inform senior staff and parents
- For other lesions, carefully follow written plan made by senior staff before delivery, including need to contact seniors and specialist staff in Children's Hospital before and after delivery
- Communicate any new information obtained after birth to the consultant as this may change plan of care required
- Maintain regular contact with specialist teams as indicated by them
- Arrange postnatal transfer if required when bed available
- Keep parents informed of actions taken, and contact from specialist teams
- Consider syndrome or group for babies with more than one lesion, discuss with senior staff as soon as possible
- if not provided antenatally, provide, when, available written information from 'Contact a family' book or website www.contactafamily.co.uk

Specific lesions

See **Renal abnormalities on ultrasound scan, Gastroschisis, and Duct-dependent cardiac lesions** guidelines

DEFINITION

Apnoea

Pause(s) in breathing for more than 20 seconds (or less, when associated with bradycardia or cyanosis)

Bradycardia

Heart rate <100/min, associated with desaturation

Types

- Central
- caused by poorly developed neurological control
- respiratory movements absent
- Obstructive
- caused by upper airway obstruction, usually at pharyngeal level
- respiratory movements continue
- Mixed
- initially central, followed by obstructive apnoea

Significance

- Most infants born <34 weeks gestation have primary apnoea of prematurity (PAP)
- multiple aetiologic factors can exacerbate apnoea in preterm infants
- sudden increase in frequency warrants immediate action
- Causes other than apnoea of prematurity must be considered if occurs:
- in term or near-term infant (>34 weeks gestation)
- on first day after birth in preterm infant

Causes

- Sepsis
- septicaemia
- necrotizing enterocolitis
- meningitis

- Respiratory
- inadequate respiratory support
- upper airway obstruction
- surfactant deficiency

- CNS
- intracranial haemorrhage
- seizure

- CVS
- patent ductus arteriosus
- anaemia

- GI
- gastro-oesophageal reflux
- Metabolic abnormalities, especially hypoglycaemia

MANAGEMENT

- If apnoea not self-limiting, perform the following in sequence to terminate episode:
- stimulate baby by tickling feet or stroking abdomen
- if aspiration or secretions in pharynx suspected, apply brief oropharyngeal suction
- face mask ventilation
- consider emergency intubation
- Once stable, perform thorough clinical examination to confirm/evaluate cause
- **Screen for sepsis** as apnoea and bradycardia can be sole presenting sign

Issue 02
Issued: October 2007
Expires: September 2009

TREATMENT

- Treat specific cause, if present
- Primary apnoea of prematurity is a diagnosis of exclusion and may not require treatment unless pauses are:
  - frequent (>8 in 12 hrs) or
  - severe (>2 episodes/day requiring positive pressure ventilation)
- Pharmacological treatment
  - caffeine citrate 20 mg/kg loading dose (PO/IV) followed, in 24 hr, by 5 mg/kg increasing to 10 mg/kg if required maintenance dose once daily (PO/IV)
- Non-pharmacological treatment
  - CPAP (continuous positive pressure ventilation) – see **CPAP** guideline
  - intubation and ventilation – if CPAP fails

PERIPHERAL ARTERIAL LINES

INDICATIONS

- Frequent monitoring of blood gases
- Direct monitoring of arterial blood pressure
- Premature removal (or failure to site) an umbilical artery catheter

CONTRAINDICATIONS

- Bleeding disorder
- Inadequate patency of the ulnar artery on transillumination (if cannulating the radial artery) or vice-versa
- Pre-existing evidence of circulatory insufficiency in limb
- Local skin infection
- Malformation of upper extremity

Possible sites of arterial entry

- Radial (most commonly used) - only procedure discussed in this guideline
- Posterior tibial
- Dorsalis pedis
- Ulnar (usually only if ipsilateral radial artery cannulation has not been attempted)

EQUIPMENT

- Gloves
- Alcohol-free antiseptic wipes/solution
- 24-gauge cannula
- T-connector with luer lock
- Adhesive tape
- Splint
- Saline flush in 2 mL syringe, primed through T-connector
- Transillumination fibre-optic light source equipment
- Three-way tap

PROCEDURE USING RADIAL ARTERY

Preparation

- Wash hands
- Check patency of ipsilateral ulnar artery and proceed only if patent
- Put on gloves
- Extend baby's wrist with palm of hand upwards
- Transilluminate radial artery with fibre-optic light source behind baby's wrist **OR** palpate pulse, situated at midpoint of lateral third of wrist
- In preterm infants, holding fibre-optic light source behind the baby's wrist will make artery clearly visible
- Clean skin with antiseptic

Procedure

- Enter artery with 24-gauge cannula just proximal to wrist crease at angle of 25-30°
- Remove stylet from cannula and advance cannula into artery
- Connect cannula to T-connector primed with saline, and flush gently
- Secure cannula with tape, ensuring fingers are visible for frequent inspection, and apply splint
- Connect T-connector to infusion line (sodium chloride 0.9% with heparin 1 unit/mL), with three-way tap in situ for blood sampling

Documentation

- Document clearly in notes all attempts at cannulation, including those that are unsuccessful

AFTERCARE

Monitor

- Inspect distal digits regularly for circulatory status: if blanching does not recover after 5 min, remove line
- Avoid excessive hyperextension of the wrist, as this can result in occlusion of artery
- Ensure a continuous pressure waveform tracing is displayed on monitor screen at all times: if flushing line does not restore lost tracing, change position of limb/dressing

Usage

- Do not administer rapid boluses of fluid as this can lead to retrograde embolization of clot or air – use minimal volume when flushing after sampling and inject slowly
- Use cannula only for sampling, and infuse only sodium chloride 0.9% with heparin 1 unit/mL
- Remove cannula as soon as it is no longer required

Removal

- Removal of arterial line: aseptic, apply pressure for at least 5 min (longer until no bleeding or bruising if coagulopathy/low platelets)
- dressings do not prevent bleeding or bruising
- do not send tip for culture routinely

COMPLICATIONS

- Thromboembolism/vasospasm/ thrombosis
- Blanching and partial loss of digits (radial artery)
- Necrosis
- Skin ulceration
- Reversible occlusion of artery
- Extravasation of sodium chloride infusate
- Infection (rarely associated with line infection)
- Haematoma
- Haemorrhage
- Air embolism

INDICATIONS

- Blood gas analysis
- Biochemical/and haematological investigations

CONTRAINDICATIONS

- Infusions of glucose solution preclude sampling for blood glucose estimation
- Blood drawn from an arterial line may not be suitable for clotting studies

COMPLICATIONS

Haemorrhage

- Ensure all connections secure, luer locks tight and 3-way taps appropriately adjusted

Infection

- Maintain sterile technique during sampling to reduce risk of infection
- Clean hands with alcohol gel and don gloves (clean, not from sealed pack)

Artery spasm

- Limb appears blanched. Stop procedure and allow time for recovery. Warming of opposite limb can elicit reflex vasodilation

Thromboembolism

- Flush catheter with 0.5 mL sodium chloride 0.9% with 10 units heparin/mL each time sample taken. If catheter is not sampling, clot formation may be in progress. Request urgent registrar review of the arterial line so they can make a prompt decision to remove

Inaccuracy of blood gas results

- Analyse sample immediately. After blood is withdrawn from an artery, it continues to consume O_2 and produce CO_2
- Excess heparin in syringe may result in a falsely low pH and $PaCO_2$. Remove excess heparin from syringe before obtaining sample
- Do not use if air bubbles in sample: take fresh specimen

EQUIPMENT

- Gloves
- Paper towel
- Alcohol swabs x 2
- Syringes
- (A) 2 mL syringe for clearing line
- (B) 2 mL syringe for other blood samples as necessary
- (C) 1 mL pre-heparinised syringe for blood gas analysis
- (D) 0.5-1mL heparinised sodium chloride 0.9% 10 units/mL
- Appropriate blood sample bottles and request forms

PROCEDURE

Preparation

- Record SpO_2 and $TcPO_2/TcPCO_2$ at time of taking blood to allow comparison with blood gas
- Wash hands and put on gloves
- Place paper towel beneath 3-way tap collection port (maintain asepsis by non-touch technique rather than sterile gloves and towel)
- Ensure 3-way tap closed to port hole

Procedure

- Remove luer lock cap, clean with alcohol swab and allow to dry, or prepare bioconnector
- Connect 2 mL syringe (A)
- Turn 3-way tap so it is closed to infusion and open to syringe and arterial catheter
- Withdraw 2 mL blood slowly. It must clear the deadspace
- Turn 3-way tap so it is closed to arterial catheter to prevent blood loss from baby
- Attach appropriate syringe (B/C) needed for required blood sample
- Turn 3-way tap to open to syringe and arterial catheter and withdraw required amount of blood for blood samples. Do not withdraw more than required amount
- Turn 3-way tap off to arterial catheter in between syringes B and C if both required, after taking required samples with syringes
- Reattach syringe (A)
- Clear the connection of air
- Slowly return to baby any blood in line not required for samples
- Turn 3-way tap off to arterial catheter
- Attach syringe (D) of heparinised sodium chloride 0.9% 10 units/mL
- Turn 3-way tap so it is open to syringe and arterial line, clear line of air and slowly flush line to clear it of blood
- Turn 3-way tap so it is closed to syringe, remove syringe (D), swab port hole with alcohol wipe and cover with luer lock cap
- Record amount of blood removed and volume of flush on infant's daily fluid record

AFTERCARE

- Ensure all connections are tight and 3-way tap turned off to syringe port to prevent haemorrhage
- If sampling from a UAC ensure lower limbs are pink and well perfused on completion of procedure
- If sampling from percutaneous arterial line check colour and perfusion of line site and limb housing the arterial line
- Ensure line patency by recommencing infusion pump
- Ensure arterial wave form present and all alarms set before leaving infant

Issue 02
Issued: October 2007
Expires: September 2009

INDICATIONS

Give BCG to neonates who have any one of the following indications:

- Specific request from parents for immunisation
- Anticipated exposure to others with TB (other than smear-positive pulmonary tuberculosis)
- Parent or grandparent born in, or intending to stay for more than one month in, an area where annual incidence of TB is >40/100,000, such as:
- Eastern Europe
- Africa
- Asia
- Latin America
- parts of UK – Bradford, Derby, Manchester, Leicester, Birmingham, Luton, Oldbury, Slough and parts of London

If in doubt see www.hpa.org.uk for incidence by PCT or http://globalatlas.who.int for other countries

Tuberculin testing is not necessary unless baby has been in recent contact with tuberculosis or has resided in high-incidence country for more than 3 months

CONTRAINDICATIONS

- Temperature >38°C
- Severe eczema
- Neonate in household where an active TB case is suspected or confirmed
- Immunodeficient or on high dose steroids
- HIV positive, living in UK
- if mother HIV positive, give vaccine only after infant has had 3 negative proviral DNA PCR tests for HIV

- Received another live vaccine within past 4 weeks:
- can be given simultaneously with other vaccines (not in same arm)
- no need to delay routine vaccinations
- no further immunisation should be given in same arm for at least 3 months

Babies born to mothers with infectious tuberculosis (sputum AFB positive)

- Give isoniazid 5 mg/kg daily for 6 months
- Tuberculin test after 3 months
- if negative give BCG
- if positive assess baby for active TB. If assessment negative, continue isoniazid for 6 months
- Babies may breast feed

EQUIPMENT

- Consent form
- Alcohol hand gel
- Kidney dish
- BCG vaccine
- Solvent (comes with BCG vaccine)
- 1 mL syringe
- Orange needle (3/8 in 25 FG 0.5 x 10 mm or 26 FG 0.45 x 10 mm)
- Green needle 21 FG 1 in
- Cotton wool balls
- Foil dish for cotton wool balls
- Non-woven gauze
- Sharps container
- Bags for clinical waste

Issue 02
Issued: October 2007
Expires: September 2009

PROCEDURE

Consent

- Ensure infant within inclusion group
- Give mother information on vaccine
- Give appropriate language leaflet **BCG and your baby; protecting babies against TB**, available from www.immunisation.org.uk order line tel: 08701 555 455 email: dh@prolog.uk.com
- DH guidelines state written consent not required but follow local practice

Injection

- **Only staff with training to give intradermal injections**
- At the insertion of the deltoid muscle near the middle of left upper arm
- The dose for infants under 12 months is 0.05 mL

Documentation

- Complete 'Unscheduled vaccine form' or letter with batch number, vaccine name and site of immunisation
- Send to local TB Service/Public Health Department
- Keep a local record
- Enter in Red Book on relevant page

Sequelae

- Scar
- within 2-6 wk a small papule will appear
- sometimes, this ulcerates and can ooze
- site need not be protected from water
- do not cover with an impervious dressing
- can take several months to heal
- occasionally persists as keloid (particularly if given higher than insertion of deltoid)

- Adenitis:
- a minor degree of adenitis can occur in the weeks following BCG
- local abscess
- no treatment indicated

- Rare sequelae:
- chronic suppurative lymphadenopathy
- disseminated disease, if immunocompromised
- osteitis
- refer to infectious diseases specialist

> *Aim to avoid kernicterus and severe anaemia*
>
> *Keep consultant in charge informed*

POSTNATAL MONITORING

Newborns at risk

- Those with mothers with known blood group antibodies including:
- D (Rhesus), c, C, s, E, Duffy
- Kell – causes bone marrow suppression in addition to haemolysis

Management of newborns at risk of haemolysis

- Antenatally: prepare a plan based on antibody levels, middle cerebral artery Dopplers and evidence of hydrops
- order blood in advance for exchange transfusion if anticipated
- Send cord blood **urgently** for Hb, blood group, direct Coombs' test (DCT) and bilirubin – chase results
- in all newborns who have had an in-utero blood transfusion (IUT), send cord blood also for a Kleihauer test
- If pale with abnormal cardiorespiratory signs (e.g. tachycardia), admit to NNU
- In babies with a positive DCT or had an IUT (regardless of DCT and blood group):
- inform middle-grade doctor
- check serum bilirubin at 4 hr of age
- monitor serum bilirubin, usually at 4 hrly intervals but frequency depends on rate of rise
- chart a graph of rate of rise
- keep parents informed
- discuss progress regularly with middle-grade doctor or consultant. Consider whether newborn needs phototherapy or exchange transfusion-see below

- In babies with no IUT and negative DCT, no further action required; the newborn is not affected

Management of newborns with haemolysis diagnosed or suspected postnatally

- Newborns with
- blood group incompatibility with a positive DCT, manage as above
- red cell enzyme defect, inform consultant on-call

PHOTOTHERAPY

Indications/treatment thresholds

> *Prophylactic phototherapy (e.g. from birth) is not beneficial*
>
> *Treatment thresholds are lower in haemolysis because bilirubin is more freely available*

- Term (≥37 weeks gestation) – serum bilirubin >240 micromol/L
- Preterm – serum bilirubin level >[(17 x gestational age in weeks)/2] – 100
- e.g. at 33 weeks, start phototherapy if >180 micromol/L
- Inform middle-grade doctor when a baby requires phototherapy

Management

- Plot bilirubin values on a chart
- Check bilirubin 4 hr after the onset of phototherapy
- Monitor serum bilirubin at least 12 hrly, determining the frequency of measurement from the response at 4 hr
- Encourage mother to continue feeding using her chosen method, but emphasise need for adequate hydration

- Continue phototherapy until value falls consistently (e.g. two consecutive bilirubin values) below the phototherapy level on the chart
- Once phototherapy has been discontinued check serum bilirubin within 12 hr
- Communicate plan of management clearly to parents and document:
- discuss any communication difficulties with on-call consultant

EXCHANGE TRANSFUSION

Indications– always discuss with consultant

Anaemia

- A newborn who has **not** had an in-utero blood transfusion with a cord Hb <12 g/dL needs an urgent exchange transfusion to remove antibodies and correct anaemia. Simple packed-cell blood transfusions should be avoided
- In a newborn who has had in-utero transfusions and the Kleihauer test demonstrates a predominance of adult Hb, anaemia can be managed using a top-up transfusion of irradiated, CMV-negative blood. This test may not be available in your hospital
- Irradiated blood has a shelf-life of 24 hr only

Hyperbilirubinaemia

- The levels at which a consultant would need to make a decision for exchange are:
- term: serum bilirubin >340 micromol/L
- preterm: serum bilirubin >(17 x gestational age in weeks)/2
- predict possible need for an exchange transfusion if rate of rise of bilirubin is >10 micromol/L per hour despite phototherapy

- cord bilirubin acts as reference to compare with 4 hr bilirubin. There is no current cord bilirubin concentration that would indicate immediate need for exchange transfusion

FOLLOW-UP AND TREATMENT OF LATE ANAEMIA

- All newborns with haemolytic anaemia need:
- Hb check at 2 and 6 weeks
- discuss results urgently with neonatal consultant

- Indication for top-up transfusion for late anaemia:
- at request of neonatal consultant
- symptomatic anaemia
- Hb <7.5 g/dL

- Outpatient clinic at 3 months and hearing test for any infant:
- with possible/definite red cell anomalies
- who has undergone an exchange transfusion
- who has had an in-utero transfusion
- with serum bilirubin at or above exchange transfusion threshold

DEFINITION

- Injury to brachial plexus nerves sustained due to stretching of nerves during delivery

RECOGNITION AND ASSESSMENT

- Can be difficult because injury recovery patterns vary in severity
- Suspect if baby not moving arm
- Examine arm for swelling, bruising, tone, posture and any movement
- Assess for breathing difficulties and Horner's syndrome
- Document findings clearly in case notes
- Explain to parents that recovery probable but may not be complete
- Inform consultant obstetrician and paediatrician

MANAGEMENT

Birth

- If limb completely flaccid and Horner's syndrome present, refer immediately to regional paediatric surgeons[1]
- If some arm movement present, refer to physiotherapist and arrange early review in outpatient clinic in three weeks
- X-ray to exclude fracture humerus/clavicle

Three weeks

- Examine limb for shoulder abduction, flexion and extension of elbow, wrist and finger movements
- If no neurological improvement, refer to regional paediatric surgeons for early review by six weeks
- If neurological function improving, review at six weeks
- Continue physiotherapy

Six weeks

- If no further neurological improvement, refer to regional paediatric surgeons
- If neurological function improving, review at six months
- Continue physiotherapy

Six months

- If recovery incomplete, refer to regional obstetric brachial plexus clinic
- Even with good recovery shoulder abduction can be limited
- Surgical intervention of shoulder may be helpful at 18 months

[1]Local contacts
West Midlands: Miss Lester's Obstetric Brachial Plexus clinic, BCH – fax a written referral.
Fax: 0121 3338131/Ph: 0121 333 8136

Issue 02
Issued: October 2007
Expires: September 2009

RATIONALE

- Human milk is important in establishing enteral nutrition
- Any amount of mother's fresh breast milk is better than none
- Physician advocacy has a strong influence on intention to feed

IMPLEMENTATION

- In pregnancy at high-risk of premature delivery, discuss feeding during antenatal period
- During mother's first visit to NICU, discuss value/benefits
- Document discussion in medical record
- Separate decision to provide a few weeks of pumped breast milk from the commitment to long-term, exclusive breastfeeding
- Praise efforts to provide expressed breast milk
- Ensure adequate discussion and written information on hand-expression, and use and frequency of a pump

CONTRAINDICATIONS TO BREASTFEEDING

Infants with galactosaemia should not receive breast milk

Human immunodeficiency virus (HIV) in the UK

- Always check maternal HIV status before breastfeeding
- Breastfeeding absolutely contraindicated (in UK)
- If you are concerned that mother intends to breastfeed, ensure an HIV specialist explains the risk to which infant will be exposed
- If returning to a developing country where there is no access to clean water, exclusive breastfeeding is safer than mixed

Maternal medications

- Antimetabolites or cytotoxic drugs
- Radioisotope investigation (until isotope clears)

A current, reliable reference for drugs and breastfeeding must be available on the neonatal unit. The recommended references are 'Medications and mother's milk' by T W Hale and 5th edition Neonatal Formulary

BREASTFEEDING WHERE SPECIAL PRECAUTIONS REQUIRED

Tuberculosis

- Maternal sputum-positive TB is not a contraindication to breastfeeding
- Give infant isoniazid 5 mg/kg/daily, unless maternal isolate known to be resistant
- Tuberculin test at 3 months
- if negative, give BCG
- if positive, assess for active TB. If assessment negative, continue isoniazid for 6 months total

Cytomegalovirus (CMV)

- Ascertain mother's CMV antibody status (no risk if seronegative)
- Never feed breast milk from CMV-positive mothers to unprotected non-immune infants
- Pasteurisation of milk inactivates CMV

Hepatitis B

- Mothers who are HbsAg positive, particularly if also HbeAg +ve and e ab negative, are at risk of infecting their infant through breastfeeding
- Risk of transmission can be almost totally eliminated by a combination of active and passive immunisation

- Encourage HBsAg +ve and HBeAg +ve mothers to breastfeed
- See **Hepatitis B** guideline

Hepatitis C

- Transmission by breastfeeding theoretically possible but has not been documented
- Breastfeeding not contraindicated but inform mother that risks are unknown

Varicella-zoster virus (VZV)

- Infants of mothers with active VZV may breastfeed once mother is no longer infectious, unless the infant already exposed, but explain risk to mother
- Premature babies <1 kg, <28 weeks are considered high risk and should be given VZIG (see **Varicella** guideline)

Herpes simplex type 1

- Stop women with herpetic lesions on breast from breastfeeding or feeding expressed breast milk from affected side (until lesions have healed)
- cover active lesions elsewhere
- careful hand hygiene essential
- encourage to pump and discard breast milk until lesions are clear

Phenylketonuria (PKU)

- Breastfeeding not contraindicated in infants with PKU
- Screening service will contact paediatric dietitians directly
- Careful dietetic management necessary
- All infants should be under care of paediatric dietitians

Radioactive diagnostic agents

- Women receiving radioactive diagnostic agents need to pump and discard milk for varying periods of time
- although most agents have very short plasma half-lives, seek advice from hospital nuclear medicine department

Medications

- Few contraindicate breastfeeding (see BNF Appendix 5)
- safe agents include magnesium sulphate, tocolytics, antihypertensives, analgesics, antibiotics (caution with ciprofloxacin), psychotropic drugs and methadone (use lowest possible dose)

Social drugs

- **Alcohol**
- discourage more than limited consumption
- **Nicotine**
- nicotine concentration in breast milk increases immediately after smoking
- discourage mothers from smoking directly before breastfeeding or expressing

Issue 02
Issued: October 2007
Expires: September 2009

Improperly collected or stored breast milk can become contaminated and cause sepsis in infants particularly susceptible to infection

All staff must adhere to local policies/guidelines on the collection of human milk and hand washing

GENERAL

- Advise mothers to bath or shower daily
- it is not advisable to wash breasts with bactericidal detergent or soap
- Before expressing milk, it is essential to wash hands thoroughly with soap and water and dry with a disposable towel
- Give all breastfeeding mothers the BLISS 'Preterm Breastfeeding' leaflet

COLLECTION OF BREAST MILK

- Give mother sterile collection kit
- Ensure a dedicated fridge and freezer for storage of milk on ward
- Clearly label milk from individual mothers and store separately in fridge
- Blood and other pigments can discolour milk causing appearance to vary considerably
- unless it appears rancid and smells offensive, the appearance of milk is of no clinical concern and it can be safely fed to the baby
- Emphasise to mothers the importance of washing all breast milk collecting equipment properly before disinfection
- wash equipment with detergent and hot water using bottle brush (not shared) and rinse well before disinfection
- discard bottle brushes on discharge

STORAGE AND USE

Where

- Store in refrigerator at 4°C. Freshly expressed breast milk can be stored for 48 hr before freezing
- Freeze breast milk at –20°C. It can be stored for 3 months in freezer without a defrost cycle
- Monitor fridge and freezer temperature using maximum/minimum thermometer that has been calibrated every 6 months

How

- Place milk in sterile container with airtight lid
- Ensure bottles labelled appropriately
- Store labelled bottles in separate containers in fridge/freezer (individual containers must not hold bottles from more than one mother)
- Wash containers in fridge daily in warm soapy water, rinse well and dry thoroughly
- Clean container between each use
- Refrigerated milk separates with hind milk forming top layer
- shake milk containers vigorously before use

Defrosting

- Use frozen milk in sequence of storage
- Defrost frozen milk in fridge
- If frozen milk needs to be thawed quickly, hold bottle under cold or tepid water
- shake frequently and do not allow water to enter bottle via cap
- Discard thawed milk (stored in a refrigerator) after 12 hr

Issue 02
Issued: October 2007
Expires: September 2009

Use

- Once removed from fridge, fresh or defrosted milk must be used within 4 hr
- Fresh milk is preferable to thawed milk
- Change continuous tube feeding (tubing between nasogastric tube and pump) every 4 hr
- to minimise fat loss, ensure syringe delivering feed in semi-upright position

TRANSPORTATION OF MILK

Milk is often transported from:

- Mother's home to hospital
- transport in an insulated container that can be easily cleaned
- encourage mothers to use coolant block to maintain stable temperature
- Hospital to hospital
- use rigid container for easy cleaning (e.g. cool box) and fill empty space with bubble wrap

PRECAUTIONS

- Wash hands thoroughly
- Cover cuts and abrasions and wear gloves if necessary

RECORD KEEPING

- Label all bottles with baby's printed hospital label containing:
- name and hospital number
- date and time of expression
- If mother is expressing milk at home, provide supply of printed hospital labels
- Before giving breast milk, two members of staff must check label and cross–reference with baby's identity bracelet to ensure milk is not given to wrong child
- See **Breastfeeding preterm infants (advocacy and contraindication guideline)**

STORAGE FOLLOWING DISCHARGE

- If in date, immediately transfer any milk left in unit refrigerator to freezer
- Discard milk stored in neonatal unit freezer one month after discharge

PERIPHERAL VENOUS CANNULATION

INDICATIONS

- Access for intravenous infusion and medications

CONTRAINDICATIONS

- Sore or broken skin

EQUIPMENT

- Cleaning solution
- Appropriately labelled blood bottles and request cards
- Non-sterile latex gloves
- 24 gauge cannula
- T-piece connected to a syringe of sodium chloride 0.9%, flushed and ready
- Tape and splint to secure cannula

EMLA cream and alcohol swabs are not used in neonates

PROCEDURE

Preparation

- Identify suitable site:
- arms: antecubital fossa or back of hand
- legs: long saphenous vein or foot
- scalp: shave area if using scalp vein
- Identify suitable vein, which should be clearly visible – unlike in adults, neonatal veins are rarely palpable

When infant likely to need numerous cannulations, avoid using potential long line veins

- It can be helpful to flush cannula with sodium chloride 0.9% to assist in identification of point at which cannula enters vein. (If blood samples taken at time of cannula insertion, discard first 0.5–1 mL of blood)
- Wash hands and put on gloves

Insertion

- Apply hand pressure around limb to distend vein
- Place thumb on skin slightly distal to proposed puncture site
- Hold cannula at 10-20° angle and puncture skin
- Advance cannula toward vein
- resistance may diminish slightly as it enters vein and a speck of blood may be seen in hub of needle (this is easier to see if cannula has been flushed with sodium chloride 0.9%). Do **not** advance needle further as it can pierce back wall of vein
- Advance cannula looking for blood flowing into cannula hub
- When this occurs, hold needle steady and advance cannula a short distance within vein
- Withdraw needle from cannula
- Connect T-piece and flush cannula gently with sodium chloride 0.9% to confirm it is in the vein
- Secure cannula with tape and connect to infusion

Issue 02
Issued: October 2007
Expires: September 2009

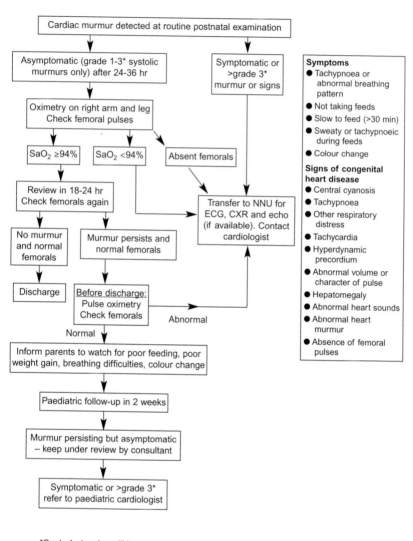

Cardiac murmur detected at routine postnatal examination

Asymptomatic (grade 1-3* systolic murmurs only) after 24-36 hr

Symptomatic or >grade 3* murmur or signs

Oximetry on right arm and leg
Check femoral pulses

SaO₂ ≥94%   SaO₂ <94%   Absent femorals

Review in 18-24 hr
Check femorals again

Transfer to NNU for ECG, CXR and echo (if available). Contact cardiologist

No murmur and normal femorals

Murmur persists and normal femorals

Discharge

Before discharge:
Pulse oximetry
Check femorals

Abnormal

Normal

Inform parents to watch for poor feeding, poor weight gain, breathing difficulties, colour change

Paediatric follow-up in 2 weeks

Murmur persisting but asymptomatic – keep under review by consultant

Symptomatic or >grade 3* refer to paediatric cardiologist

Symptoms
- Tachypnoea or abnormal breathing pattern
- Not taking feeds
- Slow to feed (>30 min)
- Sweaty or tachypnoeic during feeds
- Colour change

Signs of congenital heart disease
- Central cyanosis
- Tachypnoea
- Other respiratory distress
- Tachycardia
- Hyperdynamic precordium
- Abnormal volume or character of pulse
- Hepatomegaly
- Abnormal heart sounds
- Abnormal heart murmur
- Absence of femoral pulses

*Grade 1 - barely audible
Grade 2 - soft but easily audible
Grade 3 - moderately loud, no thrill
Grade 4 - louder, with thrill
Grade 5 - audible with stethoscope barely on the chest
Grade 6 - audible with stethoscope off the chest

Issue 02
Issued: October 2007
Expires: September 2009

INDICATIONS

- Treatment of pneumothorax or pleural effusion

EQUIPMENT

- Sterile dressing pack
- Chlorhexidine gluconate 0.05% solution
- Lidocaine 1%, with syringe and needle for preparation and injection
- Chest drains size FG 8,10,12 (use largest possible depending on size of infant)
- Low pressure suction unit
- Scalpel and fine straight blade
- Fine blunt forceps
- Underwater seal chest drainage bottle and tubing
- or flutter valve for transport
- Steristrips and transparent dressing (e.g. opsite)

Avoid area close to nipple to prevent damage to breast tissue

Take great care when inserting chest drain to avoid injury to lungs

Avoid sutures as far as possible, especially purse string sutures as they lead to cicatrized scars

SITES

- Site of insertion depends on position of pneumothorax
- preferred site is in anterior axillary line, between fourth and sixth intercostal space, to conceal subsequent scarring and avoid interference with breast development
- alternative site is just lateral to midclavicular line, in second or third intercostal space
- if pneumothorax does not drain satisfactorily, it may be necessary to insert more than one drain
- for pleural effusion, use midaxillary line between fourth and fifth intercostal spaces, and direct drain posteriorly

PROCEDURE

Obtain consent (see **Consent** guideline)

Preparation and position of baby

- Use 10-12 FG pleural catheter (small babies may need 8 FG)
- Position baby supine and flat with affected side slightly tilted up (for example, by using a folded blanket)
- Prepare skin with full aseptic technique
- Infiltrate with lidocaine 1%, even in babies receiving systemic analgesia

Insertion of tube

- Make small incision in skin with scalpel
- Dissect bluntly with fine forceps through intercostal muscle and pleura
- Use fine forceps to gently advance tip of catheter into pleural space
- Push and twist tube gently through incision into pleural space
- Use of trochar not generally recommended. If used (in bigger baby), protect lung by clamping artery forceps on to trochar 1 cm from the tip
- Connect tube to prepared underwater seal or flutter valve (according to local practice)
- Manipulate tube gently so that tip lies anteriorly in thoracic cavity for pneumothorax, and posteriorly for effusion
- Secure tube with steristrips, and cover with gauze dressing
- Secure tube to chest wall using suitable tape

Issue 02
Issued: October 2007
Expires: September 2009

AFTERCARE

- Check bubbling or oscillation of water column seen with every inspiration

- Check tube position with chest X-ray

- If bubbling poor and X-ray confirms that drain is in correct position but pneumothorax not fully draining on X-ray or cold light, apply continuous suction of 10-15 cm of water. Thoracic suction is better suited for this purpose than routine wall suction. Occasionally, a second drain may be necessary

- Record presence of bubbling (continuous/intermittent/none) in nursing care chart

- As alternative to underwater chest drain system, especially during transport a flutter valve can be used

- Record with nursing observations, bubbling and/or oscillation of water column, or fluttering of valve seen with every inspiration

REMOVAL OF CHEST DRAIN

- Remove tubing when no bubbling has occurred for 24 hr. Do not clamp chest drain

- While removing drain, ask an assistant to hold wound edges close together

- After removing drain, close wound with steristrips – a suture is seldom necessary

- Close clinical observation after removal of drain is sufficient to diagnose reaccumulation of the air leak – routine chest X-ray is not warranted

Issue 02
Issued: October 2007
Expires: September 2009

RECOGNITION AND ASSESSMENT

Definition

- Oxygen dependency at 36 weeks of postmenstrual age to maintain SpO_2 >90%
- Consistent chest X-ray findings

Symptoms and Signs

- Oxygen dependency on or off the ventilator
- Signs of respiratory distress

Investigations

- Chest X-ray – homogenous opacification of lung fields developing after the first week of life (Type 1) or coarse streaky opacities with cystic translucencies in the lung fields (Type 2)
- Exclude infections by appropriate investigations, including endotracheal culture of secretions for bacteriology, virology and urea plasma
- Exclude PDA clinically or with echocardiography, depending on local expertise available

TREATMENT

Corticosteroids

- Consider between 7 and 14 days of age if ventilator dependent and requiring increasing, or persistently high, oxygen intake
- Only a consultant decides to treat with corticosteroids
- Inform parents of potential short term and long term side effects
- Short term:
- risk of infection
- poor growth
- reversible ventricular hypertrophy
- gastrointestinal perforation and bleeding
- adrenal suppression
- glucose intolerance
- risk of nephrocalcinosis if being treated with diuretics
- Long term:
- neurodisability
- Obtain oral consent and record in notes
- Use Neonatal Formulary for dexamethasone dosage regimen
- Consider repeating the course if respiratory status worsens after initial improvement – again decision made by a consultant

Diuretics

- If baby >3 weeks old and either ventilator dependent or requiring >40% supplemental oxygen, give chlorothiazide 10 mg/kg orally 12 hrly and spironolactone 1 mg/kg orally 12 hrly

SUBSEQUENT MANAGEMENT

- Ensure adequate calorie intake (up to 130 kcal/kg/day)
- If growth unsatisfactory, involve dietitian

MONITORING TREATMENT

Continuous

- Pulse oximetry – aim for 89-94%
- Beware of infections, particularly fungal

Daily

- BP
- Urinary glucose
- Blood gases

Weekly

- Electrolytes
- Weight and head growth

Issue 02
Issued: October 2007
Expires: September 2009

DISCHARGE POLICY

- If still oxygen dependent at time of discharge, arrange multidisciplinary discharge planning meeting

- Will need open access to paediatric wards in view of increased respiratory morbidity

- If age criteria met, passive immunisation with palivizumab plus influenza in the season

- If >6 months old, influenza vaccination

- Long term neuro-developmental and respiratory follow-up

Issue 02
Issued: October 2007
Expires: September 2009

Transmission can occur following primary or recurrent maternal infection

ANTENATAL DIAGNOSIS

Indications for testing mother

- Intrauterine growth retardation (IUGR)
- Fetal hydrops
- Maternal HIV

Maternal tests

CMV IgM

- A negative result excludes current infection
- A positive result is significant of recent infection only if there is a rise during pregnancy – look at IgG avidity (titre) from two specimens >10 days apart

Ultrasound

Features include:

- Intrauterine growth retardation (IUGR)
- Hydrocephalus (ventricular dilation), intracranial calcification, microcephaly
- Ascites, hydrops fetalis
- Pleural or pericardial effusions
- Oligo- or polyhydramnios
- Hepatomegaly
- Abdominal calcification
- Pseudomeconium ileus
- Thickened placenta

INFANT DIAGNOSIS

Main clinical signs

- Small for gestational age
- Petechiae/purpura
- Hepatosplenomegaly
- Jaundice
- Pneumonia

Investigation results

- CMV IgM positive
- CMV PCR urine positive
- Haemolytic anaemia
- Thrombocytopenia
- Conjugated hyperbilirubinaemia
- Raised liver enzymes
- Repeat maternal or baby's HIV antibody test

If any of above results is positive, continue with further investigations

Further Investigations

- CSF
- raised CSF protein
- Ophthalmology
- chorioretinitis
- Audiology
- sensorineural hearing loss
- Head US
- hydrocephalus, cysts
- CT of brain
- intracranial calcification
- ventriculomegaly
- cerebral atrophy

TREATMENT

Asymptomatic (CMV IgM or PCR positive)

- Seek expert advice from paediatric infectious disease specialist regarding offering valganciclovir (possibly as part of an on-going international trial)
- advantages – reduced risk of deafness
- disadvantages – immunosuppression

Symptomatic

- IV ganciclovir 6 mg/kg 12 hrly over 1 hour prepared by pharmacy (cytotoxic) for 6 weeks (discuss with specialist in paediatric infectious diseases)

FEEDING

- Do not discourage infected women from breast feeding their own uninfected, term infants – CMV can be transmitted via breastfeeding, but benefits of feeding outweigh risks posed by breastfeeding as a source of transmission
- Avoid breastfeeding of premature neonates if the mother is positive and the baby asymptomatic

Issue 02
Issued: October 2007
Expires: September 2009

- Haemostasis is immature during the neonatal period and does not attain full function until 6 months of age
- prolonged prothrombin time (PT) and activated partial thromboplastin time (APTT) are associated with intraventricular haemorrhage (IVH) in unstable (e.g. hypotensive or hypoxic) or bruised extremely preterm babies
- 75% of cases of IVH occur within first 24 hr of life and 90% within first 7 days
- it is not necessary to correct abnormal coagulation in preterm babies with stable blood pressure, oxygen requirement etc
- prophylactic fresh frozen plasma (FFP) does not prevent IVH in stable preterm babies

INVESTIGATIONS

Check clotting in:

- Any bleeding neonate
- Moderate-to-severe encephalopathy
- Septicaemia
- Necrotizing enterocolitis
- Extremely preterm (<28 weeks gestation) with bruising, or unstable
- Metabolic disease – urea cycle disorder, galactosaemia, tyrosinaemia, organic acidaemia
- Liver dysfunction
- Neonates undergoing surgery or tissue biopsy who have had previous bleeding problems
- Family history of inherited bleeding disorder (after discussion with consultant haematologist)

Sampling

- Ensure a free-flowing venous sample
- Use fresh coagulation tubes from refrigerator
- Fill exactly to black mark on tube (usually 1.3 mL)
- If sample clots (this does not confirm normal coagulation), take another

- When venous samples are unavailable, obtain sample from an indwelling arterial catheter after taking 1 mL blood which can be given back to baby before the flush

Request

- Prothrombin time (PT)
- Activated prothrombin time (APTT)
- Fibrinogen
- If features of DIC (Disseminating Intravascular Coagulation) e.g. bruising, bleeding, sepsis, request:
- fibrin degradation products and D-dimer
- Consider further tests depending on results of initial profile and after discussion with consultant haematologist

Reference values for PT and APTT:

	Preterm	Term
PT (sec)	12-17	14-22
APTT (sec)	25-45	35-50
Fibrinogen (g/L)	1.5-3.0	1.5-3.0

See www.transfusionguidelines.org.uk

IMMEDIATE TREATMENT

- Give vitamin K (phytomenadione) 100 microgram/kg IV (maximum dose 1 mg) to all infants if not already administered IM
- If PT/APTT beyond upper limit of reference range, give FFP 10 mL/kg
- Repeat coagulation screen
- If coagulopathy not responding to FFP, or fibrinogen low, use cryoprecipitate 5 mL/kg

MONITORING

- Repeat coagulation profile every 12 hr if indication persists
- Look for and treat causes of abnormal coagulation:
- sepsis
- shock

- haemorrhage
- severe hypothermia
- hypoxia
- If abnormal coagulation persists for >24 hr in the absence of any precipitating factors, seek advice from tertiary centre paediatric haematologists about factor assays and 50:50 mixture correction test

Issue 02
Issued: October 2007
Expires: September 2009

RECOGNITION AND ASSESSMENT

Definition

- Conjunctival redness
- Swelling of conjunctiva and eyelids
- Purulent discharge
- Potentially blinding condition with associated systemic manifestations
- **Differentiate from:**
  - sticky eye with blocked tear duct in which there is no inflammation of conjunctiva
  - conjunctival glaucoma in which there is corneal opacity

AETIOLOGY

- Bacterial
  - *chlamydia trachomatis*
  - *staphylococcus aureus*
  - streptococcus
  - *haemophilus influenzae*
  - gonococcus
- Chemical
  - silver nitrate
- Viral
  - herpes simplex virus

MANAGEMENT

Sticky Eye/blocked tear duct

- **No inflammation**
  - 4-6 hrly eye toilet using sterile saline

Suspected conjunctivitis (see signs above)

- Swab for :
  - Gram stain and bacterial culture and sensitivities
  - viral immunofluorescence and culture
- Chlamydia swab (viral transport medium)
- Presentation within first 24 hr suggests gonococcal infection
  - inform senior paediatrician
- Treat with:
  - frequent eye toilet as necessary
  - chloramphenicol 0.5% eye drops

SUBSEQUENT MANAGEMENT

In severe non-resolving cases

- Take throat and eye swabs for viral culture (viral transport medium)
- If herpes detected, look for other signs of herpetic infection
- Treat suspected herpes with IV aciclovir for 14 days
- Refer to ophthalmology

Gonococcus suspected

- Request Gram stain and culture
- Assess neonate for systemic infection

Gonococcus confirmed

- Give single dose ceftriaxone 125 mg IV if IV access is present, otherwise IM (40 mg/kg for low birth weight babies)
- Give course of IV treatment if signs of systemic infection (e.g. sepsis, meningitis)
- Refer to ophthalmology

Chlamydia result positive

- Treat with azithromycin 20 mg/kg single dose or erythromycin 15 mg/kg/dose orally 8 hrly for 2 weeks. This will treat the conjunctivitis and prevent most cases of chlamydia pneumonitis

Gonococcal or chlamydia infection detected

● Refer mother and partner to genito-urinary medicine for immediate treatment

Gonococcal versus chlamydial conjunctivitis

Gonococcal	Chlamydial
2-5 days incubation	5-14 days incubation
Transmission vaginal or from contaminated fingers after birth	Transmission vaginal or from contaminated fingers after birth
Mild inflammation with sero-sanguineous discharge Progression to thick, purulent discharge with tense oedema of eyelids	Varies from mild inflammation to severe swelling of eyelids with copious purulent discharge
Complications include corneal ulceration and perforation Meningitis and sepsis	Corneas rarely affected 1 in 5 untreated will develop chlamydial pneumonitis

Issue 02
Issued: October 2007
Expires: September 2009

FOR COMMON NEONATAL INVESTIGATIONS, INTERVENTIONS AND TREATMENTS

BACKGROUND

The following guidance is taken from 'Good practice framework for consent in neonatal clinical care' produced by the British Association of Perinatal Medicine (BAPM)

● It is a legal and ethical requirement to gain valid consent before examining and initiating any investigation or treatment for any patient
● Consent is obtained from someone with parental responsibilities:
● parents, if married
● mother, but not father, if not married unless father has acquired parental responsibility via a court order, being registered on birth certificate or parental responsibility agreement
● a legally appointed guardian
● a local authority designated in a care order or holding an emergency protection order
● Consent is valid only when information has been understood by the parent(s) and explains why intervention is recommended, its risks and implications, and other options should consent be withheld

Documentation of information given and parent's understanding and agreement to proceed is the most important validation of consent. A signature does not in itself confirm informed consent

● Consent should be witnessed wherever possible, and name of witness recorded
● In neonatal practice, there are frequent occasions when no one is available to provide valid consent and treatment is initiated in its absence (e.g. emergency ABC resuscitation, stabilisation or chest drainage, when delayed treatment would not be in the patient's best interests, or following maternal general anaesthetic when mother is unmarried to the baby's father)

GOOD PRACTICE

● Give parents of all babies admitted to neonatal unit written information (BLISS booklet) describing low risk procedures such as venesection, for which explicit consent is not normally sought
● Give all parents information leaflet for MANNERS data collection allowing them to opt out

Written explicit consent

Purpose and risks of an intervention are formally explained and consent obtained and recorded prior to the intervention

Explicit consent, recorded in patient notes, and supported by a signature required for:

Investigation/intervention	
Clinical photographs and video-recordings	Use consent form specific for this purpose
Any biopsy or aspiration	e.g. skin, liver, bone marrow
Exchange transfusion	
Treatment for retinopathy	Obtained by ophthalmologist
Surgical procedures	Consent taken by surgical team. If telephone consent required, and mother still an inpatient, midwife on postnatal ward or neonatal team to act as witness
Post-mortem	See **Death** guideline and use specific form

Oral explicit consent

Explicit consent as defined above, documented, *but not supported by a signature,* required for the following:

Explicit oral consent	
Investigations	Screening babies +/or mothers in high-risk situations with no knowledge of maternal status (e.g. suspected HIV, substance misuse)
	Genetic testing
	Gut imaging involving contrast
	MR/CT imaging
Practical procedure	Therapeutic LP or ventricular tap in absence of reservoir*
	Peripherally-placed long-lines*
	Chest drain insertion/replacement*
	Abdominal drainage for perforation and ascites*
	Irrigation following extravasation*
Immunisation (see Immunisation guideline)	
Treatments	Vitamin K for normal term babies
	Nitric oxide
	Postnatal dexamethasone for chronic lung disease
Transport	Emergency transfers
	Routine transfers for outpatients or back-transfers

* It is accepted that in some circumstances these procedures are performed in an emergency in baby's best interests, and may be performed without oral consent; owing to the risks associated with procedures or conditions in which they are necessary, it is considered best practice to inform parents as soon as possible and to document this in patient's notes

Others – implicit consent

● Where nature and risk of procedure is such that a less formal transfer of information is considered sufficient, and is often retrospective
● The list of investigations, procedures and treatments is long, see table
● If unsure, seek senior advice

> *Explain all investigations, procedures and treatments to parents at earliest opportunity*

Issue 02
Issued: October 2007
Expires: September 2009

Implicit consent	
Examination and investigations	Examining and assessing patient
	Routine blood sampling
	Septic screens
	Diagnostic LP (possible infectious or metabolic illness)
	Suprapubic aspiration of urine
	Screening for infection in response to positive results of maternal screening (e.g. known maternal HIV or substance abuse)
	CMV, toxoplasmosis, rubella and herpes screening
	X-ray and ultrasound
	ECG
	Retinopathy of prematurity (ROP) screening
Practical procedures	Umbilical line insertion
	Percutaneous arterial lines (radial, posterior tibial only)
	Peripheral venous lines
	Nasogastric tube insertion
	Tracheal intubation
	Ventilation/CPAP
	Urethral catheterisation
Treatments - *haematology*	Blood transfusion
	Use of pooled blood products e.g. FFP
	Partial exchange transfusion
Treatments - *drugs*	Antibiotics
	Vitamins/minerals
	Surfactant
	Anticonvulsants
	Sedation for intubation and ventilation
	Inotropes
	Indometacin or ibuprofen for PDA
	Prophylactic indometacin
	Postnatal dexamethasone for laryngeal oedema
Nutrition/Fluids	Breast milk fortification
	Intravenous fluids
	Parenteral nutrition

AUDIT MEASURES

● Documentation, supported by a signature for written explicit consent
● Documentation of oral explicit consent
● Provision to parents of BLISS booklet and MANNERS information sheet

DEFINITION

Method of maintaining low pressure distension of lungs during inspiration and expiration when infant breathing spontaneously

Benefits

- Improves oxygenation
- Maintains lung volume
- Lowers upper airway resistance
- Conserves surfactant and reduces alveolar fluid

INDICATIONS

- Early onset respiratory distress in preterm infants (≤34 weeks gestation) with good respiratory effort
- Can be helpful in respiratory distress in infants of >34 weeks gestation, especially with clinical features of RDS. Perform a chest X-ray to confirm RDS and exclude pneumothorax
- Recurrent apnoeas in preterm infants
- Atelectasis
- Tracheomalacia
- Respiratory support following extubation (see below)

CPAP following extubation

- Use for the majority of infants of **<32 weeks**, after loading infants with caffeine
- Use **'Rescue' CPAP** for other infants who have apnoeas or desaturations and an increasing oxygen requirement within first few hours after extubation
- Apnoea and desaturations appearing later than first few hours after extubation can be an indication for CPAP but also consider an additional underlying clinical condition (e.g. sepsis)

CONTRAINDICATIONS

- Any infant fulfilling the criteria for ventilation
- Irregular respirations
- Congenital anomalies:
  - diaphragmatic hernia
  - choanal atresia
  - tracheo-oesophageal fistula
  - gastroschisis
- Pneumothorax without chest drain
- Nasal trauma/deformity so severe that it might be exacerbated by use of nasal prongs
- Cardiovascular instability is a relative contraindication as intubation and ventilation may allow better stabilisation
- Larger babies often do not tolerate application of CPAP devices well, resulting in restlessness and labile oxygen requirement

When in doubt about CPAP indications or contraindications, discuss with consultant

TYPES OF CPAP

1. **Standard CPAP**
2. **Assisted CPAP via infant flow driver** (if available locally)
3. **Bubble CPAP** (if available locally)

1. STANDARD CPAP

Equipment

- Short binasal prongs and/or nasal mask
- Circuit
- Humidification
- CPAP generating device with gas mixing and pressure monitoring
- All require high gas flow and can pose problems for transportation

Fixing nasal CPAP devices- Short binasal prongs (preferred)

- To avoid loss of pressure, use largest prongs that fit nostrils comfortably
- Ensure device is straight and not pressed hard against nasal septum to avoid damage to nasal septum and lateral walls of nostrils. Excessive pressure can cause septal erosion

Fixing nasal CPAP devices- Nasal masks

- Fit securely over nose
- consider alternating with binasal prongs, particularly if infant developing excoriation or erosion of nasal septum

> *Masks can give a poor seal and tend to obstruct*
>
> *They can result in trauma, usually at junction between nasal septum and philtrum*

Flow rates

- The usual starting rate is 8 litres per minute. Aim to keep flow to a minimum, but too low a flow rate increases the work of breathing
- With both prongs and masks, flow required is affected by degree of 'leak' of gas from nose and mouth. Aim to keep mouth closed to maintain pressure in pharynx. Support chin and/or use a preterm pacifier to try to keep mouth closed

PROCEDURE

Position baby

- Prone position is preferable, as it reduces central and mixed apnoeas
- Avoid excessive flexion, extension or rotation of the head

Set up equipment

- Connect humidification to CPAP – see manufacturer's instructions
- Connect CPAP circuit with prongs to CPAP device
- Place CPAP hat on baby
- Attach CPAP circuit to CPAP hat and place prongs in nostrils as above
- Turn on CPAP flow and set pressure – see **below**

Pressure range

- Optimum pressure depends on illness type and severity, but use 5 cmH_2O initially
- Increase by 1 cmH_2O increments
- Watch baby, and use lowest pressure required to improve work of breathing

> *High pressures (≥10 cmH_2O) may restrict pulmonary blood flow, increase air leak risk, and cause overdistension and later hypercapnia*

CPAP 'FAILURE'

CPAP 'failure' implies a need for ventilation. Consider intubation and surfactant for preterm infant (≤34 weeks gestation) on CPAP as initial therapy if:

- Early chest X-ray shows RDS and one or more of the following apply:
- FiO_2 consistently >0.6
- marked respiratory distress e.g. marked intercostal and subcostal recession, suggesting infant likely to tire quickly
- persistent respiratory acidosis with arterial pH <7.25 and $PaCO_2$ >8.3 kPa/60 mmHg
- recurrent serious apnoeas
- irregular breathing

Checks

- Before accepting apparent CPAP 'failure' exclude:
- insufficient pressure
- insufficient circuit flow
- inappropriate prong size or placement
- airway obstruction from secretions
- open mouth
- pneumothorax

COMPLICATIONS

- Erosion of nasal septum – reduced by careful prong placement
- Gastric distension – benign, reduced by leaving nasogastric tube open

WEANING CPAP

When

- Do not wean CPAP until infant consistently requiring FiO_2 <0.35 on CPAP of 5 cmH_2O
- it may be necessary for infants developing excoriation and/or erosion of nasal septum to come off CPAP for short periods at regular intervals before weaning to enable healing

How

- Infants of >29 weeks gestation at birth and >1250 g may be weaned off nasal CPAP into nasal cannula oxygen or air. Other infants may need to cycle on and off CPAP
- The following regimen of cycling CPAP can be adapted to individual cases, as rate of weaning will depend on individual baby
- Slow weaning is advised for preterm infants with atelectasis and/or apnoeas, or poor growth. Such infants would spend longer at each stage of the weaning regime

Day 1	1 hr off twice a day (1 off, 11 on)
Day 2	2 hr off twice a day (2 off, 10 on)
Day 3	3 hr off twice a day (3 off, 9 on)
Day 4	4 hr off twice a day (4 off, 8 on)
Day 5 (not always needed)	6 hr off twice a day (6 off, 6 on)
Day 6	Off CPAP

- Alternatively, wean from CPAP by reducing CPAP pressure. This is more physiological, although it can increase the work of breathing if the pressure is too low
- wean pressures in steps of 1 cmH_2O every 12 hr. If no deterioration, reduce to 3 cmH_2O before stopping CPAP

Failure of weaning

- If nasal cannula oxygen >0.2 L/min required or marked respiratory distress develops, assess and put back onto CPAP, regardless of weaning regimen unless infant stable with chronic lung disease

2. ASSISTED CPAP (if available locally)

An alternative method of CPAP, whereby a varying number of 'assisted breaths' can be delivered to baby via CPAP driver. The rate, pressure and inspiratory time of these 'assisted breaths' are set by the operator

Definitions

CPAP + Apnoea (AP)

- Apnoea monitoring via a sensor attached to abdomen

CPAP + Pressure Assist (PA)

- Increased pressure delivered intermittently, not synchronized with respiratory effort

- Can be applied at a variable rate (R) and for varying times (Ti)

- Can be used with or without apnoea monitoring

CPAP + Trigger Pressure Assist (trPA)

- Increased pressure delivered intermittently, synchronized with respiratory effort for varying lengths of time (Ti) through an abdominal sensor

- Back up rate (Rb) can be varied but will trigger every sensed breath

- Apnoea monitoring built into this model

Available settings

- Flow approximately 8 L/min to generate a pressure of 5 cmH_2O
- Variable additional flow 0-5 L/min

INDICATIONS

- **CPAP + trPA** should generally be reserved for infants who:
  - are extremely preterm (e.g. 24-25 week gestation), or
  - have previously 'failed' extubation owing to apnoea of prematurity and/or hypoventilation, but in whom it is considered very important to try to extubate (e.g. evolving chronic lung disease)

- Use trPA, rather than PA as trPA is synchronized with respiratory rate
  - set back-up rate at 10 if possible – some infants may need higher rate of 20-30 initially

- If infant does not tolerate trPA, consider PA (non-triggered) at a back-up rate of up to 30
  - wean back-up rate down by 10 at a time, as quickly as tolerated
  - once infant on a back-up rate of 10, wean onto CPAP + AP

	Default setting	Set ranges
Apnoea alarm delay	20 sec	10, 15, 20, 25, 30 sec
Ti	0.3 sec	0.1-1.0 sec
R (unsynchronized PA)	30/min	1-120/min
Rb (trPA)	10/min	10-30/min

Initial settings

- **CPAP + AP**
  - 5 cmH_2O
  - apnoea alarm delay 20 seconds

- **CPAP + PA or trPA**
  - pressure   10/5
  - Rb (trPA)   10
  - R (PA)   30

Issue 02
Issued: October 2007
Expires: September 2009

3. BUBBLE CPAP (if available locally)

This is an alternative method of CPAP that may reduce work of breathing through facilitated diffusion

Equipment

● Fisher & Paykel Bubble CPAP system:
○ delivery system
  - humidifier chamber
  - pressure manifold
  - heated circuit
  - CPAP generator
○ patient interface:
  - nasal tubing
  - nasal prongs (9 sizes)
  - infant bonnet (4 sizes)
  - chin strap

Procedure

๑ Connect bubble CPAP system to patient as per manufacturer's instructions

● Ensure appropriate size nasal prongs used

● Bubble CPAP **nasal prongs are designed not to rest on nasal septum** to prevent septal damage. Ensure prongs are not resting on the philtrum nor twisted to cause lateral pressure on septum, and allow a small gap between septum and prongs

● Commence at pressures of 5 cmH$_2$O. Follow **Pressure range** in **1. STANDARD CPAP**

BUBBLE CPAP FAILURE

● See **CPAP failure** in **1. STANDARD CPAP**

Before inferring Bubble CPAP failure

● Ensure baby has been receiving bubble CPAP appropriately by checking for continuous bubbling in CPAP generator – lack of bubbling can result from pressure leaks in the circuit or baby

Issue 02
Issued: October 2007
Expires: September 2009

PURPOSE

● To detect brain injury in at-risk babies in order to provide appropriate medical management

● To detect lesions associated with long-term adverse neurodevelopmental outcome

INDICATIONS

● Prematurity

● Neonatal encephalopathy

● Neonatal seizures

● Abnormal neurological signs (e.g. floppy child, large head)

● Multiple congenital abnormalities (except trisomy 21)

● Unexplained poor feeding at term

● Unexplained hypoglycaemia – looking for pituitary and midline structures

● Meningitis

● Congenital viral infection

● Metabolic disorders

● In term infants, at consultant discretion, MR scan is the diagnostic method of choice for:
● ischaemic brain injury
● suspected malformations

Ultrasound scanning provides rapid and useful information

SCANNING PROTOCOL FOR PRETERM INFANTS

Initiation

There is no universal agreement on target group, optimal timing and frequency of brain ultrasound scanning of preterm infants. The following is suggested as a minimum.

Further scanning, particularly on day 1, and serial scans in very preterm babies are suggested

● **≤29 weeks**
● initial scan day 4-7
● 2nd scan day 10-14
● 3rd scan between 36-40 weeks of postmenstrual age

● **30-32 weeks**
● initial scan day 3-7
● 2nd scan at term equivalent age, or discharge if earlier

● **>32 weeks**
● only if clinically indicated – discuss on ward round

Follow-up

● If initial scan shows intraventricular haemorrhage (IVH) or hydrocephalus, haemorrhagic parenchymal infarction, or any other abnormality
● consider serial scanning – discuss with consultant

● If scan abnormal at six weeks:
● consider further imaging – discuss with consultant
● usually an MR scan

● Perform additional scans following a significant clinical event:
● necrotizing enterocolitis
● major collapse on neonatal unit (NNU)
● repeated episodes of apnoea and bradycardia
● unexplained sharp fall in haemoglobin
● change in neurological status
● abnormal head growth
● pre- and post-operatively

Issue 02
Issued: October 2007
Expires: September 2009

SCANNING PROTOCOL FOR TERM OR NEAR-TERM INFANTS

Neonatal encephalopathy

- Perform ultrasound scan. Although ultrasound scanning has limited role in assessment of encephalopathic term infant, it is rapid, easily available, and helps exclude non- hypoxic-ischaemic causes of encephalopathy such as structural, metabolic, and established antenatal brain damage
  - initial scan within 24 hr
  - 2nd scan 3-4 days
  - 3rd scan 7-14 days
- In encephalopathic infants with significant birth trauma and low haematocrit, request non-contrast CT scan
- For babies with moderate to severe encephalopathy between 3-8 days of age, MR scan recommended but availability limited and instability of a baby may contraindicate

Seizures

- In term infants with seizures, MR scan is preferred. However, in experienced hands, ultrasound can detect focal infarction and should be performed on admission, 2 and 7 days later

PROCEDURE

The operator (sonographer, neonatologist or radiologist) must have achieved an acceptable level of competence before performing and reporting scans independently. Technical competence and training is essential to recognise the appearance of common ultrasound pathological findings, in preterm and term babies

- Record a minimum set of coronal (6+ images):
  - anterior to the frontal horns of the lateral ventricles
  - at the anterior horns of the lateral ventricles and Sylvian fissures
  - at the third ventricle and thalami
  - at the posterior horns of the lateral ventricles (with choroids)
  - posterior to the choroids (posterior brain substance)
  - if there is lateral ventricular dilatation, make an index measurement of the lateral ventricles at the level of the third ventricle at the foramina of Munro (ventricular index)
- Record a minimum set of sagittal (5+ images):
  - midline through the 3rd ventricle, septum cavum pellucidum, cerebellum with 4th ventricle and foramen magnum
  - through each lateral ventricle showing the anterior and posterior horns, with the caudothalamic notch imaged if possible
  - through each hemisphere lateral to the ventricle for deep white matter
- Supplemental oblique, surface and axial images may be necessary to record pathology
- For detection of cerebellar lesions, scanning through posterior fontanelle (junction of lambdoid and sagittal sutures) and mastoid fontanelle (junction of posterior parietal, temporal and occipital bones) can be useful

DIFFERENTIAL DIAGNOSIS

- Radiologists or appropriately trained staff must interpret cranial ultrasound scans
- Scans must be reported using categories/terminology in Table 1

Table 1

Intraventricular haemorrhage	● None
	● Localised IVH without dilatation (germinal matrix haemorrhage, subependymal haemorrhage)
	● IVH with ventricular dilatation
	● Parenchymal haemorrhage
Ventricular size	● Normal
	● Enlarged
Parenchymal lesions	● None
	● Periventricular flare
	● Cystic lesions
	single large – porencephalic cyst
	multiple cysts – (cystic periventricular leukomalacia)

COMMUNICATION

● Any member of neonatal team may communicate a normal result to parents but **note** that a normal scan does not equate to normal development and follow-up is essential

● Discuss an abnormal result with a neonatal consultant before discussion with parents

DOCUMENTATION

● Documentation is extremely important. Digital copies of scans must be archived suitably

● Record following information on the investigation chart:

  ◦ date scan requested

  ◦ date scan carried out

● Record ultrasound result (or file a written report) in the baby's notes (neonatal staff)

● Record any discussion with parents, especially of abnormal scans, in notes

● Include results of all scans – even if normal – in discharge summary

● If eligible baby transferred to another hospital before scanning, communicate need for scan in the transfer summary

DEFINITION

'Blue' refers to central cyanosis (e.g. colour of tongue and gums). It is very difficult to see with the naked eye before the ductus arteriosus reaches a critical closing point. Any baby presenting as blue has a critically small or closed duct and is a neonatal emergency requiring consultant input. These babies can deteriorate very quickly

Differential diagnosis

Without echocardiography, the clinical distinction between persistent pulmonary hypertension and a duct-dependent pulmonary circulation can be extremely challenging

Lungs

- Persistent pulmonary hypertension of newborn
- Congenital diaphragmatic hernia
- Congenital lung lesions (e.g. pulmonary lymphangiectasia)

Heart

- Obstruction of blood flow from heart to lungs
- Obstruction of blood flow from lungs to heart
- Mixing oxygenated and deoxygenated blood
- Total disconnection of pulmonary and systemic circulations

SYMPTOMS AND SIGNS IN CARDIAC DISEASE

- Central cyanosis
- Usually limited signs of respiratory distress
- Murmur, in the minority
- Hepatomegaly
- Poor perfusion seen as white peripheries

INVESTIGATIONS

- Chest X-ray
  - oligaemia/plethora/congenital anomaly
  - 'classic' appearance (e.g. 'boot shaped' heart) is unusual
- Echocardiogram
- 4-limb BP (>20 mmHg difference between an upper and lower limb is abnormal)
- Pre- and postductal saturations (>15% difference is abnormal)
- Nitrogen washout test (carries risk of duct closure: discuss with consultant first) to differentiate between respiratory (parenchymal) and cardiac cause of cyanosis
  - baseline saturation (and blood gas if arterial line in situ)
  - place baby in 100% ambient oxygen for 10 min
  - if there is respiratory pathology, saturations should rise to >95%

IMMEDIATE MANAGEMENT- RESUSCITATION

Call consultant – a cardiac baby presenting collapsed and/or cyanosed is a challenging neonatal emergency

Airway

- Intubate and ventilate all babies presenting profoundly cyanosed or collapsed
- Desaturated stable babies who are not acidotic do not require intubation

Issue 02
Issued: October 2007
Expires: September 2009

Stable babies found to be desaturated on monitoring for a murmur do not require intubation

● If apnoea occurs secondary to a prostaglandin infusion, intubate baby but do not alter infusion

Breathing

● If ventilation required for prostaglandin-induced apnoeas, ventilate in air with PEEP 4-6 cm plus compliant lung ventilation PIP, inspiratory times and rate. See **Ventilation** guideline

● Adjust ventilation to maintain
● $PaCO_2$ 5-6 kPa
● systemic SaO_2 75-85%
● pH ≤7.4

Circulation

● Vascular access with 2 IV cannulae or UVC. See **Umbilical venous catheterisation** guideline

Presence of cyanosis and a murmur suggest baby likely to respond to prostaglandin infusion

● Prostaglandin infusion to maintain ductal patency
● open duct with prostaglandin E_2 (dinoprostone, Prostin E_2) – see **Neonatal Formulary**. Start at 5 nanogram/kg/min, may be increased to 40 nanogram/kg/min – but only on advice of cardiologist

● Monitor blood pressure invasively using a peripheral arterial cannula, not UAC

● Titrate infusion to keep to SaO_2 >75% and BP mean not above the gestation in weeks for first 48 hr (a 34 week baby should have a mean BP of 34 mmHg)

● need to balance pulmonary and systemic circulations:
 – SaO_2 too high compromises LV output and worsens hypotension
 – BP too high may reduce pulmonary blood flow and SaO_2

● Assess cardiac output, it is likely to be low when:
● tachycardia persists
● BP remains low
● acidosis persists
● peripheral perfusion poor (white peripheries)
● ensure prostaglandin infusion adequate

● When cardiac output low:
● ensure adequate intravascular volume
● correct anaemia
● inotropes may be required for hypotension

SUBSEQUENT MANAGEMENT-TRANSFER

It is imperative that baby is kept warm and normoglycaemic

● Discuss further management and transfer with regional cardiac centre

● Babies who respond to a prostaglandin infusion do not need transferring out-of-hours

● Appropriately skilled medical and nursing staff are necessary for transfer

Intubation

An intubated baby requires a cardiac centre ITU bed – do not intubate routinely for transfer

● Intubate if:
● continuing metabolic acidosis and poor perfusion
● long-distance transfer necessary
● inotropic support needed
● apnoea occurring
● recommended by cardiac team

DISCHARGE FROM CARDIAC CENTRE

Patient may go home or return to a paediatric ward or neonatal unit, possibly on a prostaglandin infusion whilst awaiting surgery or for continuing care after a palliative procedure (e.g. septostomy)

Management Plan

● Regardless of outcome, obtain a management plan from cardiac centre, defining:

○ acceptable vital signs (e.g. saturations)

○ medication, including dosage

○ follow-up arrangements

Issue 02
Issued: October 2007
Expires: September 2009

If relatives disagree profoundly with the clinical assessment made by medical and nursing staff, involve consultant at early stage

GUIDANCE

Preparation

- If a baby (especially a very pre-term neonate) appears likely to die, discuss with on-call consultant

- On-call consultant will assess the situation clinically and write in notes, especially with regard to prognosis

Discussion with parents

- Discuss clinical situation, and baby's best interests, with parents
- ensure nurse present and document discussion in notes
- Most parents will accept situation but will be upset, and may display denial, guilt or anger
- Ask parents whether they wish a religious or spiritual person to be involved

Second opinion

- In difficult clinical situations, where parents are unable to accept consultant's assessment, seek second opinion from consultant on Neonatal Unit

Further support

- If parents do not accept second clinical assessment:
- discuss with medical director or deputy
- discuss with parents the option of a further opinion from consultant neonatologist from another unit in neonatal network

- inform communications manager regarding possible press coverage
- Seek advice from your Trust's legal advisers via medico-legal department or on-call manager
- Timescale for events may vary with individual babies from under 24 hr to over 1-2 weeks

Good documentation is essential

DEATH

When a baby dies there are formalities to be completed, but these should be handled as sensitively as possible to minimise the emotional trauma to parents, whose wishes (within reason) should be respected and who should be guided carefully through the necessary procedures

Ensure baby's correct registered name on all documentation

Formal arrangements

- Hospital general office/bereavement office will offer advice about registration and funeral arrangements and issue death certificate
- Check whether death must be reported to the coroner (see local policy)
- if uncertain, check with local coroner
- If the death need not be reported to coroner, complete appropriate death certificate (according to baby's age) so that it can accompany the baby or can be given to parents (according to local policy)
- Parents will make appointment with Registrar of Births and Deaths to deliver death certificate

- Registrar of Births and Deaths will issue certificate of authority for burial or cremation, which should be given to:
- hospital general office, if hospital is burying baby
- funeral director handling burial, if parents are making their own arrangements

Saying goodbye

- Parents may request a blessing or naming ceremony by a religious representative

- Ensure all the family are allowed time and privacy with the baby

- Provide a keep-sake box, which may include photos, hand and foot prints, lock of hair, cot card, etc

- if parental ethnicity and religious beliefs allow, offer parents opportunity to wash, dress and prepare baby

- A small toy or other memento may accompany baby to mortuary

Baby transfer

- Special arrangements will be made to transport baby to mortuary according to local hospital policy (baby must be refrigerated within 5 hr of death if autopsy required)

- allow parents to accompany baby if they wish

- some may prefer to see their baby on the neonatal unit or chapel of rest

- Parents may take baby's body directly from the neonatal unit, once appropriate documentation has been completed. Where babies are taken will depend upon religious belief of parents or to designated funeral director. In all cases strict adherence of local hospital policy must apply

Parent support

- Offer bereavement support information (e.g. Stillbirth and Neonatal Death Society; SANDS) or counsellor

- Offer parents follow-up by consultant or trained nurse

- Consultant in charge will see baby's parents the day after death or as soon as possible and may discuss consent for post-mortem examination (see www.hta.gov.uk for guidance)

Communication

- Inform obstetrician, referring hospital (if appropriate), GP and health visitor that death has occurred

Issue 02
Issued: October 2007
Expires: September 2009

DECISION TO DISCHARGE

- Responsibility of consultant in charge of unit
- Medical and nursing staff to agree discharge date with parents or persons with parental responsibility
- Nursing team perform majority of discharge requirements

DISCHARGE CHECKLIST

Where appropriate, the following must be achieved before discharge:

Parental competencies

- Administration of medications when required
- Baby cares (e.g. nappy changes, top and tailing, bathing etc)
- Feeding
- Nasogastric tube feeding where necessary

Parent education (according to local practice)

- In addition to above, it is best practice to offer parents education on:
- basic infant resuscitation (practical demonstration)
- respiratory syncytial virus (give BLISS leaflet)
- immunisations, if not already received (give national leaflet)

Communication

- If local practice, complete red book and give to parents
- Give parents copy of discharge summary and time to ask questions after they have read it
- Inform:
- health visitor (HV) of discharge
- community midwife if baby <10 days old
- GP
- community neonatal or paediatric team as required locally

Procedures/investigations check

- Newborn blood spot taken (6 days)
- Newborn blood spot repeated at 36 weeks corrected age or due date
- Inform community team of need to repeat newborn blood spot if required
- When immunisation (2, 3 and 4 month) not complete in preterm infants, inform GP and health visitor
- Arrange appointment for BCG vaccination if required – see **BCG immunisation** guideline
- Complete audiology screening
- Where required, confirm ophthalmology appointment date – see **Retinopathy of prematurity (ROP) screening** guideline

General

- Check home and discharge addresses and confirm name of GP with parents
- Complete admission book entries
- Ensure breast pump returned

Medical team

- Complete discharge summary by date of discharge
- Complete MANNERS dataset by date of discharge
- Answer parents' questions after they have read summary
- Ensure all follow-up appointments made (see over)
- Perform discharge examination and record

Issue 02
Issued: October 2007
Expires: September 2009

Follow-up appointments

- Ensure these are written on discharge summary and in red book
- Likely appointments could include:
- neonatal/paediatric consultant out-patients
- ophthalmology screening
- audiology referral
- cranial ultrasound
- brain MR scan
- physiotherapy
- dietitian
- community paediatrician
- child development centre
- BCG immunisation or palivizumab
- open access to children's wards
- planned future admission (e.g. for immunizations)
- planned future review for blood taking, wound review
- tertiary consultant out-patients

Issue 02
Issued: October 2007
Expires: September 2009

RECOGNITION AND ASSESSMENT

Definition

- New nomenclature – disorders of sexual development (DSD)
- Congenital conditions in which development of chromosomal, gonadal or anatomical sex is atypical, most commonly:
- congenital adrenal hyperplasia
- gonadal dysgenesis
- partial androgen insensitivity
- For DSD classification – see **Supporting information**

Factors suggesting DSD

- Overt genital ambiguity (e.g. chloacal extrosphy)
- Apparent female genitalia with enlarged clitoris, posterior labial fusion or inguinal/labial masses
- Apparent male genitalia with bilateral undescended testes, isolated perineal hypospadias, mild hypospadias with undescended testis
- Family history of DSD [e.g. complete androgen insensitivity syndrome (CAIS)]
- Discordance between genital appearance and pre-postnatal karyotype

> **Beware of pseudo-ambiguity (atrophic vulva and clitoral oedema) in growth-restricted or preterm female infants**

PRINCIPLES OF MANAGEMENT

> *This is a medical emergency: involve consultant immediately*

- Avoid gender assignment before expert evaluation
- Consultant to discuss with parents
- always use the term 'baby' and avoid using 'he', 'she' or, most importantly, 'it'
- advise parents about delaying registration and informing wider family and friends until gender assignment complete
- Link with expert centre for appropriate evaluation
- Communicate openly with family
- Respect family concerns and culture
- DSD is not shameful
- potential for well-adjusted individual and a functioning member of society
- best course of action may not be clear initially
- parents need time to understand sexual development

First line investigations

- Karyotype (urgent)
- Imaging
- abdominal and pelvic ultrasound by an experienced paediatric sonographer
- 17 hydroxyprogesterone (delay until day 4-5 to allow maternal hormonal effects to decline)
- Testosterone and oestradiol
- LH, FSH
- U&E
- Cortisol

Further investigations (locally and/or in conjunction with specialist advice)

- dHT (dihydrotestosterone)
- DHEA (dihydroepiandrostenedione)
- Androstenedione
- Urine steroid analysis
- ACTH
- LHRH hCG stimulation
- ACTH stimulation test
- AMH (anti-mullerian hormone) imaging studies
- Biopsy of gonad
- Molecular genetic studies (e.g. for CAIS)

TREATMENT

- Check electrolytes and glucose
- Specific treatment is dependent on many factors and the diagnosis
- discuss with specialist

Issue 02
Issued: October 2007
Expires: September 2009

INDICATIONS

Routine discharge check

A thorough physical examination of every newborn baby is good practice and forms a core item of the UK Child Health Surveillance programme

- Ideally performed >24 hr old to:
- confirm apparent normality
- detect abnormalities/anomalies
- provide a plan of care
- provide reassurance to parents and opportunity for discussion

EQUIPMENT

- Maternal and baby notes
- Stethoscope
- Ophthalmoscope

AIMS

- Identify congenital malformations
- Identify common neonatal problems and initiate management
- Continue with screening, begun antenatally, to identify need for specific interventions (e.g. immunisation)

PRE-PROCEDURE

- Before undertaking clinical examination, familiarise yourself with maternal history and pregnancy records, including:
- maternal medical, obstetric and social history
- paternal medical history, if appropriate
- family health, history of congenital diseases
- identify drugs mother may have taken during pregnancy and in labour
- health of siblings
- identify pregnancy complications, blood tests, ultrasound scans, admissions to hospital
- identify maternal blood group, presence of antibodies, serology results for sexually transmitted diseases
- duration of labour, type of delivery, duration of rupture or membranes, condition of liquor
- check 3 blood vessels identified in umbilical cord (requires renal USS)
- Apgar scores and whether resuscitation required
- birth weight, gestational age, head circumference

Consent and preparation

- Introduce yourself to mother and gain verbal consent. Ask about particular concerns
- Ensure baby kept warm and examined in quiet environment

PROCEDURE

Skin examination

- Texture
- Hydration
- Rashes – including erythema toxicum, milia, miliaria, staphylococcal skin infection, candida
- Pigmented lesions: naevi, Mongolian blue spots, birth marks, café au lait
- Bruises – traumatic lesions, petechiae
- Cutis aplasia
- Tufts of hair not on head
- Vascular lesions: haemangioma, port wine stain, simple naevus
- Colour – pink/cyanosis/jaundice/pallor/plethora
- Acrocyanosis
- Cutis marmorata

Facial examination

- General facial appearance to identify common syndromes
- **Eyes:**
- shape
- slant
- size
- position
- strabismus
- nystagmus
- **red reflex**
- presence colobomata
- discharges

- **Nose:**
- position, straight septum
- nasal flaring

- **Ears:**
- shape
- position
- tags or pits

- **Mouth:**
- size
- symmetry of movement
- swellings, Epstein's pearls, ranula, tongue tie (for parental reassurance)
- teeth
- cleft palate, hard/soft palate, cleft lip
- sucking
- candida

Skull

- Palpate:
- skull for sutures and shape/craniosynostosis
- swellings on scalp, especially crossing suture lines, cephalhaematoma
- signs of trauma associated with birth – chignon from vacuum extraction
- sutures for ridging or undue separation

Neck

- Swellings
- Movement
- Webbing
- Traumatic lesions from forceps delivery
- Petechiae

Clavicles

- For fracture

Arms and legs

- Position and symmetry of movement
- Swelling and bruising

Hands and feet

- Extra digits
- Syndactyly
- Palmer creases
- Skin tags
- Infected nail beds
- Position and configuration of feet looking for fixed/positional talipes

Hips

- Developmental dysplasia using Ortolani and Barlow's manoeuvres, symmetry of gluteal skin folds (if abnormal or close family history of CDH: refer for hip scan)

Spine

- Curvatures
- Dimples
- Sacrococcygeal pits
- Hairy patches/naevi
- Stigmata on spine

Issue 02
Issued: October 2007
Expires: September 2009

Systems

Examine (inspection, palpation, auscultation) each system

Respiratory system

- Chest shape, asymmetry of rib cage, swellings
- Respiratory rate
- Presence/absence of recession
- Grunting
- Chest movement
- Nasal flaring
- Nipple position, swelling/discharge/extra nipples
- Auscultate for breath sounds

Cardiovascular system

- Skin colour/cyanosis
- Palpate:
- precordium for thrills
- peripheral and femoral pulses for rate and volume
- central perfusion
- Auscultate for heart sounds, murmur(s), rate, rhythm

Gastrointestinal tract

Ask mother how well baby is feeding and whether any vomiting, colour of vomit

- Abdominal shape
- Presence of distension
- Cord stump for discharge or inflammation/umbilical hernia
- Presence and position of anus and patency
- a wink can be produced by touching anal margin to assess anal tone

- Stools passed
- Palpate abdomen for tenderness, masses and palpable liver
- presence or absence of spleen
- Auscultation is not routinely undertaken unless there are abdominal concerns

Genito-urinary system

Ask mother if baby has passed urine, and how frequently

- Inspect appearance of genitalia – ambiguous?

Male genito-urinary system

- Penis size
- Position of urethral meatus. Look for hypospadias
- Inguinal hernia
- Cordee
- Urinary stream
- Scrotum for colour
- Palpate scrotum for presence of two testes and presence of hydrocoele

Female genito-urinary system

- Presence of vaginal discharge (reassure parents about pseudomenstruation)
- Skin tags
- Inguinal hernia
- Proximity of genitalia to anal sphincter
- Routine palpation of kidneys is not always necessary as antenatal scans will have assessed presence

Neurological system

- Before beginning examination, observe baby's posture

- Assess:
- muscle tone, grasp, responses to stimulation
- behaviour
- ability to suck
- limb movements
- cry
- head size in relation to body weight
- spine, presence of sacral pits, midline spinal skin lesions/tufts of hair

- If neurological concerns, initiate Moro and stepping reflexes

- Responses to passive movements:
- pull-to-sit
- ventral suspension

- Palpate anterior fontanelle size (<3 cm x 3 cm) and tone

OUTCOME

Documentation

- Complete neonatal examination record in medical notes and sign and date it. Also complete child health record

- Record any discussion or advice given to parents

Normal examination

- If no concerns raised, reassure parents of apparent normality and advise to seek advice if concerns arise at home

- GP will re-examine baby at 6 weeks old

Abnormal examination

- In first instance, seek advice from neonatal registrar doctor/consultant

- Refer to postnatal ward guidelines for ongoing management

- Refer abnormalities to relevant senior doctor

Issue 02
Issued: October 2007
Expires: September 2009

Exchange transfusion replaces withdrawn baby blood with an equal volume of donor blood

> ***Discuss all cases with neonatal consultant***

INDICATIONS

- Anaemia at birth from blood group incompatibilities
- if no transfusion given in-utero, to remove antibodies and correct anaemia when cord Hb <12 g/dL
- after transfusion in-utero, when Kleihauer test shows predominance of fetal Hb and cord Hb <12 g/dL
- Hyperbilirubinaemia **with haemolysis** – discuss with consultant promptly if bilirubin values approaching guidelines below; a senior decision is required
- term infants – serum bilirubin >340 μmol/L
- preterm infants – serum bilirubin >[(17 x gestational age in weeks)/2] – 100
- anticipate need for exchange transfusion if bilirubin rises faster than 10 μmol/L/hr despite phototherapy
- Hyperbilirubinaemia without haemolysis
- inform consultant when serum bilirubin >gestational age x 10 (exchange transfusion can be withheld below bilirubin values of 510 μmol/L)
- should be used only if phototherapy failing to bring levels under control
- Chronic feto-maternal transfusion
- Disseminated intravascular coagulation

COMPLICATIONS

- Cardiac arrhythmias
- Air embolism
- Necrotizing enterocolitis
- Coagulopathy
- Apnoeas and bradycardia
- Sepsis
- Electrolyte disturbances
- Acidosis due to non-fresh blood
- Thrombocytopenia
- Late hyporegenerative anaemia

PROCEDURE

Prepare

- Ensure full intensive care space and equipment available and ready
- Allocate one doctor/practitioner and one other member of nursing staff, both experienced in exchange transfusion, to care for each baby during the procedure – document their names in baby's notes
- Obtain written consent when possible, and document in baby's notes
- Phototherapy can usually be interrupted during exchange
- Calculate volume of blood to be exchanged – 160 mL/kg (double blood volume) removes 90% of baby red cells and 50% of available intravascular bilirubin
- Order appropriate volume (usually 2 units) of blood from blood bank, stipulating that it must be:
- cross-matched against mother's blood group and antibody status, and (if requested by your blood bank) baby blood group
- CMV-negative
- irradiated (shelf-life 24 hr) for any baby who has had an in-utero blood transfusion
- as fresh as possible, and certainly no more than 4 days old
- for 'exchange transfusion' (haematocrit 0.5-0.6), not SAG-M blood

Issue 02
Issued: October 2007
Expires: September 2009

Prepare baby

- Empty stomach using nasogastric tube
- Allow nil by mouth and start appropriate intravenous infusion
- Pay attention to thermoregulation, particularly if procedure to be performed under radiant heater
- Commence continuous cardiac, temperature and saturation monitoring

Monitor and document

- Blood pressure every 15 min throughout exchange

> **If there is any change in baby's cardiorespiratory status, pause the exchange by priming catheter with donor blood, which will not clot. Discuss with consultant**

Prepare blood

- Set up blood warmer early (aim for 37°C)
- Check blood units as per hospital policy
- Connect donor blood to filter and prime blood giving set
- Connect to 4-way (if using UVC) or 3-way tap (outside the warmer) as indicated
- Ensure donor blood well mixed before and throughout exchange

Technique

- Ensure working area sterile

Either

- Insert UVC (see **Umbilical venous catheterisation** guideline) and confirm position. Use **UVC 'push-pull' technique** below for exchange

OR

- Insert peripheral venous ('in route') and arterial ('out route') catheters. Use **peripheral venous and arterial catheters – 'continuous' technique** below for exchange

UVC 'push-pull' technique

- Connect catheter bag (using Vygon connector) and donor blood to 4-way tap and 4-way tap to UVC
- Remove 10 mL baby blood from UVC using syringe
- Send first sample for serum bilirubin, full blood count, blood culture, blood glucose, calcium, electrolytes, coagulation and liver function tests
- when exchange performed for reasons other than known blood group antibodies, send blood for G6PD screening and viral serology
- Replace precise volume removed with donor blood, slowly using a syringe
- Each out-in cycle should replace no more than 8.5 mL/kg and take at least 5 min; start with smaller aliquots (10 mL) and increase to 20 mL (if baby stable and weight allows) only after 30 min. As a guide:
  - birth weight <1000 g use 5 mL aliquots
  - birth weight 1000-2000 g use 10 mL aliquots
  - birth weight >2000 g use 20 mL aliquots
- Discard 'out' baby blood into catheter bag
- Continue out-in cycles every 5 min (maximum aliquot with each cycle) until complete
- Send last 'out' baby blood sample for serum bilirubin, full blood count, blood culture, blood glucose, calcium and electrolytes

Peripheral venous and arterial catheters – 'continuous' technique

● Connect catheter bag, using Vygon connector, to 3-way tap attached to arterial line extension

Never leave arterial line open to the catheter bag

● Connect donor blood to the venous catheter

● Remove 10 mL of baby's blood from arterial line and send for tests as listed above under **UVC 'push-pull' technique**

● Start venous infusion as fast as peripheral cannulae will allow up to maximum flow rate of 10 x 8.5 mL/kg/hr

● Remove 'out' aliquots of baby's blood from arterial line every 5 min to match volume of donor blood being infused into venous line

● Observe limb distal to arterial line at all times and document appearance. **If concerned, pause exchange and discuss with consultant**

● Continue steps as above but note that continuous 'in' cycle requires removal of 'out' aliquots only every 5 min

● Umbilical artery catheter may be used as a last resort

● If exchange stopped >2-3 min, discontinue procedure and ensure all lines are flushed

AFTERCARE

Immediate

● When Hb and bilirubin in final 'out' sample known, check with consultant before removing all lines

● Complete documentation (volumes in/out, and all observations)

● Recommence phototherapy

● Recommence feeds 4-6 hr after completion

● Monitor blood sugar 4 hrly until acceptable on 2 consecutive occasions

● Update parents

Intermediate

● In babies receiving antibiotics, a repeat dose may be required – discuss with consultant

● Delayed Guthrie spot collection will be indicated, as directed by regional centre

Follow-up

● All babies who have undergone exchange transfusion should have developmental follow up

EXTRAVASATION INJURIES • 1/2

RECOGNITION AND ASSESSMENT

- Extravasation injuries occur when there is leakage of intravenous infusates into surrounding tissues, and can lead to tissue necrosis. The degree of injury depends on the nature of fluid extravasated

- Fluids commonly causing tissue damage include:

- intravenous glucose >10% concentration

- fluids containing calcium, potassium, THAM (trometamol) or sodium bicarbonate (e.g. total parenteral nutrition)

- Preterm babies are at particular risk owing to immature nature of skin and reduced integrity of venous walls

SYMPTOMS AND SIGNS

- Swelling and/or induration and/or discolouration and/or pain

- Tenderness at IV access site

- Raised infusion pressure if pressure sensitive pump used

PREVENTION

- Use central line for administering fluids likely to cause tissue damage on extravasation

- Use pressure-sensitive pumps and set appropriate alarm limits

- Monitor IV access sites hrly

- Determine whether additives are needed if using peripheral infusions. Do not use unnecessary additives

- Use transparent dressings to secure percutaneous devices

- Avoid name tags in limbs with IV line to avoid tourniquet effect in event of extravasation

TREATMENT

- Stop infusions

- Aspirate fluid if possible through cannula

- Then remove percutaneous device

- Apply a warm compress to disperse extravasated fluid

- Examine site for injury and document findings accurately in notes, including:

- time

- site

- size

- areas of necrosis

- risk of infection

- status of limb proximal and distal to the site

- Obtain photographs of wound, with scale if possible

- Complete incident form

- Discuss with parents at earliest opportunity

- In term and older infants, involve plastic surgeons at an early stage

Dressing

- Use Duoderm to dress wound

- Dressing must not impair limb movement and must cover affected area only

- Apply Hydrogel to wound to reduce scarring

- Document status of wound with each dressing change

Hyaluronidase

- Not recommended for extravasation of vasoconstrictive medications or if site infected

- Use only by consultant or senior middle grade staff, and within 1-2 hr of extravasation

Issue 02
Issued: October 2007
Expires: September 2009

- Dissolve 1 ampoule (1500 units per ampoule) with 1 mL water for injection to make solution of 1500 units/mL

- Using aseptic technique, inject 500-1000 units beneath area of damaged skin

- For large lesions:

- using a scalpel, make 4 small incisions around periphery of extravasated site

- insert a blunt Verres needle, or a pink cannula with the needle removed, into each incision in turn, inject hyaluronidase and irrigate the damaged tissue with 25-100 mL of sodium chloride 0.9% per incision

- sodium chloride should flow freely out of the other incisions

- massage out any excess fluid using gentle manipulation

- cover with paraffin gauze for 24-48 hr

INTRODUCTION

- Outcomes for premature babies at borderline of viability generally improve with each additional week of gestational age

- estimation of gestational age confirmed by ultrasound when carried out in first trimester of pregnancy

- Discussion with parents, before birth if possible, to precede any action

MANAGEMENT

- An experienced paediatrician to be present at delivery of extremely premature babies (<28 completed weeks gestation) and make confirmatory assessment of gestational age and condition of baby

25 weeks gestation and above

- Unless baby has a severe abnormality incompatible with any significant period of survival, initiate intensive care and admit to neonatal intensive care unit

<25 weeks gestation

- Discuss with parents national and local statistical evidence for survival in babies with range of disabilities found in this age group

- explain that statistics indicate most babies born <25 weeks gestation will die

Between 24 weeks, 0 days and 24 weeks, 6 days gestation

- Unless parents and clinicians agree that, in view of baby's condition (or likely condition), it is not in his/her best interests to start intensive care, provide full, invasive, intensive care and support from birth and admit to neonatal intensive care unit

Between 23 weeks, 0 days and 23 weeks, 6 days gestation

- Give precedence to parents' wishes regarding resuscitation and invasive intensive care treatment. However, when condition indicates baby will not survive for long, clinicians are not legally obliged to proceed with treatment that is wholly contrary to their clinical judgement, if they consider treatment would be futile

- as a first step, determine whether baby is suffering, whether any suffering can be alleviated, and likely burden placed on baby by intensive care treatment

- where parents would prefer clinical team to make decision about initiation of intensive care, clinicians must determine what constitutes appropriate care

- where it has not been possible to discuss a baby's treatment with the mother and, where appropriate, her partner, before the birth, clinical team should consider offering full invasive intensive care until baby's condition and treatment can be discussed with parents

Issue 02
Issued: October 2007
Expires: September 2009

Between 22 weeks, 0 days and 22 weeks, 6 days gestation

- Standard practice should be not to resuscitate a baby and this would normally **not** be considered or proposed

- If parents request resuscitation, and reiterate this request, discuss risks and long-term outcomes with an experienced paediatrician before attempting resuscitation and offering intensive care

- Treating clinicians must all agree that this is an exceptional case where resuscitation is in a baby's best interests

Below 22 weeks gestation

- Resuscitation should never occur in routine clinical practice

- any attempt to resuscitate babies born at this gestational age should take place only within the context of an approved research study

> *When intensive care not given, clinical team must provide palliative care until baby dies*

Further information

For full Nuffield council on bioethics report critical care decisions in fetal and neonatal medicine: ethical issues see
http://www.nuffieldbioethics.org

INDICATIONS

- Birth weight ≤1500 g
- Gestation <32 weeks
- Requiring IPPV or CPAP for more than a few hours
- Significant cranial ultrasound abnormality
- cystic PVL or IVH with significant ventricular dilation defined by consultant following final scan on NICU
- Acute neonatal encephalopathy grade 2 or 3
- Seizures – of whatever cause
- Neonatal meningitis
- Exchange transfusion for any reason
- Major congenital anomalies
- Consultant discretion

PROCEDURE

Refer to neonatal (NICU) clinic

Minimum follow up:

- EDD + 6 weeks
  neurological examination
  Ht, Wt, OFC
- EDD + 4 months
  developmental examination
  Ht, Wt, OFC
- EDD + 8 months
  developmental examination
  Ht, Wt, OFC
- EDD + 12 months
  developmental examination
  Ht, Wt, OFC
- EDD + 18 months
  developmental examination
  Ht, Wt, OFC
- EDD + 2 years
  developmental examination
  Ht, Wt, OFC

- Some babies may require additional appointments.

FURTHER MANAGEMENT AT CLINIC

Neurodevelopmental problems identified

- Refer to child development centre
- Refer to patch consultant community paediatrician
- referral may be made at time problem identified or later if this is more appropriate for the family
- arrange back-up appointment for NICU clinic for parents to cancel if they have received community appointment
- If child >18 months old, refer also to pre-school forum
- copy of most recent neonatal clinic letter and brief covering letter are sufficient
- Consider referral for social work advice about benefits, etc.

Babies with problems identifiable early

- **For babies with** Down's syndrome, severe hypoxic ischaemic encephalopathy or at consultant discretion, involve patch community paediatric consultant and preschool therapy team early, before discharge if appropriate
- For babies with concurrent medical problems (e.g. cardiac problem, chronic lung disease), arrange joint follow up with neonatal consultant – decided on individual basis following discussions between community and neonatal consultants
- Refer visually- and hearing-impaired children to community paediatric consultant

Issue 02
Issued: October 2007
Expires: September 2009

High-risk patients reaching 2 years without an identified neurodevelopmental problem

● If ≤32 weeks gestation or ≤1000 g birth weight, and/or significant cranial ultrasound abnormality, refer to patch community consultant for Griffiths' developmental assessment, if available

GASTRO-OESOPHAGEAL REFLUX (GOR)
• 1/2

Definition

- Passive transfer of gastric contents into the oesophagus owing to transient or chronic relaxation of the lower oesophageal sphincter

Symptoms

- Frequent vomiting after feeds in otherwise healthy baby
- Recurrent desaturations in ventilated babies (exclude BPD spells)
- Chronic lung disease of prematurity may be worsened by recurrent aspiration caused by GOR

Risk factors

- Immaturity of the lower oesophageal sphincter
- Chronic relaxation of the sphincter
- Increased abdominal pressure
- Gastric distension
- Hiatus hernia
- Oesophageal dysmotility
- Neuro-developmental abnormalities

Differential diagnosis

- Suspect cow's milk protein intolerance (CMPI) in babies who are formula bottle fed and have recurrent vomiting and irritability despite appropriate management of GOR

INVESTIGATIONS

- Litmus test (pH paper - on two occasions) for acid in oropharyngeal secretions (OPS) but not after stimulation for apnoea or bradycardia which can cause a GOR episode and not immediately after a feed

- 24 hr pH monitoring is of limited value in preterm babies. Perform in cases where repeated apnoea/bradycardia is resistant to other measures

MANAGEMENT

Position

- Head upwards – at an angle of 30°
- Nurse baby prone or in left lateral position

Feeding

- Frequent low volume feeds
- Avoid overfeeding
- Infant Gaviscon (half dual sachet)
- breastfed: give during or after a feed (add 5 mL sterile water/milk to make a paste, then add another 5-10 mL and give with a spoon)
- bottle fed: add to at least 115 mL of milk
- NG fed: make up with 5 mL water and give 1 mL per 25 mL of feed

Caution: Gaviscon contains sodium 0.92 mmol/half a dual sachet

- If symptoms persist, change to Instant Carobel (will thicken cold or with hand-warm milk). Add 2 scoops to 100 mL shake well and leave for 3-4 min to thicken. Shake feed again and give immediately. Take care that thickened liquid does not block fine bore nasogastric tube

Warning: do not give Gaviscon and Carobel together as both these agents will cause the milk to become too thick leading to unnecessary complications such as milk curd (mechanical) intestinal obstruction or NEC

Issue 02
Issued: October 2007
Expires: September 2009

Drugs

- If above measures fail, add domperidone 300 micrograms/kg 4-8 hrly

- If pain secondary to reflux oesophagitis causes irritability/refusal to feed, add ranitidine 2 mg/kg 8 hrly orally or 0.5 mg/kg IV 12 hrly <32 wks or 6 hrly ≥32 wks (as infusion over 10-15 min)

Caution - ranitidine can increase incidence of NEC

Other measures

- If symptoms persist, consider other measures in discussion with senior consultant e.g.

- omeprazole 0.7 mg/kg/day

- erythromycin 4 mg/kg four times daily

- cow's milk protein-free formula (in artificially fed infants)

- some neonates with suspected CMPI, are also allergic to hydrolysate formula and will respond to an amino acid-based formula

DEFINITION

- Herniation of intra-abdominal contents (mostly bowel) via a full thickness abdominal wall defect, situated immediately adjacent to the umbilicus

ANTENATAL

- Usually an isolated abnormality
- Fetus is at risk of:
- in-utero growth retardation
- non-reassuring fetal heart trace
- other organ anomalies (uncommonly)
- Counsel mothers antenatally and decide place of delivery and preferred surgical unit
- discuss possibility of alternative surgical units

Labour and delivery

- Not a contraindication to vaginal delivery
- If a woman presents in labour and not able/not planned for in-utero transfer, inform neonatal consultant on-call
- Contact surgical centre when mother in labour or in unlikely event of planned section
- Introduce yourself to parents
- Prepare for delivery – see below

POSTNATAL

On labour ward

- Resuscitate if necessary
- Examine baby
- Pass large bore NG tube, aspirate gastric contents to decompress the stomach and leave on free drainage
- Examine intestines:
- note colour of bowel
- note presence of any narrowing/strictures

- straighten mesentery to avoid twisting that will limit vascular supply
- Cover and support intestines with cling film from upper chest to lower abdomen, holding intestines in central position
- ensure intestines are visible
- do not wrap cling film tightly as this will reduce perfusion
- alternatively, use gastroschisis bag, if available in your unit
- Place baby in right lateral position (to prevent intestinal ischaemia)
- Transfer to NNU

> **If you have any concern about the bowel, seek senior advice**

On neonatal unit

- Start IV fluids: glucose 10% and sodium chloride 0.18% 90 mL/kg/day
- Replace nasogastric tube losses with sodium chloride 0.9%
- Give sodium chloride 0.9% 20 mL/kg over 30 min. Repeat if bowel remains or becomes dusky/blue
- Start antibiotics:
- cefuroxime 25 mg/kg IV 12 hrly
- metronidazole – loading dose 15 mg/kg IV over 10 min, then 7.5 mg/kg IV 12 hrly
- Vitamin K IM – See **Neonatal Formulary** for doses
- Inform surgical team of delivery and status of bowel

COMMUNICATION AND FOLLOW-UP

- Keep parents informed at all times
- When stable, transfer promptly to paediatric surgical unit with transfer letter detailing neonatal consultant name for contact
- send copy of neonatal unit transfer summary to on-call neonatologist and obstetrician

Issue 02
Issued: October 2007
Expires: September 2009

RECOGNITION AND ASSESSMENT

Definition

Group B streptococcus (GBS) disease is classified as follows:

- Early onset within first 7 days of life:
- often with rapid onset in first hours after birth
- risk can be reduced by giving maternal intrapartum antibiotics
- Late onset cannot be prevented

- Signs of early GBS infection are non specific and could include
- grunting/tachypnoea/respiratory distress
- pallor/cyanosis
- lethargy
- irritability
- poor feeding
- tachycardia/bradycardia
- hypotension

Risk factors for maternal treatment

- Previous infant with invasive GBS disease

or

- GBS bacteriuria this pregnancy

or

- 2 or more of the following present:
- GBS on vaginal swab in this pregnancy
- fever ≥38°C during labour
- prematurity <37 weeks
- rupture of membranes >18 hr

PRE DELIVERY MANAGEMENT

- Vaginal delivery: give **mother** benzylpenicillin 3 g IV, then 1.5 g 4 hrly during labour
- if allergic to penicillin, give clindamycin 900 mg IV 8 hrly until delivery
- give intrapartum antibiotics as soon as possible after the onset of labour and at least 2 hours before delivery
- Caesarean section: no investigation or treatment necessary if:
- intact membranes, no suspicion of chorio-amnionitis and no maternal fever
- chorio-amnionitis is treated with broad-spectrum antibiotics which will cover GBS

POST DELIVERY MANAGEMENT

- If one baby from multiple birth has GBS disease, treat other babies empirically
- **If signs of neonatal sepsis**, at any gestation, perform a septic screen which includes FBC, CRP, blood culture, urine culture, CXR and lumbar puncture if baby will tolerate it. Give empirical treatment with benzylpenicillin and gentamicin (see **Infection** guideline). Duration of therapy based on clinical assessment, results and local policy
- Routine post natal antibiotic prophylaxis is not indicated
- In a term baby, if maternal antibiotics were indicated but not given appropriately (e.g. at least 2 hrs prior to delivery), observe for 12 hr, then discharge if baby remains well
- observation does not need admission to neonatal unit
- In the preterm neonate whose maternal antibiotics were indicated but not given appropriately (local guidelines may vary), do limited septic screen (FBC, CRP, blood culture), start penicillin and

gentamicin, and review after 48 hours with culture results

● Breastfeeding does not increase the risk of neonatal GBS disease

● **The following are NOT indications for starting antibiotics:**

● vaginal GBS before labour if mother asymptomatic

● vaginal GBS in previous pregnancy

● term rupture of membranes when not in labour

● a well baby more than 12 hr after delivery even if risk factors present. 90% of babies with early GBS sepsis will have signs within 12 hours of delivery

INTRODUCTION

- It is important to identify children with hearing loss as early in life as possible. The NHS Newborn Hearing Screening Programme (NHSP) ensures this happens for all newborn babies in England

INDICATIONS

Well babies

- Unless unequivocal evidence of hearing impairment (e.g. unilateral or bilateral atresia), all babies must undergo newborn hearing screening

- for babies with unequivocal evidence of hearing impairment, arrange appointment for audiological assessment

- local co-ordinator is responsible for discussing with parent(s) in conjunction with paediatricians and midwives

- For well babies in an area that undertakes newborn hearing screening in hospital, complete as far as possible before discharge

- if process not completed in hospital, arrange outpatient appointment/primary care clinic appointment/home visit to complete

- Well babies in an area that undertakes newborn hearing screening in the community will be offered screening in a clinic/home visit

- Complete screening, as a rule, within 1 visit

Babies on NICU or SCBU for >48 hr

- Unless unequivocal evidence of hearing impairment (e.g. unilateral or bilateral atresia), all babies on NICU to receive newborn hearing screening using NICU protocol

- Babies in 'transitional care' should undergo NICU protocol only if they have been on NICU or SCBU >48 hrs; otherwise, follow the 'well baby' protocol

TIMING OF SCREENING

- Screen as close to discharge as possible, when well enough to test and preferably once any major medical treatment, ototoxic or other drug treatment complete

- may not always be possible (e.g. babies on reducing doses of morphine may require testing on last day of drug treatment)

- Never screen at <34 weeks gestational age

- Do not screen babies transferring to another NICU/SCBU unless they meet criteria described in **Indications**

- Complete screening of babies on SCBU or NICU >48 hr by 44 weeks gestational age

CONSENT AND INFORMATION

- Before screening, person performing screening or staff with national or local NHSP training should:

- give NICU leaflet to parent(s) and provide information orally

- obtain informed written consent

- file consent and decline forms in baby's notes

- Offer parent(s) opportunity to be present and arrange suitable time

- Where parent(s) do not wish to be present, arrange a time to relay results in person

- if screener unable to give results in person, they may be given by another member of staff with national or local NHSP training who is able to contact local co-ordinator if further information required

FURTHER INFORMATION

● Detailed information available from
NHSP website:
http://www.nhsp.info/index.php

Local details

Russells Hall Hospital, Dudley **Staffordshire General Hospital** **Shrewsbury & Telford Hospitals** **New Cross Hospital, Wolverhampton**	Carried out by health visitor in the community
Manor Hospital, Walsall **University Hospital of North** **Staffordshire**	Within hospital while inpatient, usually at bedside

Issue 02
Issued: October 2007
Expires: September 2009

DEFINITION

- Congestive cardiac failure occurs when the heart is unable to pump sufficient blood to meet metabolic demands of body tissues
- cause can be cardiac or non-cardiac

Differential diagnosis

Non-cardiac

- Sepsis
- Asphyxia
- Anaemia
- Polycythaemia
- Fluid overload
- AV malformation
- BPD (bronchopulmonary dysplasia)

Cardiac

- LVOT obstruction
- Left-to-right shunt
- Arrhythmia

Left ventricular outflow tract obstruction (LVOT)

- Hypoplastic left heart syndrome
- Critical aortic stenosis
- Coarctation
- Interrupted aortic arch

Clinical differentiation between an obstructed systemic circulation and severe sepsis is extremely difficult as a murmur and weak pulses can be common to both.

In infant in extremis, presence of abnormal pulses alone is sufficient indication to start a prostaglandin infusion until a cardiac lesion has been excluded by echocardiography

SYMPTOMS AND SIGNS OF CARDIAC FAILURE

- Tachycardia
- Tachypnoea
- Hepatomegaly
- Excessive weight gain
- Hypotension
- Murmur
- Abnormal femoral pulses
- in obstructive left heart lesions, femoral pulses may not be absent if duct still patent
- weak femoral pulses are significant

INVESTIGATIONS

- Chest X-ray
- fluid overload
- Echo
- Four-limb BP (a difference of >20mmHg between an upper and lower limb is significant)
- Pre- and postductal saturations
- postductal saturations can be considerably lower than preductal in aortic arch defects (a difference of >15% is significant)

INVESTIGATIONS

If left sided obstructive lesion suspected, do not give diuretics, treat with inotropes and volume support

Resuscitation

Airway

- Intubate and ventilate babies presenting collapsed or with obvious cyanosis in association with cardiac failure

- Routine intubation not indicated
- If apnoea occurs secondary to a prostaglandin infusion, intubate baby but do not alter infusion

Breathing

- See **Ventilation** guideline
- Ventilate with PEEP 4-6 cm
- Adjust ventilation to maintain:
- $PaCO_2$ 5-6 kPa
- pH $\leq$7.4

Circulation

- Vascular access with 2 IV cannulae or UVC. See **Umbilical venous catheterisation** guideline

> **Presence of cyanosis and a murmur suggest baby likely to respond to prostaglandin infusion**

- Prostaglandin infusion to maintain ductal patency
- open duct with prostaglandin E_2 (dinoprostone, Prostin E_2) – See **Neonatal Formulary**. Start at 5 nanogram/kg/min, may be increased to 40 nanogram/kg/min – but only on advice of cardiologist
- Monitor blood pressure invasively using a peripheral arterial cannula, not UAC
- Titrate infusion to keep to SaO_2 >75% and BP mean not above the gestation in weeks for first 48 hr (a 34 week baby should have a mean BP of 34 mmHg)
- need to balance pulmonary and systemic circulations:
  – SaO_2 too high compromises LV output and worsens hypotension
  – BP too high may reduce pulmonary blood flow and SaO_2
- Assess cardiac output, it is likely to be low when:
- tachycardia persists

- BP remains low
- acidosis persists
- peripheral perfusion poor (white peripheries)
- ensure prostaglandin infusion adequate
- When cardiac output low:
- ensure adequate intravascular volume
- correct anaemia
- inotropes may be required for hypotension

SUBSEQUENT MANAGEMENT-TRANSFER

> **It is imperative that baby is kept warm and normoglycaemic**

- Discuss further management and transfer with regional cardiac centre
- Babies who respond to a prostaglandin infusion do not need transferring out-of-hours
- Appropriately skilled medical and nursing staff are necessary for transfer

Intubation

> **An intubated baby requires a cardiac centre ITU bed – do not intubate routinely for transfer**

- Intubate if:
- continuing metabolic acidosis and poor perfusion
- long-distance transfer necessary
- inotropic support needed
- apnoea occurring
- recommended by cardiac team

Issue 02
Issued: October 2007
Expires: September 2009

DISCHARGE FROM CARDIAC CENTRE

Patient may go home or return to a paediatric ward or neonatal unit, possibly on a prostaglandin infusion whilst awaiting surgery or for continuing care after a palliative procedure (e.g. septostomy)

Management Plan

- Regardless of outcome, obtain a management plan from cardiac centre, defining:
- acceptable vital signs (e.g. saturations)
- medication, including dosage
- follow-up arrangements

INCREASED LEFT TO RIGHT SHUNT

RECOGNITION AND ASSESSMENT

Definition

- Any lesion causing increased pulmonary blood flow
- Usually presents when pulmonary resistance falls after 48 hr
- Size and type of lesion will influence time of presentation

Differential diagnosis

- AVSD
- Partial AVSD
- VSD

Investigations

- CXR looking for fluid overload
- ECHO

MANAGEMENT

- If in cardiac failure give immediate dose of diuretic
- May require maintenance diuretics
- usually furosemide and amiloride – see **Neonatal Formulary** for dose and administration
- Discuss with cardiac centre for definitive management and follow-up

HEPATITIS B • 1/2

AIMS

- Immediate postnatal treatment of neonates exposed to maternal Hepatitis B (acute infection or chronic carrier)
- Prevention of infection in infants at high risk of exposure

PREPARATION

As vaccination is ideally best given immediately after birth, know mother's hepatitis B status **before birth**

Antenatal

- If aware antenatally, inform obstetrician, neonatologist, public health team and GP of plan to immunize
- Hepatitis B immunoglobulin (HBIG) is issued by the Health Protection Agency (HPA) via local consultant microbiologist. Order well in advance of birth

Labour

- Labour ward must inform on-call neonatal team when a mother who is HBsAg +ve arrives in labour or for caesarean section

Postnatal

- For all newborns, check antenatal screening results for mother's tests
- If antenatal testing not done (e.g. concealed pregnancy) request urgent maternal hepatitis B virus surface antigen (HBsAg) test

COMMUNICATION

- Give mother information about hepatitis B, modes of transmission and prevention of spread
- Mother can breastfeed

IMMEDIATE POSTNATAL TREATMENT OF THE BABY

To which babies

Maternal status	Vaccine required by baby	Immunoglobulin required by baby
HBsAg positive, HBeAg positive	Y	Y
HBsAg positive, HBeAg negative, HBe antibody (anti-HBe) negative	Y	Y
HBsAg positive where e markers have not been determined	Y	Y
Acute hepatitis B during pregnancy	Y	Y
HBsAg positive <u>and</u> baby <1.5 kg	Y	Y
HBsAg positive, anti-HBe positive	Y	N
Other high risk group	Y	N

- Hepatitis B vaccine is effective in babies <1.8 kg – give full dose
- Give HBIG and hepatitis B vaccine to babies with birth weight <1.5 kg born to mother with hepatitis B, regardless of mother's HBeAg status
- Hepatitis B vaccine can be given to HIV exposed/infected neonates

Issue 02
Issued: October 2007
Expires: September 2009

When

- Give within 24 hr of birth, ideally as soon as possible after delivery

What

- Give hepatitis B vaccine (e.g. Engerix B) 0.5 mL (10 microgram)
- caution: other brands have different doses (e.g. HBVaxPro Paediatric ® 5 microgram)
- HBIG 2 mL (whole ampoule) 200 units is additionally given for babies of highly infectious mothers (see table above)

How

- Use two separate injection sites for hepatitis B vaccine and HBIG, in anterolateral thighs (not buttocks)
- Give hepatitis B vaccine IM, except in bleeding disorder where it may be given deep subcutaneously

Relationship to other immunisations

- No need to delay BCG following HBIG
- Hepatitis B vaccine can be given with other vaccines, but use separate site – if same limb used, give vaccines >2.5 cm apart

SUBSEQUENT MANAGEMENT

Further doses

- GP to give subsequent doses of hepatitis B vaccine:
- second dose at 1 month
- third dose at 2 months
- fourth dose at 12 months

1 year follow up

- Check child's HBsAg status at one year old (to assess if chronic carrier, or vaccine was effective). This testing can be carried out at the same time as fourth dose
- if a carrier, refer for further management

ROUTINE HEPATITIS IMMUNISATION

To whom

- Hepatitis B immunization is recommended with other routine immunizations for high risk babies born to mothers:
- with partners who are hepatitis B surface antigen (HBsAg) positive
- with partners who are intravenous drug users (even if HBsAg negative)
- who change sexual partners frequently (e.g. commercial sex workers)
- with close family contacts known to be HBsAg positive
- who intend to live in a country with high prevalence of hepatitis B (Africa, Asia, Eastern Europe, Northern Canada, Alaska)

Dose regimen

- Vaccine is given at 0, 1 and 2 months
- A further 12 month dose is recommended for those at continued risk

ANTENATAL

- Discuss infant testing with mothers who have hepatitis C during the antenatal period
- give mother choice of hepatitis C antibody (anti-HCV) testing at 18 months only or hepatitis C virus (HCV) polymerase chain reaction (PCR) at 3 months followed by repeat tests as below
- treatment is not started under 18 months

DOCUMENTATION

- Document Hepatitis C follow-up visits in Red book to ensure health visitor is aware and baby is followed up

BREASTFEEDING

- Mother can breastfeed

POSTNATAL

Mother anti-HCV positive and/or Hepatitis C RNA +ve

Test infant at age 3 months HCV RNA by PCR

-ve → HCV RNA Negative / Infection unlikely

+ve → HCV RNA positive / HCV infection

Test anti-HCV at age 18 months

Repeat test to confirm at 12 months

-ve → Test anti-HCV at age 18 months

+ve → Discuss with regional liver unit

HCV infection +ve → Discuss with regional liver unit

Test anti-HCV at age 18 months:
- +ve → Discuss with regional liver unit
- -ve → Discharge

Issue 02
Issued: October 2007
Expires: September 2009

Decision to initiate HFOV must be made by a consultant. Do not start HFOV unless you have been trained and have demonstrated your competence to do so

INDICATIONS

- Rescue following failure of conventional ventilation
- To reduce barotrauma when conventional ventilator settings are high
- Pulmonary haemorrhage

Less effective in non-homogenous lung disease

Terminology

Frequency	High frequency ventilation rate (Hz, cycles per second)
MAP	Mean airway pressure (cmH$_2$O)
Amplitude	Delta P or power is the variation around the MAP

Mechanism

Oxygenation is dependent on MAP and FiO$_2$	MAP provides constant distending pressure equivalent to CPAP, inflating the lung to constant and optimal lung volume, maximizing area for gas exchange and preventing alveolar collapse in the expiratory phase
Ventilation (CO$_2$ removal)	Ventilation is dependent on amplitude and, to a lesser degree, frequency. Thus, when using HFOV, CO$_2$ elimination and oxygenation are independent

MANAGEMENT

Preparation for HFOV

- If there is significant leak around the ET tube, insert a larger one
- Optimize blood pressure and perfusion – complete any necessary volume replacement and start inotropes, if necessary, before starting HFOV
- Ensure sedation adequate
- Muscle relaxants are not necessary unless already in use

Initial settings on HFOV

Optimal (high) lung volume strategy (aim to maximize recruitment of alveoli)	● If changing from conventional ventilation, set MAP 2-4 cmH$_2$O above MAP on conventional ventilation ● If starting immediately on HFOV, start with MAP of 8 cmH$_2$O and increase in 1-2 cmH$_2$O increments until optimal SaO$_2$ achieved ● Set frequency to 10 Hz
Low volume strategy (aim to minimize lung trauma)	● Set MAP equal to MAP on conventional ventilation ● Set frequency to 10 Hz ● Adjust amplitude to get an adequate chest wall vibration

● Optimal (high) volume strategy preferred but consider low volume strategy when air leaks

● Obtain early blood gas (within 20 min) and adjust settings as appropriate

● **Change frequency only after discussion with consultant**

Making adjustments once HFOV established

	Poor oxygenation	Overoxygenation	Underventilation	Overventilation
1	Increase FiO$_2$	Decrease FiO$_2$	Increase amplitude	Decrease amplitude
2	Increase MAP (1-2 cmH$_2$O)	Decrease MAP (1-2 cmH$_2$O)	Decrease frequency (1-2 Hz) only if amplitude maximal	Increase frequency (1-2 Hz) only if amplitude minimal

MONITORING

● Amplitude maximal when chest 'wobbling', minimal when movement imperceptible. Frequent blood gas monitoring (every 30-60 min) in early stages of treatment as PaO$_2$ and PaCO$_2$ can change rapidly

● **Chest X-ray**

● within 1 hr to determine baseline lung volume on HFOV (aim for 8-9 ribs) posteriorly above diaphragm

● repeat after 4-6 hr to assess expansion, and again if condition changes acutely

TROUBLE SHOOTING ON HFOV

Chest wall movement

● Suction indicated for diminished chest wall movement indicating airway or ET tube obstruction

● Avoid suction in the first 24 hr of HFOV, unless clinically indicated, and always use an in-line suction device to maintain PEEP

● increase FiO$_2$ following suctioning procedure

● MAP can be temporarily increased by 2-3 cmH$_2$O until oxygenation improves

Issue 02
Issued: October 2007
Expires: September 2009

Low PaO$_2$

- Suboptimal lung recruitment
- increase MAP
- consider CXR
- Over-inflated lung
- check blood pressure
- reduce MAP – does oxygenation improve?
- consider CXR
- ET tube patency
- check head position and exclude kinks in tube
- check for chest movement and breath sounds
- check that there is no water in the ETT/T piece
- Air leak/pneumothorax
- transillumination
- urgent CXR

High PaCO$_2$

- ET tube patency and air leaks (as above)
- Increase amplitude – does chest wall movement increase?
- Increased airway resistance (MAS or BPD) or non-homogenous lung disease – is HFOV appropriate?

Persisting acidosis/hypotension

- Over-distension
- reduce MAP – does oxygenation improve?
- consider CXR

Spontaneous breathing

- Usually not a problem but can indicate suboptimal ventilation (e.g. kinking of ETT)

WEANING

- Reduce FiO$_2$ to <0.4 before weaning MAP (except when overinflation evident)
- Reduce MAP when chest X-ray shows evidence of overinflation (>9 ribs)
- Reduce MAP in 1-2 cm decrements to 8-9 cm 1-2 hrly or as tolerated
- If oxygenation lost during weaning, increase MAP by 3-4 cm and begin weaning again more gradually
- In air leak syndromes (low volume strategy), reducing MAP takes priority over weaning the FiO$_2$
- Wean the amplitude in 4 cmH$_2$O increments
- Do not wean the frequency
- Consider switching to conventional ventilation or extubation to CPAP when MAP <10 cmH$_2$O, amplitude 20-25 and blood gases satisfactory

Maternal to child transmission of HIV can be prevented only if maternal HIV status is known

RECOGNITION AND ASSESSMENT

Maternal blood tests

- Check every mother's HIV antibody test results
- if no result, recommend mother is tested urgently

Neonatal blood tests

- Within 72 hr after birth
- Must arrive at virology laboratory by 1600 hr Mon-Thurs
- At weekends, delay until next working day
- Virology 1.3 mL EDTA (purple top) do not use cord blood for this test
- Send 5 mL EDTA from mother with first specimen
- Send maternal and neonatal samples with single request form
- Request 'Pro-viral retroviral DNA PCR (Colindale)'
- Label forms with 'Danger of infection' stickers

Define RISK to neonate

High risk

- Mother's viral load >50 copies/mL or not known
- Associated risk factors [e.g. prolonged rupture of membranes, premature delivery (<36/40)]; breastfeeding, chorio-amnionitis, placental abruption and fetal scalp monitoring

Low risk group

- Maternal viral load <50 copies/mL

TREATMENT OF NEONATE

Low risk group

- Use NRTI antiretroviral which:
- mother is taking
- is available as syrup
- zidovudine (AZT) or lamivudine (3TC) is suitable
- Ensure supply on labour ward
- Do not delay treatment for blood tests or any other reason
- Start as soon as possible after birth
- Formula feed – provide bottles/sterilizer if necessary

High risk group

- Use zidovudine, and lamivudine for 4 weeks, and nevirapine for 2 weeks

Dosing schedule

Zidovudine

>34 weeks and feeding	4 mg/kg orally 12 hrly
>34 weeks and not tolerating feeds	1.5 mg/kg IV over 30 min 6 hrly
30-34 weeks and on feeds	2 mg/kg orally/NG 12 hrly for the first 2 weeks **THEN** 2 mg/kg orally/NG 8 hrly to completion
<30 weeks and on feeds	zidovudine 2 mg/kg orally/NG 12 hrly for the first 4 weeks
<34 weeks and not tolerating feeds	1.5 mg/kg IV over 30 min 12 hrly

- Lamivudine 2 mg/kg orally 12 hrly for 4 weeks
- Nevirapine 2 mg/kg orally daily for 1 week then 4 mg/kg daily for 1 week, then stop

Other medications: seek specialist help

- Mother presents pregnant on effective treatment that does not include zidovudine or lamivudine
- Concerns that the mother has HIV resistant to zidovudine or lamivudine
- Mother has viral load >10,000 copies/mL despite antiretroviral treatment but no resistance data
- Discuss with infectious diseases team locally or, if unavailable:
- contact infectious diseases team at St Mary's (0207 886 6666) or St George's (0208 725 3262)

MONITORING TREATMENT

- At birth and at 4-6 weeks, FBC, U&E, LFT, lactate, glucose, amylase, urine for CMV

DISCHARGE POLICY

- Ensure mother confident to give antiretrovirals to infant
- Dispense 4 weeks' supply on discharge
- Notify consultant paediatrician with interest in HIV who will notify BPSU

- Follow-up appointment with paediatrician with interest in HIV at 4-6 weeks
- Ensure all involved have record of perinatal care: mother, paediatrician, obstetrician, infectious diseases consultant
- Hepatitis B vaccine to all neonates born to mothers with HIV (first dose within 24 hrs if mother HBsAg +ve, otherwise before discharge)

SUBSEQUENT MANAGEMENT

- HIV proviral DNA PCR at 6 weeks and 3 months (and 4 months in high-risk group)
- HIV antibody after 18 months

High risk group

- Co-trimoxazole 120 mg (infants >2 kg) or 60 mg (infants <2 kg)
- once daily 3 times a week (Monday, Wednesday, Friday)
- from 4 weeks (stop if HIV proviral DNA PCR still negative at 3 months)

Immunisations

- Delay BCG vaccination of infant until results of 3 month PCR tests negative
- Recommend all other vaccinations as per routine schedule (including MMR)

DEFINITION

- Blood glucose >12 mmol/L, and/or presence of ≥2+ glycosuria on dipstick testing

> *Do not take sample from an infusion line that has glucose running through it*

CLINICAL FEATURES

- Dehydration
- Acidosis
- ketoacidosis does not occur in babies
- Poor weight gain

Babies at high risk

- Ill, unstable
- Preterm (especially <28 weeks)
- Small for gestational age (<3rd centile)
- Receiving TPN
- Receiving corticosteroids, caffeine

MONITORING

Twice daily monitoring

- Check blood glucose at least twice a day in:
- unstable or acutely ill babies (RDS, septicaemia, NEC)

Daily monitoring

- Check blood glucose at least once a day in babies:
- <32 weeks gestation for first week
- receiving TPN
- with severe unexpected dehydration or metabolic acidosis
- with poor weight gain while receiving >120 kcal/kg/d

Babies on corticosteroids

- Check urine for glycosuria daily in babies on corticosteroids
- Check blood glucose if ≥2+ glucose in urine

TREATMENT

- Discontinue or decrease medications that worsen hyperglycaemia

Infection

- Hyperglycaemia in baby with previously stable blood glucose may be early indicator of infection
- Treat suspected infection after taking appropriate cultures

Fluids

- Correct dehydration by increasing daily fluid intake – use sodium chloride 0.9%
- If baby receiving >6 mg glucose/kg/min, decrease concentration of glucose infused or replace some of the glucose intake with sodium chloride 0.9%
- these measures often bring blood glucose down substantially
- hypoglycaemia can occur following overzealous glucose restriction

Insulin

- **If laboratory blood glucose confirms markedly raised concentration,** consider insulin:
- when control not obtained with above methods or
- a higher carbohydrate intake than infant will tolerate is necessary for nutritional reasons
- Seek senior advice before commencing insulin therapy
- Follow **Neonatal Formulary** for insulin infusion rates
- Check blood glucose concentrations regularly during insulin infusion – treating clinician to decide on frequency, based on stability of glycaemia
- If unable to wean off insulin after 2 weeks, transient neonatal diabetes is likely; consult a paediatric endocrinologist

Significant hyperglycaemia

- In babies with significant hyperglycaemia – request cranial ultrasound scan

Issue 02
Issued: October 2007
Expires: September 2009

RECOGNITION AND ASSESSMENT

Definition

- Serum potassium >6 mmol/L (normal 3.0-5.5)
- Neonates often tolerate concentrations up to 7.5-8.0 mmol/L without ECG changes

SYMPTOMS AND SIGNS

- Cardiac arrest
- ECG abnormalities:
- tall peaked T waves
- widened QRS complex
- sine waves
- bradycardias

Causes

- Renal failure – secondary to hypoxic ischaemic encephalopathy (HIE), sepsis and hypotension, or structural abnormalities
- Very low-birth-weight babies without renal failure (non-oliguric hyperkalaemia) – first 12-48 hr
- Excess K^+ in IV solutions

INVESTIGATIONS

- Ensure sample not haemolysed, repeat and send free-flowing venous sample or arterial sample
- If potassium >6.5 mmol/L, connect to cardiac monitor

IMMEDIATE TREATMENT

Serum potassium >6.0 mmol/L (stable with normal ECG)

- Stop all K^+ IV solutions or oral supplements
- Reconfirm hyperkalaemia
- Institute continuous ECG monitoring

Serum potassium >7.5 mmol/L without ECG changes

- As above
- Give salbutamol 4 microgram/kg IV in glucose 10% over 5-10 min – effect evident within 30 min but sustained benefit may require a repeat infusion after a least 2 hr
- if IV access difficult, give nebulized salbutamol 2.5 mg as a single dose (difficult to administer if ventilated and not formally evaluated in neonates) and repeat if necessary
- Give intravenous insulin and glucose (12 units of soluble insulin in 100 mL of 25% glucose – 5 mL/kg given over 30 min) – very effective and has an additive effect with salbutamol
- Repeat U&E
- Repeat infusion as necessary until K^+ <7 mmol/L
- **Monitor blood glucose every 15 min for first 2 hr during and after infusion**
- aim for blood glucose 4-7 mmol/L

Serum potassium >7.5 mmol/L with ECG changes

- Give 10% calcium gluconate 2 mL/kg IV (diluted with equal volume glucose 10%) over 5-10 min
- Flush line with sodium chloride 0.9%
- Give intravenous sodium bicarbonate (1 mmol/kg) – effective even in patients who are not acidotic (2 mL of 4.2 % sodium bicarbonate = 1 mmol)
- Follow rest of the management as above

Further treatments - discuss with consultant

- A cation-exchange resin, such as calcium resonium (500 mg/kg rectally, with removal by colonic irrigation 8-12 hrly, repeat every 12 hrs. Dose can be doubled at least once to 1 g/kg in severe hyperkalaemia), is useful for sustained reduction in serum potassium but takes many hours to act and is best avoided **in sick preterms who are at risk of NEC** (Necrotizing enterocolitis)

- If severe hyperkalaemia persists despite the above measures in term babies with otherwise good prognosis, contact renal team for consideration of dialysis
- Exchange transfusion using fresh blood or washed red blood cells provides another strategy for sustained and reliable reduction in serum K^+ concentration

SUBSEQUENT MANAGEMENT

- Recheck 4-6 hrly – if arrhythmias present with renal failure, monitor hrly
- Monitor urine output and maintain good fluid balance
- If urine output <1 mL/kg/hr, unless baby volume depleted, give furosemide IV 1 mg/kg until volume corrected
- Treat any underlying cause (e.g. renal failure)

Consequences

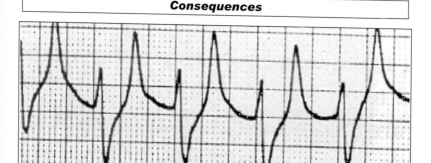

Figure: Hyperkalaemia leads to tall, peaked T waves, ventricular arrhythmias, widening of QRS, then sine wave QRS complex (before cardiac arrest)

Issue 02
Issued: October 2007
Expires: September 2009

DEFINITION

Asymptomatic hypoglycaemia

- Low glucose common in preterm and small for gestational age infants
- No simple correlation between blood glucose concentration and neuroglycopenia
- Blood glucose ≥2.6 mmol/L is safe

Symptomatic hypoglycaemia

- Blood glucose <2.6 mmol/L + any of the following symptoms, provided these resolve once hypoglycaemia has been corrected:
- convulsions
- abnormal neurological behaviour, including hypotonia and poor response to stimulation
- apnoea

Symptoms cannot be attributed to hypoglycaemia if they persist after adequate treatment. Jitteriness alone does not constitute symptomatic hypoglycaemia

PREVENTION

- Keep all infants warm
- Feed all high risk infants within 2 hr of birth if possible
- In all starved high risk infants, institute IV infusion of glucose 10% (see below)

At risk infants

Perform blood glucose estimation in following cases:

- Small for dates
- Preterm
- Any ill infant
- Infant of diabetic mother
- Haemolytic disease of the newborn
- Severe fluid restriction

Monitor all at risk patients using near-patient monitoring

- First 24 hr, 3-4 hrly
- Second 24 hr, 4-6 hrly
- Then as necessary
- Babies on TPN, at least daily
- Babies fed enterally, immediately before feeds

Always verify a low near-patient test result (<2.6 mmol/L) in a symptomatic baby by sending a sample for laboratory blood glucose estimation

MANAGEMENT

Never use concentrated (>20%) glucose solutions in babies

Asymptomatic hypoglycaemia in at-risk infant

- Correct hypothermia (see **Hypothermia** guideline)
- Increase frequency and/or volume of feeds

Milk is more beneficial than glucose 10% as it is more energy dense (70 kcal/100 mL v 40 kcal/100 mL) and contains fats that promote ketoneogenesis and glucose uptake

- Repeat glucose measurement after 1 hr. If low, check laboratory blood glucose

Issue 02
Issued: October 2007
Expires: September 2009

- Consider giving IV glucose if:
- unable to increase/tolerate feed frequency or volume **or**
- intensive feeding does not produce normoglycaemia
- Give glucose 6 mg/kg/min (glucose 10% at 90 mL/kg/day) by IV infusion
- If infant develops symptoms or becomes profoundly hypoglycaemic (<1.1 mmol/L), follow **Symptomatic hypoglycaemia** protocol (see below) immediately
- Continue enteral feeding during IV infusion

Give glucose 20% centrally as extremely hypertonic.
If UVC used, ensure tip not near liver

Failure to respond

- If >12 mg/kg/min of glucose required to achieve normoglycaemia, hyperinsulinaemic state is very likely. Obtain blood sample **at the time of hypoglycaemia** for simultaneous measurement of:
- blood glucose
- plasma insulin and C-peptide
- free fatty acids
- ketones
- cortisol
- growth hormone
- acylcarnitines
- collect next passed urine for organic acid analysis

Step down

- Once normoglycaemia achieved, wean from infusion as tolerated

Symptomatic hypoglycaemia

- Aim for blood glucose ≥2.6 mmol/L
- Give glucose 10% 2.5 mL/kg by IV bolus into peripheral vein and follow with an infusion of at least 90 mL/kg/day (~6 mg/kg/min), which may be increased if necessary. Continue enteral feeds
- Record whether symptoms respond to treatment within 30 min – very important for definitive diagnosis of symptomatic hypoglycaemia
- Recheck blood glucose after 30 min. If still low, give another 2.5 mL/kg bolus and increase infusion rate to 120 mL/kg/day (8.3 mg/kg/min)
- Record response and repeat glucose measurement in 1 hr. If still low, check blood glucose by laboratory estimation, and if hypoglycaemia confirmed, increase delivered glucose content by increasing either volume (to 150 mL/kg/day), or concentration (12.5-20%)

- Administer glucagon 200 microgram/kg (maximum 1 mg) IM, SC, or IV. Check blood glucose within 30 min of glucagon administration, and hrly thereafter until stable
- If persistent hyperinsulinism suspected, seek advice from paediatric endocrinologist/metabolic paediatrician, and consider early transfer to a unit specialising in the management of such infants

Routine addition of glucose polymers such as Maxijul is not recommended.
If a decision is made to use Maxijul, discuss with paediatric dietitian.
Beware risk of necrotizing enterocolitis

Issue 02
Issued: October 2007
Expires: September 2009

Prescription to make up 50 mL of varying concentrations of glucose solution

Infusion concentration (%)	Volume of 10% glucose (mL)	Volume of 50% glucose (mL)
12	47.5	2.5
15	44.0	6.0
17	41.0	9.0
20	37.5	12.5

Step down

● Once blood glucose normal, wean infant on to milk feeds either continuously or by hrly boluses

MONITORING

● Hypoglycaemic patients:
- if symptomatic, every 30 min
- if asymptomatic, every hr
- continue until normoglycaemic
● Once normoglycaemic, 3-4 hrly until 24 hr has elapsed since last hypoglycaemic episode

SEVERE PERSISTENT OR RECURRENT HYPOGLYCAEMIA

Causes of recurrent, persistent neonatal hypoglycaemia

● Hyperinsulinism
● Endocrine deficiency, especially panhypopituitarism
● Disorder of fatty acid metabolism
● Disorder of carbohydrate metabolism
● Disorder of amino acid metabolism

● Rate of glucose infusion required is good guide to likely cause

Substrate or endocrine deficiency	<5 mL/kg/hr of glucose 10% required (<8 mg/kg/min)
Hyperinsulinism	>6 mL/kg/hr of glucose 10% required (>10 mg/kg/min)

When to investigate further

● Persistent recurrent hypoglycaemia, especially in 'low risk' baby
● Unexpectedly profound hypoglycaemia in a well baby
● Hypoglycaemia in association with metabolic acidosis
● Hypoglycaemia in association with other abnormalities:
- midline defects
- micropenis
- exomphalos
- erratic temperature control
● Family history of SIDS, Reye's syndrome, or developmental delay

Investigations

● Paired insulin and glucose estimations while hypoglycaemic (hyperinsulinism confirmed if insulin >10 picomol/L when glucose <2 mmol/L or glucose:insulin ratio <0.3)
● Urinary ketones and organic acids
● Plasma cortisol and growth hormone
● Plasma amino acids
● Plasma acylcarnitine, free fatty acids and betahydroxybuturate

Issue 02
Issued: October 2007
Expires: September 2009

HYPOPLASTIC LEFT HEART SYNDROME AND OTHER DUCT-DEPENDENT LESIONS DIAGNOSED ANTENATALLY • 1/2

BACKGROUND

- Malformation affecting left ventricle, aorta and valves

- Degree of hypoplasia varies considerably and, in many cases, lesion is dynamic with progression during pregnancy

- Recently palliative/corrective surgery (Norwood procedure and its modifications) has become increasingly successful in prolonging survival with a view to later heart transplantation

MANAGEMENT OF DUCT-DEPENDENT CARDIAC LESION, INCLUDING HLHS DIAGNOSED IN-UTERO

- Record management plan in mother's notes and in antenatal counselling letter (with additional copy of both on neonatal unit)

- After delivery and stabilisation at local maternity unit, arrange non-urgent transfer to regional cardiac surgery centre for full cardiology assessment

- If closed or small (restrictive) atrial septum puts fetus at risk of severe pulmonary congestion and hypoxaemia shortly after birth, urgent septostomy immediately after delivery at maternity unit may be recommended, despite a generally poor outcome

Postnatal diagnosis

- Some babies will present when duct closes, anytime during neonatal period and early infancy, particularly where a left heart lesion has developed later in gestation – see **Cyanotic congenital heart disease (blue baby)** and **Heart failure** guidelines

It is important to consider the diagnosis of HLHS in any baby presenting with 'shock'

- Diagnosis is made by echocardiography

- Whenever possible, all diagnoses of HLHS and other duct-dependent lesions must be confirmed by paediatric cardiologists

Investigations

- Echocardiography by trained, experienced personnel

- Cranial ultrasound

- recommended because of increased risk of cerebral injury, but should not delay transfer

MANAGEMENT

Aim is to maintain patency of (or open a closed) ductus arteriosus, and optimise systemic perfusion

- In HLHS, single right ventricle supplies blood to systemic and pulmonary circulations running in parallel – excess flow in one circulation will lead to a significant decrease in blood supplied to other circulation

- Greatest risk is excessive blood flow through pulmonary circulation with systemic underperfusion, presenting with:

- tachypnoea;

- poor peripheral perfusion; and

- metabolic acidosis

- Poor peripheral perfusion can lead to cerebral injury and necrotizing enterocolitis (NEC)

Resuscitation

- Neonatal team must be present at delivery to ensure baby establishes effective respirations and becomes pink

- Although there is no increased requirement for resuscitation, it is extremely important to **avoid hypoxia and hyperoxia**

Issue 02
Issued: October 2007
Expires: September 2009

- If stable, allow short cuddle with parents before transfer to neonatal unit, but keep warm to **avoid hypothermia**
- Admit to unit for routine monitoring and investigations including blood gases and **avoid acidosis**

Maintain ductal patency

- Open duct with prostaglandin E_2 (dinoprostone, Prostin E_2)
- 5-10 nanograms/kg per min IV infusion to start; see **local formulary**
- increase dosage if necessary on advice of cardiac team
- if dinoprostone not available, use prostaglandin E_1 (Alprostadil); see **local formulary**
- Make fresh solution every 24 hr
- Be vigilant – 10% will develop apnoeas on this low dose regimen
- if apnoeas clinically significant, ventilate

Ventilation

Indications

- Significant apnoeas
- Congestive cardiac failure
- Respiratory failure

Technique

- Avoid hyperventilation, which can increase pulmonary blood flow
- initial settings: PEEP 4-5 cm H_2O and FiO_2 0.21, adjusted accordingly
- Aim for:
- $PaCO_2$ 5-7 KPa
- PaO_2 4-6 KPa
- pH 7.35-7.40
- SaO_2 70–85%, although many will run higher in room air

Inotropes

- If signs of peripheral underperfusion persist, arrange local echocardiography (if available) to assess contractility
- if confirmed, start dobutamine 5–10 micrograms/kg/min by continuous IV infusion
- if no improvement to peripheral circulation, consider nitroprusside 0.5-8 micrograms/kg/min by continuous IV infusion after discussion with cardiac team

COMMUNICATION

- Inform cardiac team when mother presents in labour, after delivery and daily thereafter
- inform immediately of new developments (e.g. apnoeas that require ventilation, or intensive care admission on transfer)
- Inform consultant on call of any delivered baby

CARDIAC CENTRE MANAGEMENT OPTIONS FOR HLHS

- Make sure you are aware of the process the family will experience. They will already have received counselling by cardiac team, including cardiac liaison nurses, and local perinatal team

To be certain of diagnosis and provide family with most relevant advice, all babies must be seen by paediatric cardiology team

Hypovolaemia is an uncommon cause of hypotension in the preterm newborn.

Excessive volume expansion can increase mortality

DEFINITION

Thresholds for intervention

- Aim to maintain **mean arterial BP** >gestational age in weeks

- If mean BP unavailable or pulse pressure wide (e.g. PDA), aim to maintain **systolic BP** >gestational age in weeks

- Aim for even higher mean arterial blood pressure in case of persistent pulmonary hypertension of newborn (see **PPHN** guideline)

RECOGNITION AND ASSESSMENT

Assessment of BP

- Measure mean arterial pressure (MAP) by:

- direct intra-arterial BP [umbilical arterial catheter (See **Umbilical artery catheterisation** guideline) or peripheral arterial line if trace satisfactory]

- automated oscillometry (Dinamap) has limited accuracy in hypotensive preterm neonates; usually over-reads BP in the lower ranges

- Assess as many of the following indices of tissue perfusion as possible (thresholds for abnormality in brackets):

- toe-core temperature difference (>2°C)

- urine output (<1 mL/kg/hr)

- base deficit (>−10 mmol/L)

- serum lactate (>2.5 mmol/L)

Causes of hypotension or poor perfusion

- Cardiac dysfunction or hypovolaemia owing to:

- cold

- bleeding

- polyuria secondary to glucosuria

- diarrhoea

- Sepsis

IMMEDIATE TREATMENT

The aim of treatment is to improve organ perfusion, not to correct a 'BP reading'

Fluid

- **Not more than 10 mL/kg** unless there is evidence of fluid/blood loss and hypovolaemia

- Maximum: 20 mL/kg over first 24 hr in ≤28 weeks' gestation

- If clinical condition poor or BP very low, or mother has been treated with IV antihypertensive agent, give inotrope (see below) after fluid bolus

Which fluid?

- Use sodium chloride 0.9% 10 mL/kg over 30 min **EXCEPT** when there is:

- coagulopathy with bruising – give fresh frozen plasma 10 mL/kg over 30 min (see **Coagulopathy** guideline)

- acute blood loss – give packed cells 10 mL/kg over 30 min

Reassess clinically within 30 min of each bolus

- If hypotension persists after fluid bolus, seek senior advice

- start inotropes

Inotropes

- Dopamine 5 microgram/kg/min via UVC (see **Umbilical venous catheterisation** guideline)
  - if given into liver, can cause extravasation injury
  - if given peripherally, can cause extravasation injury
  - if hypotension persists after 5 min, increase dose of dopamine in 5 microgram/kg/min increments up to a maximum of 20 microgram/kg/min
- If no central access, or if hypotension still persists, add dobutamine 10 microgram/kg/min (can be given peripherally)
  - if hypotension persists, increase dobutamine to 20 microgram/kg/min
- If hypotension persists despite these measures:
  - give hydrocortisone 2 mg/kg IV followed by 1 mg/kg IV 8-12 hrly for 2-3 days
  - seek senior advice

If acidotic with severe hypotension, but not hypovolaemic

- Give adrenaline 0.1 microgram/kg/min and increase up to 1.0 microgram/kg/min in 0.1 mL/hr increments every 5 min – see **Neonatal Formulary** for instructions on making up solution
- **Monitor limb perfusion and urine output**
- Seek senior advice before starting adrenaline infusion

MONITORING

- If pneumothorax suspected, transilluminate
- Chest X-ray:
  - if intubated
  - urgent if respiratory status worsening
  - look for air leak or overinflation
- Blood gases
- Check effective delivery of drugs:
  - record volume in syringe hrly
  - check for leaks
  - ensure correct position of UVC delivering inotropes

SUBSEQUENT MANAGEMENT

- If on morphine, reduce dose of morphine if possible
- If ventilated, try to reduce mean airway pressure without compromising chest inflation and oxygenation
- If poor response to above measures:
  - echocardiogram to assess for myocardial dysfunction/congenital heart disease
- Wean inotropes in 5 microgram/kg/min increments as tolerated

DEFINITION

- Skin temperature <36.0°C on admission from delivery suite

ASSESSMENT

Babies at risk

- Preterm <30 wk gestation
- Low birth weight <1500 g
- The sick baby
- Small for dates

Consequences (<36.0°C)

- Hypoglycaemia
- Metabolic acidosis
- Hypoxia with increased oxygen demands

Consequences (<35.5°C)

- Increased metabolic rate
- Clotting disorders
- Shock
- Apnoea
- Intraventricular haemorrhage
- Persistent fetal circulation
- Decreased surfactant production

Causes of heat loss

- Radiation – heat lost to cooler objects in the room
- in cold environment, whether in incubator or not, excessive heat may be lost
- in excessively hot environment or in direct sunlight, baby could overheat in incubator
- Conduction – heat lost to cooler surfaces baby is placed on
- Convection – heat lost due to drafts
- Evaporation – heat lost through water evaporating from skin

PREVENTION

Delivery suite

- Keep room 23-28°C and free from draughts, especially when babies are due to be delivered

Babies <30 wk

- Dry head and put on hat
- Do not dry remainder of baby but
- Place in polythene bag immediately after transfer to resuscitaire and keep inside the bag until placed in pre-heated pre-humidified incubator

Other babies

- Use pre-warmed towel, dry immediately after delivery
- Discard towel and wrap in another pre-warmed towel and blanket
- The room must be adequately warm to enable skin-to-skin contact and early breast feeding
- Cover exposed skin with warm blanket

Neonatal unit

- Keep at 24-25°C to avoid cooling from radiant heat loss, and 'misting' (condensation) in incubators
- Keep incubators and cots away from windows to prevent radiation heat loss
- Nurse babies requiring intensive care in pre-warmed incubator
- Babies <29 wks must have humidification >60% for first 2 weeks

Issue 02
Issued: October 2007
Expires: September 2009

Incubator temperature during the first 3 days

Birth weight (g)	Incubator temperature (°C)
1000	35
1500	34
2000	33.5
2500	33.2
3000	33
4000	32.5

- Babies <1000 g require even higher temperatures, occasionally >37°C
- If baby's temperature remains within normal limits for 24 hrs, lower the incubator temperature by 1°C according to baby's needs
- When baby's weight reaches about 1600 g, transfer to an open cot

Rainout may occur if the difference between the temperature in the incubator and room temperature is greater than 5°C: ensure room temperature kept at locally agreed level

Babies not at risk of hypothermia

- If not requiring observation of respiratory status or excessive invasive procedures, babies may be:
- dressed
- kept wrapped
- placed in a cot

- Mild hypothermia can be managed with the addition of:
- hats
- cot lids
- heated mattresses
- If baby's temperature <36.0°C consider:
- use of incubator, if available
- increasing humidity, if appropriate for gestational age
- bubble wrap

REWARMING OF HYPOTHERMIC BABIES

- Rewarm in incubator
- >1200 g – rewarm at 1°C per hour
- <1200 g – rewarm more slowly

Take care not to overheat babies. Aim for 36.5–37.2°C

Issue 02
Issued: October 2007
Expires: September 2009

SCREENING

- Perform neonatal screening blood test at 5-8 days old for:
- congenital hypothyroidism (CH)
- phenylketonuria

and in some districts:

- sickle cell disease
- medium chain acyl-co A dehydrogenase deficiency
- cystic fibrosis
- In preterm infants, perform on day 6 and repeat at 36–40 weeks gestational age
- Screening relies on measurement of raised blood spot TSH
- duty clinical biochemist will notify designated consultant or on-call consultant if blood spot TSH >20 mU/L on first testing or ≥10 mU/L on two occasions

IMMEDIATE MANAGEMENT

Informing diagnosis

- If screening test result indicates congenital hypothyroidism, a well-informed healthcare professional (community midwife, neonatal outreach nurse, health visitor or GP) must inform parents face-to-face
- provide parents with information leaflet 'Congenital hypothyroidism suspected' (available from www.newbornscreening-bloodspot.org.uk)

Consultant meeting

- Consultant to arrange to meet parents on same, or certainly within next 3 days
- do not communicate an abnormal result on Friday, Saturday or just before a weekend if such a visit cannot be arranged within next 24 hr

- At this meeting, consultant should:
- explain abnormal result
- examine baby using screening laboratory proforma as an aide-mémoire
- look for other abnormalities (10% in CH versus 3% in normal baby) – congenital heart disease (pulmonary stenosis, ASD and VSD) is commonest anomaly
- commence baby's treatment
- stress importance of daily and life-long treatment
- provide parent information leaflet (available from www.ich.ucl.ac.uk/factsheets/families/F040274/congenital_hypothyroidism.pdf)
- Document discussion and management plan and follow up and send to GP and parents
- Complete and return the data form to clinical biochemist at screening laboratory

Obtain further diagnostic tests

- Baby
- 1 mL venous blood in heparinised container for FT_4 and TSH
- send repeat dried blood spot card to screening laboratory
- ultrasound or radionuclide scan of thyroid, preferably within 7 days of starting levothyroxine
- Mother
- take 3 mL venous blood from mother into a heparinized container for FT_4, TSH and thyroid antibodies

Issue 02
Issued: October 2007
Expires: September 2009

TREATMENT

- Start treatment with levothyroxine after obtaining the confirmatory blood tests. Do not wait for the results unless transient hypothyroidism is suspected. The treatment must start before 21 days of age, and preferably by 18 days

- after discussion with paediatric endocrinologist, consultant may withhold treatment if transient hypothyroidism suspected

- Starting dose levothyroxine 10 microgram/kg/day with a maintenance regimen to maintain serum FT_4 in upper half of normal range, particularly for infants with severe hypothyroidism (e.g. athyrotic, ectopic or those with initial FT_4 <5.5 nmol/L)

- Adjustment required depending on thyroid function test results

- Tablets are 25 microgram strength

- it is not necessary to divide tablets for intermediate dose as half life >1 week

- administer intermediate dose, such as 37.5 microgram, as 25 and 50 microgram on alternate days

- Crush required levothyroxine dose (e.g. between 2 metal spoons) and mix with a little milk or water, using teaspoon or syringe

- do not add to bottle of formula

- suspensions not advised due to variable bioavailability

- repeat dose if baby vomits or regurgitates immediately

- Record date treatment commenced

- Provide parents with 14 day prescription for levothyroxine

- Arrange continued prescription with GP, emphasising need to avoid suspensions

FOLLOW–UP

- Arrange follow up after commencement of hormone replacement therapy as follows:

- 2 weeks, 6 weeks, 3 months, 6 months, 9 months, 1 yr, 18 months, 2 yrs, 30 months, 3 yr, yearly thereafter

- At each clinic visit:

- physical examination, including height, weight and head circumference

- developmental progress

- blood sample for thyroid function test (FT_4, FT_3 and TSH, just before usual daily medication dose)

- request as **FT_4 priority, then TSH**

Interpretation of thyroid function test results

Analyte	Age	Concentration
FT_4 (pmol/L)	0-5 days	17-52
	5-14 days	12-30
	14 days-12 yr	12-25
TSH (mL/L)	0-4 days	1-10
	5 days-12 yr	3.6-8.5

- Aim for FT_4 towards upper limit of normal range

- at higher concentrations of FT_4, normal concentrations of T_3 (produced by peripheral conversion) are achieved

- if FT_4 concentration satisfactory but with significantly raised TSH, consider non-compliance

- TSH concentration does not always normalise under 6 months and may be slightly raised up to 3 yr of age in the absence of non-compliance, probably due to reset feedback mechanism
- Overtreatment may induce tachycardia, nervousness and disturbed sleep patterns, and can produce premature fusion of cranial sutures and epiphyses

AFTERCARE

- Reassure parents that baby will grow into healthy adult with normal intelligence
- Stress importance of regular treatment. As half-life is long, it is not necessary to give an extra tablet next day if a day's treatment is missed
- Give details of:
- British Thyroid Foundation, PO Box 97, Clifford, Wetherby, West Yorkshire, LS23 6XD
- Child Growth Foundation, 2 Mayfield Avenue, Chiswick, London, W4 1PW
- www.bsped.org.uk

Issue 02
Issued: October 2007
Expires: September 2009

RECOGNITION AND ASSESSMENT

Risk factors

- History of fetal distress
- Fetal heart rate abnormalities during labour
- Apgar scores can be low
- Umbilical arterial gas can be acidotic
- Continued resuscitation can be necessary

SYMPTOMS AND SIGNS

Brain

- Hypo/hyperventilation
- Altered state of consciousness
- Irritability, unresponsiveness to stimulation
- Abnormal posturing, decerebrate rigidity, extensor response to painful stimulus
- Seizures
- Hypo/hypertonia
- Weak (or no) suck

Other signs and symptoms related to effects on other organ systems

- Renal failure
- Respiratory distress syndrome, particularly if preterm
- Pulmonary haemorrhage
- Persistent pulmonary hypertension of the newborn
- Hypoxic cardiomyopathy, hypotension
- Hepatic failure
- Necrotizing enterocolitis
- Hypoglycaemia
- Fluid retention, DIC

Grades of severity in term babies

Grade I (mild)	Grade II (moderate)	Grade III (severe)
Irritable and 'hyper-alert'	Lethargic	Comatose
Mild hypotonia	Marked abnormalities in tone	Profound hypotonia
Weak suck	Requires tube feeds	Failure to maintain spontaneous respiration
No fits	Fits easily controlled	Prolonged fits that are difficult to control
Recovering by 48 hr	Recovering by 7 days	

INVESTIGATIONS

Bloods

- FBC
- Blood culture
- Clotting screen
- Renal and liver profile, calcium, magnesium
- Glucose
- Blood gas including lactate
- Urine dipsticks

Cranial USS

- Early cerebral oedema – generalised increase in echogenicity, indistinct sulci and narrow ventricles
- After 2-3 days of age, increased echogenicity of thalami and parenchymal echodensities
- After 1 wk, parenchymal cysts, ventriculomegaly and cortical atrophy
- Cerebral Doppler used early, but does not affect management
- relative increase of end-diastolic blood flow velocity compared to peak systolic blood flow velocity (Resistive Index <0.55) in anterior cerebral artery predicts poor outcome

MR scan of brain after day 5 of life for grade 2 and 3 HIE

- Hypodense areas in thalamus, basal ganglia and internal capsule indicate poor prognosis

EEG

- Normal EEG during first 3 days has good prognosis
- Lack of normal background activity associated with a poor outcome

IMMEDIATE TREATMENT

- Prompt and effective resuscitation
- Maintain body temperature – avoid hyperthermia
- IV access
- Isotonic glucose-containing IV fluids at 75% of maintenance requirements. See **Intravenous fluid therapy** guideline

SUBSEQUENT MANAGEMENT

Oxygen

- Avoid hypoxaemia. Maintain PaO_2 (10-12 kPa) and SaO_2 (>94%) within normal limits
- Episodes of hypoxaemia (possibly associated with convulsions) are indication for IPPV
- Avoid hyperoxia

Carbon dioxide

- Maintain $PaCO_2$ 5.0 to 6.5 kPa
- Hypoventilation leading to hypercapnia (>7 kPa) is indication for IPPV
- Hyperventilation contraindicated but, if baby spontaneously hyperventilating, mechanical ventilation can be necessary to control $PaCO_2$

Circulatory support

- Maintain mean arterial blood pressure at 40 mmHg or above for term infants
- If cardiac output poor (e.g. poor perfusion – blood pressure is poor predictor of cardiac output) use inotropes
- Avoid volume replacement unless evidence of hypovolaemia

Issue 02
Issued: October 2007
Expires: September 2009

Fluid balance and renal function

- Give 75% of normal maintenance fluid requirement. See **Intravenous fluid therapy** guideline

- Monitor serum sodium and potassium, and urine output

- Some infants develop inappropriate ADH secretion at 3-4 days (suggested by hypo-osmolar serum with low serum sodium associated with an inappropriately high urine sodium and osmolality) – restrict fluid to 75% maintenance

Acidosis

- Will normally correct itself once adequate respiratory and circulatory support provided – correction occasionally required during initial resuscitation

- Repeat blood gas after 30 min and provide base if spontaneous correction not proceeding spontaneously

- Aim to half-correct acidosis using infusion of sodium bicarbonate 4.2% (0.5 mmol/mL over 20 to 30 min)

Glucose

- Regular blood glucose monitoring
- Target >2.6 mmol/L
- Fluid restriction may require use of higher concentrations of glucose to maintain satisfactory blood glucose
- Avoid hyperglycaemia (>8 mmol/L)

Calcium

- Asphyxiated babies are at increased risk of hypocalcaemia
- Treat with calcium gluconate when serum corrected calcium <1.7 mmol/L

Convulsions

- Prophylactic anticonvulsants not indicated

- In paralysed infant, abrupt changes in blood pressure, SaO_2 and heart rate can indicate convulsions

- Treat persistent (>3/hr) or prolonged convulsions; see **Seizures** guideline

- Give phenobarbital

- If ineffective or contraindicated, give phenytoin. If no response give clonazepam – see **Seizures** guideline

- Convulsions associated with HIE can be notoriously difficult to control – preventing every little twitch is unrealistic

- Regular fits causing respiratory insufficiency are an indication for IPPV

- Once baby stable for 2-3 days anticonvulsants can usually be withdrawn although phenobarbital can be continued for a little longer - duration can vary depending on individual practise and clinical severity of seizures

- Avoid corticosteroids and mannitol

Thermal control

- Maintain normal body temperature (36.5–37.2°C). Avoid hyperthermia

Gastrointestinal system

- Term infants who suffer a severe asphyxial insult are at risk of developing necrotizing enterocolitis – see **Necrotizing enterocolitis** guideline

- In other infants gastric motility can be reduced – introduce enteral feeds slowly

PROGNOSIS

- The risk of long-term problems increases with the degree of encephalopathy
- Overall risk of death or significant handicap negligible for mild HIE, 26% for moderate and almost 100% for severe HIE
- Prolonged encephalopathy (e.g. moderate HIE lasting >6 days) also associated with poor outcome
- Persistent oliguria associated with poor outcome in 90%
- Prognostic factors indicative of worse outcome:
- prolonged duration of ventilation
- prolonged need for anticonvulsants
- time taken to establish oral feeding

DISCONTINUING INTENSIVE CARE

- When prognosis very poor, discuss withdrawing intensive care support
- Very poor prognostic factors include:
- need for prolonged resuscitation at birth
- evidence of severe asphyxia
- multi-organ failure
- intractable seizures
- coma
- very abnormal cranial ultrasound scan
- abnormal Doppler cerebral blood flow velocities
- Decision to withdraw care requires discussion with parents, and other nursing and medical staff. Such decisions are frequently reached after a series of discussions by the infant's consultant
- It helps if the same staff speak to parents on each occasion

- The best interests of the child are paramount
- Record summary of discussion in notes

DISCHARGE POLICY

- Arrange clinic follow-up in 4-6 weeks for babies discharged
- Repeat cranial USS before discharge (see protocol)
- Arrange hearing screen
- Arrange MR scan for grades 2 and 3 HIE as an outpatient (if not already done as an inpatient), preferably before follow-up

Issue 02
Issued: October 2007
Expires: September 2009

ROUTINE IMMUNISATIONS FOR ALL NEONATES

Plan to achieve immunity to diphtheria, tetanus, pertussis, (DTaP), polio, haemophilus (Hib) meningococcus C and pneumococcus within 4 months of birth

Do not delay immunisation in pre-term babies because of prematurity or low body weight

CONTRAINDICATIONS

- BCG can be temporarily contraindicated in the immunosuppressed:
- check maternal antenatal HIV screening result
- if on prednisolone 1 mg/kg/day for >3 weeks, give BCG if indicated 3 months after stopping steroids
- Cardiorespiratory events (apnoea, bradycardia and desaturations) are **not** contraindications to immunisation, but continue to monitor for a further 72 hr following immunisation

TREATMENT

Consent

- Inform parents of process, benefits and risks
- Provide fact sheets
- Offer parents opportunity to ask questions
- Written consent is not obligatory
- Complete the 'unscheduled immunisation form' prior to immunisation
- send form to local Child Health Information

Prescription

Use immunisation listed in the schedule below

- Keep strictly to schedule to avoid delay
- Order vaccines in advance unless held as stock on NNU
- Prescribe on treatment sheet

Schedule

2 months	DTaP/IPV/Hib	1 injection
	+ Pneumococcal	1 injection
3 months	DTaP/IPV/Hib	1 injection
	+ Men C	1 injection
4 months	DTaP/IPV/Hib	1 injection
	+ Men C	1 injection
	+ Pneumococcal	1 injection

Administration

- DTaP/IPV/Hib is a 5 in 1 preparation
- Administer by **IM** injection into the thigh
- Give Men C and Prevenar (pneumococcal vaccine) into separate injection sites in the other thigh

DOCUMENTATION

- Ensure accurate documentation so that community healthcare professionals are aware course will not be complete

- After immunisation, document the following in case notes as well as in Child Health Record (red book):
- vaccine given and reasons for any omissions
- site of injection(s) in case of any reactions
- batch number of product(s)
- expiry date of product(s)
- legible signature of doctor administering immunisations
- adverse reactions
- Sign treatment sheet
- Document all information on discharge summary and medical case notes including recommendations for future immunisations and need for any special vaccinations such as influenza, palivizumab, etc

ADVERSE REACTIONS

- Local:
- extensive area of redness or swelling
- General:
- fever $\geq 39.5°C$ within 48 hr
- anaphylaxis (see below)
- bronchospasm
- laryngeal oedema
- generalised collapse
- episodes of severe apnoea

ADDITIONAL IMMUNISATIONS

Influenza (in autumn and winter only)

Indications

- Chronic lung disease (on, or have recently had, oxygen)
- Congenital heart, renal or liver disease
- Immunodeficiency

Recommendations

- Recommend vaccination to close family members of these infants
- Give infants >6 months of age

Palivizumab

Indications

During RSV season (mid-October to mid-March), give to:

- <2 yr with severe chronic lung disease on home oxygen
- Infants <6 months of age who have left to right shunt, haemodynamically significant congenital heart disease and/or pulmonary hypertension in consultation with consultant cardiologist
- Children under 2 yr with severe congenital immunodeficiency

Procedure

- Consultant neonatologist will identify patient and sign accompanying letter to GP
- Five monthly doses in the RSV season at the middle of October, November, December, January and February
- where possible, administer first dose before commencement of RSV season
- 15 mg/kg by IM injection into the antero-lateral aspect of thigh
- Order palivizumab injection from local community or hospital pharmacy, who will obtain from manufacturer, Abbott Laboratories Ltd. This can take some days
- Palivizumab must be stored at 2-8°C. Full reconstitution and administration instructions are provided in the Summary of product characteristics (SPC). It is important to:
- avoid shaking vial

- stand at room temperature for minimum of 20 min until solution clarifies
- administer within 6 hr of preparation (palivizumab contains no preservative)
- note that final concentration, when reconstituted as recommended, is 100 mg/mL
- split between 2 sites if >1 mL

Rotarix (rotavirus vaccine)

- Give according to local policy
- Increased morbidity in low birth weight infants, highest risk morbidity in very low birth weight infants
- given at 2 and 4 months

BCG and Hepatitis B

See **BCG immunisation** and **Hepatitis B** guidelines

PREVENTION

- **Strict hand washing or alcohol hand rubs:**
- to the elbow with particular attention between digits
- on entering the unit and between each patient
- Unless absolutely essential, avoid entering incubators or touching any part of cots
- Meticulous regimen for changing drips and three way taps

DIAGNOSIS

Symptoms

- Difficult especially in babies of low birth weight
- These can be vague and non-specific
- The following are suggestive of an infection:
- poor colour
- lethargy/inactivity
- hypotonia
- irritability
- poor suck
- vomiting
- abdominal distension
- high or **low** body temperature
- jaundice
- cyanotic attacks
- tachypnoea

Nursing staff may describe babies with a mixture of these signs and symptoms as having 'gone off'

Signs

Look for:

- Septic spots in the eyes, the umbilicus, the nails and the skin
- Tenderness in joints and limbs suggestive of osteomyelitis or osteoarthritis
- Signs of pneumonia in the chest

- Bulging of the fontanelle suggesting raised intracranial pressure
- not always detectable in babies with neonatal meningitis
- Abdominal distension and tenderness
- auscultate for bowel sounds
- inspect stool for macroscopic blood
- petechiae, bleeding diathesis
- systemic signs of sepsis such as tachycardia, poor perfusion, reduced tone, quiet, sleepy

INVESTIGATIONS
(to be performed before starting antibiotics)

Swabs for culture

- Swab any suspicious lesion (e.g. skin, umbilicus or nails)
- Routine swabs are not useful

Blood cultures

- From a peripheral vein, using aseptic technique

Complete blood count

- A neutrophil count <2 or >15 x 10^9/L (supportive but not diagnostic, and marginally more sensitive than a total white cell count)
- Platelet count of <100 x 10^9/L
- Toxic granulation in neutrophils (or if measured: an Immature to Total (I:T) neutrophil ratio >0.2)

CRP

- Take 2 samples 24 hr apart
- a rise may support diagnosis of infection but failure to rise does not exclude it where other findings are supportive
- if blood culture negative and clinical condition satisfactory, failure of CRP to rise during first 24 hr is a useful indicator that antibiotics may be safely stopped

Urine

- Clean catch, supra-pubic aspiration (SPA) or in-out catheter (use U/S to check urine in bladder before SPA)
- do not send urine collected in a bag for culture

CSF

- If baby unstable, discuss advisability with consultant

Others

- **Chest X-ray**
- If abdominal distension noted, **abdominal X-ray**
- If features of intrauterine infection: urine CMV PCR, toxoplasma or syphilis serology, swab vesicles or throat for herpes simplex culture
- Clotting profile, in septicaemia

EMPIRICAL TREATMENT

Early onset sepsis

- Do not use oral antibiotics to treat infection in neonates
- Give penicillin and gentamicin (see **Neonatal Formulary** for doses and intervals)

Late onset sepsis

- Empiric treatment may vary according to local microbiology isolates. Generally:
- give penicillin and gentamicin if not already on antibiotics
- If not responding after 24 hr:
- add flucloxacillin to penicillin and gentamicin
- If not responding after 24 hr:
- give IV cefotaxime and vancomycin
- if meningitis excluded by LP give Tzocin and vancomycin
- If not responding after 24 hr:
- give meropenem and vancomycin

- When culture results available, always change to narrowest spectrum
- Give nystatin (oral and nasogastric) to all neonates treated with broad spectrum antibiotics if policy in your unit
- If the baby has improved clinically and bacteriological cultures are so far negative, stop antibiotics after 48 hr

SPECIFIC INFECTIONS

Prolonged rupture of membranes (>18 hr)

- If baby is clinically well, antibiotics are not indicated
- Take microbiology specimens and treat if there is any clinical deterioration in baby's condition

Prelabour rupture of membranes

- **Preterm (<37 weeks):** take blood culture and treat with empiric antibiotics until cultures back /48 hrs if negative
- **Term:** investigate only if clinical deterioration

Chorioamnionitis

Symptoms and Signs

- Maternal temperature >38°C
- Maternal tachycardia, elevated CRP or neutrophil count
- Foul or purulent vaginal discharge
- Fetal tachycardia
- Fundal tenderness

Management

- Empiric antibiotics for mother and immediate delivery, regardless of gestational age
- Empiric antibiotics for neonate: if cultures negative stop antibiotics, otherwise treat as appropriate for that organism

Discharging eyes

● See **Conjunctivitis** guideline

Umbilicus sepsis (omphalitis)

● Only if local induration or surrounding reddening of the skin, systemic antibiotics required

Meningitis

Empirical treatment whilst CSF results pending:

● CSF visually clear – give penicillin and gentamicin

● CSF cloudy – give cefotaxime and amoxicillin

Subsequent management

● If culture negative (and CSF taken before antibiotics), stop after 48 hr

● If high suspicion of meningitis and no growth (and CSF taken after antibiotics), stop after 21 days

● If >5 WBC in CSF, give cefotaxime and amoxicillin

● Bloody CSF taps cannot exclude meningitis; in general, consider a RBC:WBC ratio of 500:1 as within normal range

● If low clinical suspicion, CSF glucose >2/3 simultaneous blood glucose and CSF protein <1 g/L, stop antibiotics after 48 hrs if neonate remains well and cultures negative

● Group B Streptococcus isolated, give benzylpenicillin and gentamicin for 14 days

● Gram negative bacillus isolated, give cefotaxime; if resistant to cefotaxime, give meropenem. Treat for 21 days

● Other organisms isolated, treat according to microbiological sensitivity

● If other focus found, treat as for other infection

Urinary infection

Do not delay treatment, start immediately after urine collection

● Give cephalexin until cultures available; then treat according to sensitivities

● Continue antibiotic until imaging investigations completed

● Exclude obstruction by renal ultrasound scan within a few days (or as soon as available)

Subsequent management

● Prophylaxis: a single night time dose of trimethoprim (2 mg/kg/dose) for all with confirmed UTI

● For further information on management of UTIs in neonates – see **Paediatric** guidelines

Necrotizing enterocolitis

● See **Necrotizing enterocolitis** guideline

ADJUNCTIVE THERAPY

● No substantive trials show benefit yet of intravenous immunoglobulin, recombinant cytokines etc

PRINCIPLES

- Postnatal physiological weight loss is about 5-10%
- Postnatal diuresis is delayed in Respiratory Distress Syndrome (RDS)
- Preterm babies have limited capacity to excrete sodium in first 48 hr
- Liberal sodium and water intake before onset of natural diuresis is associated with an increased incidence of patent ductus arteriosus (PDA), necrotizing enterocolitis (NEC) and chronic lung disease (CLD)
- After diuresis, a positive sodium balance is necessary for tissue growth
- Preterm babies, especially born <29 weeks gestation lose excessive sodium through immature kidneys
- Babies <28 weeks have significant transepidermal water loss (TEW)
- TEW loss leads to hypothermia, loss of calories and dehydration, and causes excessive weight loss and hypernatraemia

MONITORING

Weigh

- On admission
- Once daily – twice daily in babies ≤26 weeks gestation during first week, or if fluid balance is a problem
- use in-line scales if available

Serum sodium

- On admission in babies ≤28 weeks gestation
- Once daily in babies <28 weeks gestation, babies on IV fluids, TPN or unwell
- If electrolyte problems or ≤26 weeks, measure twice daily
- admission electrolytes reflect maternal status – need not be acted upon but help to interpret trends
- serum urea not useful in monitoring fluid balance – reflects nutritional status and nitrogen load

Serum creatinine

- Daily
- Reflects renal function over longer term
- trend is most useful
- tends to rise over first 2-3 days
- gradually falls over subsequent weeks
- absence of postnatal drop is significant

Urine output

- Review 8-12 hrly
- 2-4 mL/kg/hr normal hydration
- <1 mL/kg/hr requires investigation
- >6-7 mL/kg/hr suggests impaired concentrating ability or excess fluids

NORMAL REQUIREMENTS

Humidification

- If <29 weeks, humidify incubator 80%
- If ventilated or on CPAP ventilator, set humidifier at 39°C negative 2 to ensure maximal humidification of inspired gas

Normal fluid volume requirements

Fluid volume (mL/24 hr)		
Day of life	<1000 g	>1000 g
1	90	60
2	120	90
3	150	120
4	150	150

- **Day 1**
- glucose 10%
- **Day 2**
- glucose 10% and potassium 10 mmol in 500 mL
- if birth weight <1000 g, use TPN (with potassium 2 mmol/kg/day)
- add sodium only when there is diuresis, or weight loss >6% of birth weight
- **Day 3**
- glucose 10%, sodium chloride 0.18% and potassium 10 mmol in 500 mL or TPN (with potassium 2 mmol/kg/day and sodium 4 mmol/kg/day)
- **After Day 4**
- glucose 10% (with maintenance electrolytes adjusted according to daily U&E) or TPN

Daily electrolyte requirements

- Sodium 2-4 mmol/kg/day (5 mmol = 1 mL sodium chloride 30%)
- infants ≤30 weeks need at least 4 mmol/kg/day to overcome renal tubular loss
- Potassium 2 mmol/kg/day (2 mmol = 1 mL of potassium chloride 15%)
- Calcium 0.45 mmol/kg/day (0.45 mmol = 2 mL of calcium gluconate 10%) if supplementation required

HYPONATRAEMIA (<130 MMOL/L)

Response to treatment should be proportionate to degree of hyponatraemia

Causes

- May reflect maternal electrolyte status in first 24 hr
- **Excessive free water** owing to:
- failure to excrete fetal ECF – common in first few postnatal days and failure to lose weight provides a clue to this aetiology
- inappropriate secretion of ADH in babies with major cerebral insults, or severe lung disease
- treatment with indometacin or ibuprofen
- **Excessive losses** – common beyond first few postnatal days in preterm infants and can be exacerbated by concomitant diuretic therapy, caffeine, diarrhoea, or adrenal disorders
- **Deficient intake** – preterm breast milk is poor in sodium, and breast-milk fed babies often develop hyponatremia beyond first week

Management depends on cause

Excessive IV fluids

- Reduce fluid intake by 20%

Inappropriate ADH

Clinical features

- Weight gain, oedema, poor urine output
- Serum osmolality low (<275 mosmol/kg) with urine not maximally dilute (osmolality >100 mosmol/kg)

Management

- Reduce fluid intake by approximately 20-40%
- Sodium infusion only if serum sodium <120 mmol/L

Acute renal failure

- Reduce intake to match insensible losses + urine output
- Seek advice from a senior colleague

Excessive renal sodium losses

Stop medication (diuretics, caffeine) that causes excess losses if possible

Check urinary electrolytes

● Calculate urinary sodium losses from a spot urine sample using the formula: urinary sodium loss (mmol/kg/d) = $100 \times U_{Na}/U_{creat}$

○ formula gives approximate urinary Na losses, and can be used to ensure losses are matched by oral/IV intake

Increase sodium intake and monitor trend

Consider fluid retention when dealing with low sodium – may need restriction of fluid or reduction in supplementary sodium (over supplementation also leads to fluid retention)

● Calculate sodium deficit

○ = (135 – plasma sodium) x 0.6 x weight in kg

○ replace over 24 hr unless sodium <120 or symptomatic (apnoea, fits, irritability)

○ initial treatment should bring serum sodium up to about 125 mmol/L

○ use sodium chloride 30% (5 mmol/mL) diluted – see **Neonatal Formulary**

● Once serum sodium corrected, use value from urinary Na losses (see above) to ensure adequate daily Na supplementation

● If sodium intake >5 mmol/kg/day, discuss with consultant (this amount should be sufficient to overcome normal tubular losses), and exclude other causes (e.g. medication, fluid retention and, very rarely, endocrine causes)

Adrenal insufficiency

Clinical features

● Hyperkalaemia
● Excessive weight loss
● Virilization of females
● Increased pigmentation of both sexes
● Ambiguous genitalia

Management

● Seek consultant advice

Inadequate intake

Clinical features

● Poor weight gain and decreased urinary sodium

Management

● Give increased sodium supplementation
● If taking diuretics, stop or reduce dose

Excessive sodium intake leading to water retention

Clinical features

● Inappropriate weight gain

Management

● Reduce sodium intake

HYPERNATRAEMIA (>145 MMOL/L)

Prevention

● Prevent high transepidermal water loss
○ use plastic wrap to cover babies of <30 weeks gestation at birth
○ nurse in high ambient humidity >80%
○ use bubble wrap
○ minimise interventions
○ reduce need to open incubators
○ humidify ventilator gases
○ set humidifier temperature (Fisher Paykell recommend 39°C negative 2)

Causes

- Water loss
  - transepidermal water loss
  - glycosuria
- Excessive sodium intake
  - sodium bicarbonate
  - repeated boluses of sodium chloride
- Congenital hyperaldosteronism/diabetes insipidus (very rare)

Management depends on cause

Hypernatraemia resulting from water loss

Clinical features

- Weight loss and hypernatraemia

Management

- Increase fluid intake and monitor serum sodium
- If undergoing phototherapy, increase fluid intake by 10 mL/kg/day in very preterm babies

Osmotic diuresis

- Treat hyperglycaemia with an insulin infusion (see **Hyperglycaemia** guideline)
- Rehydrate with sodium chloride 0.9%

Hypernatraemia resulting from excessive intake

- If acidosis requires treatment, use THAM instead of sodium bicarbonate
- Reduce sodium intake
- Change arterial line fluid to sodium chloride 0.45%
- Minimise number and volume of flushes of IA and IV lines

PRESCRIBING ELECTROLYTE ADDITIVES TO IV FLUIDS

- Use birth weight of baby until birth weight regained

Calculate daily fluid requirement

- Include volumes of any additional infusions (e.g. IA line, sedation) in calculations of intake

Calculate hrly infusion rate of maintenance

- Volume of IV fluid to be infused over 24 hr (V) = total to be infused – other fluids

Calculate amount of calcium gluconate

- Amount of calcium gluconate 10% to be added per 24 hr = 2 mL/kg calcium gluconate 10% (Y mL) per V mL of fluid
- Amount of calcium gluconate 10% to be added to a 500 mL bag (X) = Y x (500) divided by V mL

Worked example in a 2 kg baby on 120 mL/kg with UAC at 1 mL/kg

Y (calcium gluconate 10%) = 2 mL/kg x 2 = 4 mL
V = (120 mL/kg x 2 = 240 mL) – (UAC at 1.0 mL/hr = 24 mL) = 216 mL
X mL (calcium gluconate 10%) = 4 mL (Y) x 500, divided by 216 (V) = 9.3 mL
(round to nearest 0.5) = 9.5 mL

Issue 02
Issued: October 2007
Expires: September 2009

Calculate amount of potassium

- Use standard potassium-containing infusates

- 10 mmol/500 mL should meet daily maintenance requirements;

- for correction of hypokalaemia, use bag containing 20 mmol/500 mL

IV FLUIDS – some useful information

- Percentage solution = grams in 100 mL (e.g. glucose 10% = 10 g in 100 mL)

- One millimole = molecular weight in milligrams

Avoid addition of potassium to existing infusates wherever possible

---

Compositions of commonly available solutions

FLUID	Na mmol/L	K mmol/L	Cl mmol/L	Energy kCal/L
sodium chloride 0.9%	150	-	150	-
glucose 10%	-	-	-	400
glucose 10% / sodium chloride 0.18%	30	-	30	400
albumin 4.5%	150	1	-	-
sodium chloride 0.45%	75	-	75	-

Useful figures:

- Sodium chloride 30% = 5.13 mmol/mL each of Na and Cl

- Sodium chloride 0.9% = 0.154 mmol/mL each of Na and Cl

- Potassium chloride 15% = 2 mmol/mL *strong KCl*

- Calcium gluconate 10% = 0.225 mmol/mL

- Sodium bicarbonate 8.4% = 1 mmol Na/mL

- Sodium chloride 1 mL/hr 0.9% = 3.7 mmol Na in 24 hr

Osmolality

- Serum osmolality = 2(Na + K) + glucose + urea (normally 285–295 mosmol/kg)

- Anion gap = $(Na^+ + K^+) - (Cl^- + HCO_3^-)$ normally 7-17 mmol/L

- Normal urine: osmolality 100-300 mosmol/kg, specific gravity 1004-1015

- Neonates can dilute urine up to 100 mosmol/kg, but can concentrate only up to 700 mosmol/kg

Glucose

- To make glucose 12.5%, add 30 mL of glucose 50% to 470 mL of glucose 10%

- To make glucose 15%, add 60 mL of glucose 50% to 440 mL of glucose 10%

- Glucose 20% is commercially available

- Glucose 10% with sodium chloride 0.18% and 10 mmol potassium chloride is not commercially available but can be made up using 3 mL sodium chloride 30% and a 500 mL bag of glucose 10% with 10 mmol potassium chloride

This procedure must be undertaken or supervised by an experienced person

Do not attempt to carry out this procedure unless you are familiar with the anatomy of the upper airway and have demonstrated your competence in the use of a laryngoscope

ELECTIVE INTUBATION

● Use pre-medication

Equipment

● Suction
● Oxygen with pressure limiting device and T-piece or bag and appropriate size mask
● ETT tubes 3 sizes:

Weight of baby (g)	Size of ETT
<1000 -1500	2.5
1500-2500	3.0
>2500	3.5

● Hat for baby to secure tube, ETT fixing device, forceps and scissors
● Laryngoscopes x 2, stethoscope, oropharyngeal airway

Preparation

● Ensure cannula in place and is working
● Ensure all drugs drawn up, checked, labelled and ready to give
● Check no contraindications to drugs
● Ensure monitoring equipment attached and working reliably
● If NGT in place, aspirate stomach (particularly important if baby has been receiving enteral feeds)

Premedication

● Give 100% O_2 for 2 min before drug administration
● Continue to give 100% O_2 until laryngoscopy and between attempts if more than one attempt necessary

Drugs

Choice of drugs depends on local practice

Analgesia and muscle relaxation may make intubation more successful

Muscle relaxants

Administer muscle relaxants only if you are confident that the team can intubate the baby quickly. Do not use a muscle relaxant unless adequate analgesia has been given

PROCEDURE

● Press on cricoid bone to displace trachea downwards into field of view of clinician carrying out intubation. This can be done by clinician or nurse who is assisting procedure
● Insert ET tube
● Do not advance ETT further than end of black mark at end of tube (2.5 cm beyond cords)
● Markings of the ETT at the lips should approximately be (see Table **Length of ETT**)

Table: Length of ETT

Approximate weight of baby (kg)	Length of ETT (cm) at lips
<1	5.5
1	6.0
2	7.0
3	8.5
3.5	9.0
4	9.5

Issue 02
Issued: October 2007
Expires: September 2009

- Auscultate chest to check for bilateral equal air entry
  - if air entry unequal and louder on right side, withdraw ET tube by 0.5 cm and listen again
  - repeat until air entry equal bilaterally
  - do not leave the baby with unequal air entry
  - stabilise tube using ETT fixation method in accordance with unit practice
- Request chest X-ray

Intubation failure

- If intubation unsuccessful, seek help from someone more experienced
- If there is a risk of aspiration, maintain cricoid pressure
- Continue bag and mask ventilation with 100% oxygen after inserting an oropharyngeal airway

Issue 02
Issued: October 2007
Expires: September 2009

RECOGNITION AND ASSESSMENT

Symptoms and signs

- Yellow colouration of the skin in a pale-skinned infant observed in natural light
- Yellow conjunctivae in dark-skinned infants

Assess

- Pallor
- Poor feeding, drowsiness (neurotoxicity)
- Hepatosplenomegaly (blood-group incompatibility)
- Splenomegaly (spherocytosis)

Causes

- Physiological
- Prematurity
- Increased haemoglobin load (e.g. bruising, blood group incompatibility)
- G6PD deficiency and other red cell enzyme deficiencies
- Congenital spherocytosis
- Cephalhaematoma
- Rarely infection (e.g. UTI, congenital infection)
- Metabolic disorder

Persistent jaundice after 14 days of age

- Breast milk jaundice
- Hypothyroidism
- Liver disease (e.g. extra hepatic biliary atresia and neonatal hepatitis)
- Alpha-1-antitrypsin deficiency
- Galactosaemia
- TPN

Investigations

All

- Total bilirubin

Jaundice in first 24 hours of life or requiring treatment

- Full blood count and film
- Baby's blood group and direct Coomb's test
- Mother's blood group and antibody status (should be available from maternal case notes)
- Full infection screen (in ill babies)
- G6PD concentration (if indicated by ethnic origin – Mediterranean, Middle Eastern, South East Asian)

Persistent jaundice >14 days old

- Total and conjugated bilirubin
- Urine M,C&S
- Document stool colour

Unconjugated persistent jaundice:

- G6PD screen in African, Asian or Mediterranean patients
- Thyroid function tests – ask for 'FT$_4$ priority and then TSH'
- Blood galactose-1-phosphate
- Congenital infection screen:
- urine for CMV PCR, toxoplasma ISAGA-IgM and throat swab for HSV culture/PCR
- Metabolic investigations (e.g. urine for reducing substances)

If conjugated bilirubin elevated (>20% of total or >20 µmol/L), discuss with consultant

Issue 02
Issued: October 2007
Expires: September 2009

TREATMENT <7 DAYS

- Adequate fluid and energy intake
- Phototherapy

Jaundice presenting in first 24 hours of life

- Visible jaundice can be treated with phototherapy after sample taken for bilirubin measurement

After first 24 hours

- Commence phototherapy according to the equation:
- serum bilirubin (μmol/L) = (gestational age in completed weeks x 10) – 100

Phototherapy

- If bilirubin near exchange levels or still rising:
- increase power number of lights
- increase area exposed (e.g. biliblanket and overhead)

Exchange transfusion

- See **Exchange transfusion** guideline

MONITORING TREATMENT

- Check bilirubin level 24-hrly or more frequently depending on rate of rise
- If haemolysis present, check bilirubin 4-6 hrly until rate of rise flattens
- If bilirubin concentration approaching threshold for exchange transfusion, or rising rapidly (>10 μmol/hr), check 4 hrly

SUBSEQUENT MANAGEMENT

- When bilirubin concentration has fallen below the threshold for phototherapy (see above), discontinue phototherapy
- If jaundice persists after 14 days of age, review and treat cause

DISCHARGE POLICY

- GP follow-up with routine examination at 6-8 weeks
- If exchange transfusion necessary or considered, request development follow up and hearing test
- In babies with positive Coomb's test who require phototherapy, check haemoglobin at 2 and 4 weeks of age because of risk of continuing haemolysis

- Encourage obstetric team to warn neonatal team of expected problems
- Plan who should attend [e.g. advanced neonatal nurse practitioner (ANNP), SHO, SpR, consultant], and degree of urgency

Neonatal team should attend the following deliveries:

- Fetal distress as assessed by obstetric team
- Thick fresh meconium
- Caesarean section under general anaesthesia (see below)
- Major congenital abnormalities (minor abnormalities will wait until working hours)
- Vacuum extraction or instrumental deliveries performed for fetal reasons (see below)
- Preterm delivery <35 weeks gestation
- Multiple pregnancy
- Severe pre-eclampsia
- Antepartum haemorrhage
- Moderate-severe Rhesus disease

It is **not** necessary for the neonatal team to attend the following deliveries:

- Elective Caesarean section under regional anaesthesia
- Meconium staining of liquor
- Breech delivery (including Caesarean section under regional anaesthesia)

Inform neonatal team after the following deliveries:

(see antenatal plan in maternal notes)

- Low birth weight infant <2.5 kg
- Prolonged rupture of membranes
- Polyhydramnios
- Previous infant/perinatal death
- Illness in mother likely to affect infant:
- maternal diabetes
- hypothyroidism, hyperthyroidism and maternal Graves' disease
- systemic lupus erythematosus
- myasthenia gravis
- myotonic dystrophy
- Maternal Hepatitis B carriers
- Maternal HIV cases

Issue 02
Issued: October 2007
Expires: September 2009

DEFINITION

- Cholestasis: conjugated hyperbilirubinaemia ≥20 µmol/L and ≥20% of total bilirubin
- Acute liver failure with raised transaminase and coagulopathy unresponsive to vitamin K

Discuss all term infants with liver dysfunction urgently with liver unit team.

To exclude extra-hepatic biliary atresia, admit to liver unit

CAUSES

- Not all liver dysfunction in preterm infants is caused by parenteral nutrition. Extra hepatic biliary atresia does occur and must be diagnosed and managed in a timely fashion

SYMPTOMS AND SIGNS

- Pale or acholic stools
- Prolonged jaundice (defined as visible jaundice at day 21 or older in preterm infants)
- Bleeding, including intraventricular haemorrhage from vitamin K deficiency
- Green jaundice on any day of life
- Acute collapse with liver failure
- Failure to thrive

INVESTIGATIONS

Aim to diagnose causes of liver dysfunction that will benefit from early diagnosis whilst avoiding unnecessary transfer and investigation of small sick infants

Biliary tract disorders	Neonatal hepatitis	Metabolic
● Extra-hepatic biliary atresia	Isolated	● α_1-antitrypsin deficiency
● Bile duct stricture	● Associated with:	● Cystic fibrosis
● Choledochal cyst	○ parenteral nutrition	● Galactosaemia
● Alagille syndrome	○ maternal diabetes	● Dubin-Johnson syndrome
● Non-syndromic bile duct paucity	○ hydrops fetalis	● Bile acid disorder
	○ trisomy 21	● Haemochromatosis
Infection	**Endocrine**	**Toxins/injury**
● Cytomegalovirus	● Hypopituitarism	● Parenteral nutrition
● Toxoplasmosis	● Hypothyroidism	● Multifactorial preterm
● Sepsis		● Haemolytic disease
		● Hypoxia

First-line investigations

- Complete following as soon as possible:
- coagulation screen
- liver transaminases, bilirubin (total and conjugated), albumin, gamma GT, and alkaline phosphatase
- galactosaemia and tyrosinaemia screen
- α_1-antitrypsin concentration **and** phenotype
- serum cortisol, T_4 and TSH
- serum immunoreactive trypsin for cystic fibrosis
- stool in opaque pot for consultant review
- urine for M,C&S
- abdominal ultrasound after 4 hr fast if possible to include liver and gallbladder examination
- if clinical suspicion high, toxoplasma serology, CMV IgM and urine PCR for CMV, syphilis serology, viral culture from swabs of vesicles for *herpes simplex*
- if metabolic disorder suspected, lactate, plasma and urine amino-acids, and urine organic acids

As they become available, discuss results of liver function, coagulation, stool colour, weight gain and abdominal ultrasound with liver unit team

FURTHER INVESTIGATIONS

- Standard aggressive protocol used to investigate term infants is inappropriate in preterm infants because of:
- insufficient blood volume for blanket testing
- poor temperature control when attending for isotope scans
- limited size increases risk of liver biopsy
- Transfer to specialist centre often not possible owing to need for ongoing respiratory support and neonatal nursing care
- Preterm infants with diagnoses requiring surgery (e.g. Kasai procedure for biliary atresia) need to be more than term-corrected age or weigh at least 2 kg before surgery is considered
- Early isotope scanning not widely available and of limited value – many infants can be investigated without this procedure
- Assessment of stool colour can determine which infants with cholestasis require urgent further investigation, as shown over:

Issue 02
Issued: October 2007
Expires: September 2009

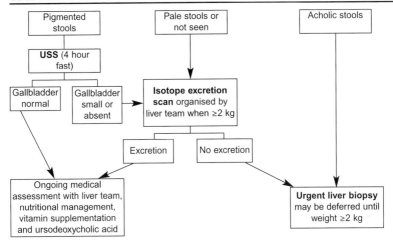

Flowchart

Pigmented stools → **USS** (4 hour fast) → Gallbladder normal / Gallbladder small or absent

Pale stools or not seen → **Isotope excretion scan** organised by liver team when ≥2 kg

Acholic stools

Isotope excretion scan → Excretion / No excretion

Excretion → Ongoing medical assessment with liver team, nutritional management, vitamin supplementation and ursodeoxycholic acid

No excretion → **Urgent liver biopsy** may be deferred until weight ≥2 kg

Acholic stools → **Urgent liver biopsy** may be deferred until weight ≥2 kg

Investigations for ongoing liver dysfunction

● Preterm infants with persistent liver dysfunction but initially normal gallbladder size or an excreting isotope scan can be further investigated locally – discuss with liver team

● If indicated by results of first-line investigations or progressive dysfunction, consider:

● ophthalmic review (other than for retinopathy of prematurity)

● karyotype for dysmorphism

● very long-chain fatty acids for neurological abnormality

● urinary bile salts

● isotope scan, liver biopsy or bone marrow aspirate

MANAGEMENT OF CHOLESTASIS

● Surgical correction if appropriate (e.g. Kasai, choledochal cyst) usually when ≥2 kg or term-corrected age – discuss individual cases

● Nutrition to overcome malabsorption of long-chain fat and fat-soluble vitamins

● if breastfeeding, continue unless weight gain or linear growth inadequate

● if breastfeeding not available or failing to thrive, provide high-calorie diet aiming for 120-150% of estimated average with increased percentage of fat as medium-chain triglycerides (such as Pepti-Junior) OR supplement breast milk with medium-chain triglyceride fat additives – seek advice from liver unit team

● if individually prescribed modular feed required, this is co-ordinated by liver unit dietitians whilst infant is inpatient on liver unit or attending their outpatients

● Prescribe vitamins during cholestasis and for 3 months following resolution of jaundice – doses required will need monitoring and adjustment if still required after discharge (co-ordinated by liver team):

● vitamin K 1-2 mg daily – monitor PT and APTT

● vitamin A 2500-5000 iu daily – monitor serum vitamin A

● vitamin E 100 mg daily – monitor serum vitamin E

● alfacalcidol 30-50 nanogram/kg daily – monitor bone biochemistry

Ursodeoxycholic acid

- Liver team will normally recommend 20-30 mg/kg/day in divided doses for most preterm infants until jaundice resolves, and to stimulate bile flow in infants and children with cystic fibrosis

Parenteral nutrition (PN)

- Wherever possible, feed enterally, as even small amounts have trophic effects on the gut, reduce bacterial colonisation and promote bile flow

- Discontinue PN as soon as possible in all preterm infants with cholestasis

Specific treatments

- Infants with cystic fibrosis, galactosaemia, tyrosinaemia type 1, hypopituitarism, hypothyroidism or bile acid disorders require additional targeted management and life-long follow-up shared by local teams and appropriate specialists

FOLLOW UP

- For infants with persistent cholestasis, arrange outpatient follow-up with liver team after discharge from neonatal unit

- If liver dysfunction has resolved, no follow-up with liver team necessary

- For all others with a specific diagnosis, follow-up will be directed by liver team, appropriate specialists and local consultant

- Long term hepatic outcome excellent – majority resolve within first year

Issue 02
Issued: October 2007
Expires: September 2009

Central venous catheters allow administration of infusions that, if given peripherally, may either cause damage to the vein and surrounding skin, or be less effective. These benefits must be weighed against the risks of line sepsis, thrombosis, embolism, and pleural and pericardial effusion

INDICATIONS

- Total/partial parenteral nutrition
- Concentrated (>10%) glucose infusions
- Inotrope infusions
- Prolonged antibiotic administration (rarely)

CONTRAINDICATIONS

- Infection at the local site
- Systemic sepsis – defer until sepsis treatment commenced and blood cultures negative

EQUIPMENT

- Sterile gown and gloves
- Aqueous chlorhexidine
- Dressing pack with swabs and plastic dish
- Sterile towels/sheets
- Non-toothed forceps
- Neonatal long line
- 5-10 mL syringe
- Heparinised saline 1 unit in 1 mL
- Steristrips
- Gauze
- Clear dressing e.g. Tegaderm
- Contrast (e.g. Hypaque or Omnipaque) solution if lines cannot be seen on X-ray or inverted X-ray (see local policy)

PROCEDURE

This procedure must be performed or directly supervised by an individual competent in the insertion of these devices

Consent and preparation

- Inform parents and obtain verbal consent as recommended by BAPM
- Identify site
- long saphenous at ankle
- medial antecubital vein, lateral antecubital vein at elbow
- scalp veins anterior to ear as a last resort
- Measure distance aiming to insert tip of catheter into superior or inferior vena cava (to xiphisternum for lower limb insertion, to upper sternum for upper limb insertion)

Aseptic Insertion

- Maintain strict asepsis throughout
- Clean site with non-alcohol containing chlorhexidine and allow to dry
- Puncture site with needle in pack and follow instructions for that catheter
- When blood flows back through needle insert line using non-toothed forceps
- The line will pass easily beyond the tip of the needle if appropriately placed
- There may be some resistance when the line passes joints, such as knee, and gentle repositioning of the baby's limb may help
- When in place, withdraw needle as stated in catheter instructions

Securing catheter in correct position

- When haemostasis achieved, fix with steristrips. Place gauze piece under blue hub, and cover with Tegaderm, making sure that all dressing and site is covered, but not encircling the limb tightly
- X-ray to determine position if necessary using 0.2-0.5 mL Hypaque/Omnipaque solution flushed through catheter simultaneously. As with all contrast dyes there is a small risk of allergic reactions

- if upper limb, ensure arm is at 90° angle to thorax during X-ray
- Determine position satisfactory
- Catheter tip should preferably be in superior or inferior vena cava just outside the right atrium, but not in the heart
- Catheter tips in axillary, cephalic and femoral veins acceptable if the benefit outweighs the increased risks
- If catheter tip beyond desired location, withdraw catheter the measured distance, and confirm new position by X-ray

> **Catheter tip must not lie within heart – risk of perforation and tamponade**

Failure of Insertion

- If second operator is required following an unsuccessful attempt at placement, use fresh dressing pack, forceps and catheter

DOCUMENTATION

- Record in case notes:
- date of insertion
- success of insertion and number of attempts
- type and gauge of catheter
- site and length of insertion
- X-ray position and alterations
- Mark on X-ray (using a sticky label) the position of catheter, and any adjustments made

AFTERCARE

Dressings and site care

- Routine dressing changes unnecessary
- Replace aseptically only if dressings lift or catheter visibly kinked or becomes insecure
- Observe site every shift for bleeding, leaking of infusate and signs of infection (redness, swelling)

Medication administration

- Plan these and infusion changes to minimise the number of line violations
- Lines should only be broken into once daily and intermittent medications given via this route only in extreme circumstances
- When breaking into the line observe hand hygiene, wear sterile gloves and swab the connection with 0.05% aqueous chlorhexidine and allow to dry
- Change giving sets every 24 hr
- Change tubing used to give blood products immediately after the transfusion

Position maintenance

- If catheter still required 7 days after placement, note tip position on subsequent X-ray to exclude line-tip migration and take appropriate action as necessary
- Never routinely resite a line
- Review continued need on daily ward rounds

COMPLICATIONS

Prevention

- Do not give blood products routinely through the long line
- Use only 5 or 10 mL syringes. Never use 1 or 2 mL syringes as catheter can rupture
- Limit line violations as above

Catheter-related sepsis

- Commonest complication
- Most common organism is coagulase negative staphylococcus (CoNS)
- Morbidity includes end-organ damage – osteomyelitis, organ abscess, endocarditis and meningitis

- Treat any suspected sepsis with antibiotics covering Gram-negative organisms and CoNS (see **local antibiotic guideline**), **after** taking a peripheral blood culture
- If baby stable, leave line in situ whilst awaiting blood culture results
- If blood culture confirms CoNS and baby stable, discuss continued need for long line with senior colleague
- If line left in situ, repeat blood culture and continue appropriate antibiotic therapy. If second culture remains positive for CoNS, re-discuss long line removal
- If there are ever any signs of complications (end-organ damage, hypotension, progressive platelet consumption/coagulopathy), remove the line without waiting for a positive blood culture

> *If blood cultures grow candida,*
> *Staphylococcus aureus or Gram*
> *negative organisms, remove line*
> *immediately*

Suspected/proven pericardial tamponade

- Suspect if any of following symptoms:
  - acute or refractory hypotension
  - acute respiratory deterioration
  - arrhythmias
  - tachycardia
  - unexplained metabolic acidosis
- Confirm by X-ray (widened mediastinum, enlarged cardiac shadow) or by the presence of pericardial fluid on echocardiogram
- Drain pericardial fluid and remove catheter

Extravasation of fluids

- Into pleural, peritoneal, pericardial (above) and subcutaneous compartments
- Seek immediate advice from senior colleagues

Embolisation of catheter fragments

- Lines can snap if anchored within a thrombus
- If undue resistance encountered during removal, do not force
- Inform your consultant: if accessible it may need surgical removal

REMOVAL

Indications

- Remove when clinical use is no longer justified
- Remove 24 hr after stopping T/PN to ensure tolerance to full enteral feeds, running sodium chloride 0.9% through line at 0.5 mL/hr to maintain patency
- Remove as indicated for complications above

Technique

- Remove using aseptic technique:
  - remove adhesive dressing very carefully
  - pull line out slowly, using gentle traction in the direction of the vein, grasping line not hub
  - ensure catheter is complete
  - if clinical suspicion of line infection, send tip for culture and sensitivity
  - apply pressure to achieve haemostasis
  - use an occlusive dressing and remove within 24 hr
  - document removal in notes

METABOLIC DISORDERS (INBORN ERRORS OF METABOLISM) • 1/5

RECOGNITION

Consider inborn errors of metabolism at same time as common acquired conditions, such as sepsis

- Early recognition of inborn errors of metabolism (IEM) and prompt management are essential to prevent death or neurodisability

- diagnosis of IEM in neonates is often delayed owing to non-specific nature of clinical presentation, and unfamiliarity with diagnostic tests

- seek advice from local and regional clinical chemistry services

Differential diagnosis

Presentation	Common conditions
Encephalopathy without metabolic acidosis	• Urea cycle disorders
	• Maple syrup urine disease (MSUD)
	• Zellweger syndrome
	• Non-ketotic hyperglycinaemia (NKHG)
	• Molybdenum cofactor deficiency
Encephalopathy with metabolic acidosis	• Organic acidaemias (propionic, methylmalonic, isovaleric)
	• Glutaric acidaemia type II
Liver dysfunction	• Galactosaemia
	• Tyrosinaemia
	• Neonatal haemochromatosis
	• Zellweger syndrome
	• α_1-antitrypsin deficiency
	• Smith-Lemli-Opitz syndrome
	• Fatty acid oxidation disorders (MCAD)
	• Congenital disorders of glycosylation – CDG 1b
Hypoglycaemia	• Fatty acid oxidation disorders
	• Galactosaemia
	• Glycogen storage disorders
	• Fructose-1, 6-bisphosphatase deficiency
Metabolic acidosis	• With raised lactate
	• Pyruvate dehydrogenase (PDH) deficiency
	• Pyruvate carboxylase deficiency
	• respiratory chain disorders
	• organic acidaemias
	• With normal lactate
	• organic acidaemias

Issue 02
Issued: October 2007
Expires: September 2009

Non-immune hydrops	● GM1 gangliosidosis ● Mucopolysaccharidosis type VII and IV ● Gaucher's ● Niemann-Pick A & C ● I-Cell disease
Odour: maple syrup (burnt sugar) sweaty feet odour	● MSUD ● Isovaleric acidaemia or ● Glutaric acidaemia type II
Cataracts	● Galactosaemia ● Zellweger syndrome ● Lowe syndrome
Dislocated lens	● Homocystinuria ● Sulphite oxidase deficiency
Congenital anomalies: hypotonia, epicanthal folds, Brushfield spots, simian creases, large fontanelle, renal cysts hypertelorism, low set ears, high forehead, abdominal wall defects, large kidneys appearance similar to fetal alcohol syndrome facial dysmorphism, cleft palate, poly- or syn-dactyly, congenital heart disease	 ● Zellweger syndrome ● Glutaric acidaemia type II ● PDH deficiency ● Smith-Lemli-Opitz syndrome
Agenesis of corpus callosum	● NKHGPDH deficiency
Apnoea or periodic breathing in term infant	● NKHG
Respiratory alkalosis in a tachypnoeic baby	● Hyperammonaemia
Jaundice (particularly conjugated) and liver dysfunction	● Galactosemia ● Tyrosinaemia ● α_1-antitrypsin deficiency
Hypoglycaemia in a low-risk infant, or persistent/recurrent, with neurological symptoms	● Fatty acid oxidation defects ● Glycogen storage disorders ● Galactosaemia
Metabolic acidosis with increased anion gap	● Organic acidaemias
Persistent vomiting	● Hyperammonaemia
Hiccoughing	● NKHG

Issue 02
Issued: October 2007
Expires: September 2009

Specific indicators

- Clinical context:
- unexplained and mysterious deterioration of baby (can be as short as 12 hr but more commonly at 48 hr)

- Family history of:
- known metabolic disorders
- unexplained neonatal or infant deaths
- parental consanguinity

- Obstetric history:
- acute fatty liver of pregnancy and HELLP syndrome in index pregnancy may point towards long chain fatty acid oxidation defect in neonate

Non-specific indicators suggestive of metabolic disorder in an encephalopathic baby

- Encephalopathy in low risk infant, or onset after period of normality
- Fluctuating consciousness and muscle tone
- Changes in muscle tone:
- axial hypotonia with limb hypertonia
- 'normal' tone in comatose baby
- Abnormal movements:
- myoclonic or boxing movements
- tongue thrusting
- lip smacking
- True seizures occur late in metabolic encephalopathies except in NKHG

INITIAL INVESTIGATIONS

- Whenever IEM suspected, perform required investigations without delay
- Seek early advice about appropriate investigations and management from inherited metabolic diseases (IMD) team at tertiary metabolic centre

Urine

- Smell
- Ketostix – presence of large amounts of urinary ketones is always abnormal in neonates and suggests IEM, especially organic acidaemias
- Reducing substances – use Clinitest – urinary dipsticks are specific for glucose and miss galactose in babies with galactosaemia
- Freeze 15-20 mL urine for amino and organic acid analysis

Blood

- Full blood count, U&Es, infection work up
- Glucose
- Blood gas
- Ammonia
- Lactate
- Total and conjugated bilirubin, liver function tests including clotting studies
- Acylcarnitines, including free and total carnitine
- Uric acid
- Amino acids

Imaging

- Cranial ultrasound
- Ophthalmic examination

SPECIFIC INVESTIGATIONS

Jaundice

Blood

- Galactosaemia screen (urinary reducing substances can be negative after short period of galactose exclusion)
- Ferritin
- Very long chain fatty acids
- α_1-antitrypsin (quantitative)
- 7-dehydrocholesterol
- Transferrin isoelectric focusing

Urine

- Succinylacetone
- Skin (and liver) biopsy after discussion with metabolic team

Encephalopathy

- Paired blood and CSF glycine
- CSF lactate
- Very long chain fatty acid profile
- Urine for orotic acid
- Urine – Sulfitest for sulphite oxidase deficiency

Hypoglycaemia (most informative when obtained at the time of hypoglycaemia)

- Plasma non-esterified fatty acids
- ß-hydroxybutyrate
- RBC galactosaemia screen
- Insulin and C-peptide
- Acylcarnitine profile, free and total carnitine
- Cortisol, growth hormone
- Urine for organic acids

Post-mortem (plan how best to use these precious samples in consultation with IMD team)

- Plasma (2-5 mL), urine (10-20 mL) and CSF (1 mL) – frozen at -20°C
- Red cells – blood (5 mL) in lithium heparin stored at 4°C (fridge)
- Blood (5 mL) in EDTA – stored at 4°C for DNA analysis
- Tissue biopsies
- skin – store in culture medium or saline at 4°C (fridge)
- muscle and liver – take within hour of death, snap freeze in liquid nitrogen
- Post-mortem examination

IMMEDIATE MANAGEMENT

Commence emergency management of suspected IEM while awaiting results of initial investigations

- Attend to Airway, Breathing and Circulation; ventilate if necessary
- Omit all protein intake, including TPN and lipid
- Commence intravenous glucose infusion to provide 6-8 mg glucose/kg/min
- start insulin infusion if hyperglycaemic (>15 mmol/L) or catabolic
- if hypertonic glucose infusion necessary, insert central line
- Correct dehydration, acid-base and electrolyte disturbances
- Cover for infection
- Control seizures (avoid sodium valproate)
- Consider transfer to tertiary metabolic centre if stable and appropriate

SPECIFIC MANAGEMENT

- Must be led by IMD team
- Use following as guide to general principles of management
- Neonatal hyperammonaemia – a medical emergency requiring prompt intervention to lower ammonia concentration
  - renal replacement therapy (haemofiltration more efficient than peritoneal dialysis)
  - sodium benzoate
  - sodium phenylbutyrate
  - L-arginine
  - L-carnitine
- Organic acidaemia
  - reduce/stop protein intake
  - hypertonic glucose infusion ± insulin
  - L-carnitine
  - glycine
  - biotin
- Fatty acid oxidation disorders
  - avoid prolonged fast
  - L-carnitine
- Lactic acidosis
  - dichloroacetate
  - biotin
  - L-carnitine
  - thiamine
- Galactosaemia
  - dietary exclusion of galactose

The procedure is the same for both nasogastric and orogastric tubes. As nasogastric tubes are more commonly used in neonates, the term nasogastric will be used throughout the guideline

INDICATIONS

- To keep stomach deflated or to instil enteral feeds when full oral feeding not possible

- Orogastric tubes are used predominantly in babies in respiratory distress or with structural abnormality of nasal cavity where full bottle feeds are contraindicated

- Nasogastric tubes are used short term for all other neonates until full oral feeding is achievable

EQUIPMENT

- Appropriately sized nasogastric tube – 6FG or 8FG most commonly used

- use tubes with markings to enable accurate measurement of depth and length

- 10 mL syringe
- pH testing paper
- Duoderm
- Adhesive tape (e.g. Transpore or Hyperfix)
- Gloves

PROCEDURE

Preparation

- To prevent risk of aspiration, pass nasogastric tube before a feed

- To reduce risk of epidermal stripping, apply Duoderm to skin of face as an attachment for adhesive tape

- Wash hands and prepare equipment
- Wrap baby securely in a sheet

- Determine length of tube to be inserted

- keeping tube in its packet, extend tip of tube from nose to ear and then from ear to stomach, aiming for the space in the middle below the ribs; note the mark on the tube or keep your fingers on the point measured

Sternum
Ribs
Navel

Insertion

- With clean hands, don gloves and pass tube slowly and steadily until required pre-measured depth is reached

- Observe baby throughout procedure for colour change, vomiting, respiratory distress or resistance

- if any distress occurs, stop and remove tube

Checking position of gastric feeding tube

- Neonatal units and carers in the community should use pH indicator strips or paper

- for recommended products go to www.pasa.nhs.uk/PASAweb

- Do NOT use radiography 'routinely' but, if baby is being X-rayed for another reason, use X-ray to confirm position is satisfactory by noting the position of tube on film

- Do not use 'Whoosh test' (auscultation of injected air entering the stomach) to determine position of nasogastric tubes as it is unreliable

Checking position using pH

- Aspirate stomach contents with a 10 mL syringe and test for an acid response using pH paper

- pH <6 indicates correct gastric placement

- even though aspirates with pH ≤5.5 indicate correct placement in most babies, including the majority of those receiving acid suppressants, some babies will consistently have pH values ≥6 despite correct placement

- If pH values ≥6, seek senior advice

- ensure you work through the **NPSA flowchart** below and record findings before making any decisions

- the multidisciplinary care team should then discuss possible actions, balancing the risk between feeding (with a possibility of the tube being in the lungs) and not feeding the baby in the short term, and record how they reached their decision

NPSA Flowchart as a basis for decision making when checking position of naso and orogastric feeding tube in babies on neonatal units

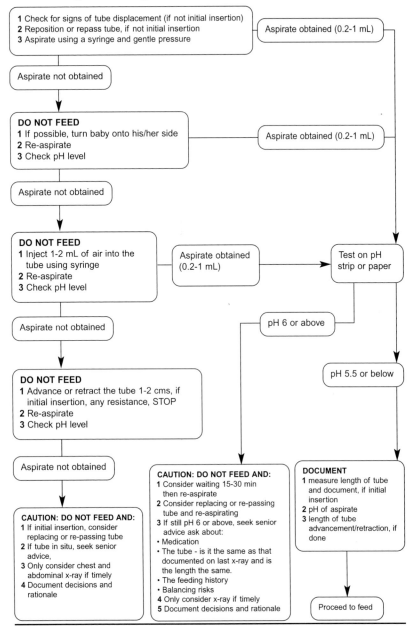

1 Check for signs of tube displacement (if not initial insertion)
2 Reposition or repass tube, if not initial insertion
3 Aspirate using a syringe and gentle pressure

Aspirate obtained (0.2-1 mL)

Aspirate not obtained

DO NOT FEED
1 If possible, turn baby onto his/her side
2 Re-aspirate
3 Check pH level

Aspirate obtained (0.2-1 mL)

Aspirate not obtained

DO NOT FEED
1 Inject 1-2 mL of air into the tube using syringe
2 Re-aspirate
3 Check pH level

Aspirate obtained (0.2-1 mL)

Test on pH strip or paper

Aspirate not obtained

pH 6 or above

DO NOT FEED
1 Advance or retract the tube 1-2 cms, if initial insertion, any resistance, STOP
2 Re-aspirate
3 Check pH level

pH 5.5 or below

Aspirate not obtained

CAUTION: DO NOT FEED AND:
1 Consider waiting 15-30 min then re-aspirate
2 Consider replacing or re-passing tube and re-aspirating
3 If still pH 6 or above, seek senior advice ask about:
• Medication
• The tube - is it the same as that documented on last x-ray and is the length the same.
• The feeding history
• Balancing risks
4 Only consider x-ray if timely
5 Document decisions and rationale

DOCUMENT
1 measure length of tube and document, if initial insertion
2 pH of aspirate
3 length of tube advancement/retraction, if done

CAUTION: DO NOT FEED AND:
1 If initial insertion, consider replacing or re-passing tube
2 If tube in situ, seek senior advice,
3 Only consider chest and abdominal x-ray if timely
4 Document decisions and rationale

Proceed to feed

Issue 02
Issued: October 2007
Expires: September 2009

Risk assessment when pH ≥6

- The following factors can contribute to a high gastric pH (≥6)
- Presence of amniotic fluid in a baby <48 hr
- Milk in baby's stomach, particularly if receiving 1-2 hrly feeds
- Use of medication to reduce stomach acid

Securing tube

- Once correct position of tube ascertained, secure to face with adhesive tape (e.g. Transpore or Hyperfix) over Duoderm

DOCUMENTATION

- Record procedure in nursing documentation, noting size of tube, length passed and, if a nasogastric tube, which nostril used

FURTHER MANAGEMENT

Monitoring

- Check integrity of skin around nostril at frequent intervals for signs of deterioration
- if signs of pressure appear, reposition tube and/or tape, or re-pass nasogastric tube via opposite nostril, or use orogastric route if necessary
- Check nasogastric tube position using pH. Follow **NPSA flowchart** above:
- following initial insertion and subsequent reinsertions
- before administering each feed
- before giving medication
- following vomiting, retching or coughing – absence of coughing does not rule out misplacement or migration

- if evidence of tube displacement (e.g. if tape loose or visible tube appears longer or kinked)
- when chest X-ray taken for another reason
- If on continuous feeds, synchronize tube checking with syringe changes
- when continuous feeding has stopped, wait 15-30 min to allow stomach to empty of milk and for pH level to fall

Changing nasogastric tubes

- When changing nasogastric tubes, follow manufacturer's recommendations
- Pass new nasogastric tube via opposite nostril wherever possible

Reporting misplaced tube incidents

- Report all misplaced feeding tube incidents using local risk management procedure

FURTHER INFORMATION

- Further details on determining correct position of oro-/nasogastric tubes in infants are available from http://www.npsa.nhs.uk/site/media/documents/1298_InterimAdvice.pdf

Issue 02
Issued: October 2007
Expires: September 2009

RECOGNITION AND ASSESSMENT

Definition

NEC is characterised by the triad of abdominal distension, gastrointestinal bleeding and pneumatosis intestinalis (intramural gas)

Modified Bell's criteria

Stage 1 – Suspected NEC

- Signs suggestive but not diagnostic
- Systemic signs:
  - temperature instability
  - apnoea
  - bradycardia
  - lethargy
- Intestinal signs:
  - elevated pre-gavage residuals
  - mild abdomen distension
  - emesis
  - haem-positive stools (exclude local pathology)
- Radiological signs:
  - normal or intestinal dilatation
  - mild ileus
- Intestinal signs:
  - bright red blood from rectum (exclude local pathology)

Stage 2 – Definite NEC (mild to moderately ill)

- Systemic signs: see **stage 1** ± mild metabolic acidosis, mild thrombocytopenia
- Intestinal signs: see **stage 1**, plus absent bowel sounds, ± abdominal tenderness, abdominal cellulitis or right lower quadrant mass

- Radiological signs: intestinal dilatation, ileus, pneumatosis intestinalis, portal vein gas, ± ascites

Stage 3 – Advanced NEC (severely ill, bowel intact or perforated)

- Systemic signs: see **stage 2** + hypotension, bradycardia, severe apnoea, combined respiratory and metabolic acidosis, DIC, neutropenia
- Intestinal signs: see **stage 2** + signs of generalised peritonitis, marked tenderness, distension of abdomen
- Radiological signs: see **stage 2** + definite ascites ± pneumoperitoneum

Risk factors

- Prematurity
- Reverse umbilical flow antenatally
- Low systemic blood flow during neonatal period
- Formula milk
- No antenatal steroids
- Infections with – klebsiella, enterobacter, anaerobes
- H_2-blocker (reduced gastric pH)

Differential diagnosis

- Sepsis with ileus
- Bowel obstruction
- Volvulus
- Malrotation
- Spontaneous intestinal perforation:
  - associated with early postnatal corticosteroids or indometacin
  - often seen at the terminal ileum with normal bowel
  - abdominal XR does not show evidence of pneumatosis intestinalis
- Systemic candidiasis:
  - clinical signs can mimic NEC with abdominal distension, metabolic disturbances, hypotension and thrombocytopenia

INVESTIGATIONS

Abdominal X-ray

- Supine AP
- + left lateral if concern about perforation

Not all infants will have radiological findings associated with NEC

Bloods

- FBC – anaemia, neutropenia and thrombocytopenia often present; early return to normal carries good prognosis
- Blood film – evidence of haemolysis and toxic changes (e.g. spherocytes, cell fragments, polychromatic cells)
- CRP
- U&E
- Blood gas – evidence of acidosis (base excess <-10)
- Coagulation screen
- Blood cultures

IMMEDIATE TREATMENT

Always discuss management with senior neonatologist

Stage 1-Suspected NEC

- Transfer baby to neonatal intensive care and nurse in incubator to avoid cross infection
- Nil by mouth
- Gastric decompression
- free drainage with large nasogastric tube (size 8) or continuous suction with 10 cm water
- IV fluids/TPN (without Intralipid in the acute stage) – total volume 150 mL/kg or less
- Long line when stable
- Pain relief – consider morphine/diamorphine infusion (see **Pain and Stress** guideline)

Stage 2-Proven NEC (confirmed radiologically)

- As for Stage 1
- Antibiotics:
  - penicillin/ampicillin + gentamicin + metronidazole
  - cefotaxime and vancomycin not routinely necessary: discuss with senior neonatologist
- If coagulation abnormal, give FFP
- If thrombocytopenia and/or anaemia occur, transfuse – see **Thrombocytopenia** guideline
- If hypotension occurs, see **Hypotension** guideline
- Discuss with surgical team – may need transfer to surgical centre

Stage 3-Advanced NEC (intestinal perforation or fulminant NEC)

- Refer to surgical team – may need laparotomy or resection of bowel in surgical centre

SUBSEQUENT MANAGEMENT

In recovery phase

- If baby fully recovered at 48 hr and NEC no longer suspected, restart feeds
- In Stage 1, if no progression after 3-5 days, consider restarting feeds slowly (see **Nutrition** guideline)

- In Stage 2, if abdominal examination normal after 10 days, consider restarting feeds
- some may need longer period of total gut rest
- In Stage 3, discuss with surgeon and dietitian before restarting feeds

Late complications

- Recurrence (in about 10%)
- Strictures (in about 10% non-surgical cases)
- Short bowel syndrome and problems related to gut resection

MONITORING TREATMENT

- Observe general condition closely and review at least 12 hrly
- Daily
- acid-base
- fluid balance
- electrolytes (twice daily if condition unstable)
- FBC and coagulation
- Repeat X-ray daily until baby becomes clinically stable. Discuss with consultant

LONG-TERM MANAGEMENT

- Advise parents about signs of bowel obstruction
- Medical ± surgical follow-up after discharge
- Contrast studies if clinically indicated for stenosis
- Appropriate developmental follow-up

INDICATIONS

- Persistent pulmonary hypertension of the newborn in term infants, proven on clinical grounds or by echocardiography – see **PPHN** guideline

- Oxygen Index >25

- Initiate treatment with nitric oxide (NO) only after discussion with on-call consultant

- Caution in preterm infants, Grade IV IVH, recent pulmonary haemorrhage, platelets <50 x 10^9/L

DOSE AND ADMINISTRATION

Starting nitric oxide

Preparation

- Ensure ventilation optimal and that other aspects of the PPHN guideline have been followed

- A sustained inflation immediately before starting NO can enhance response

Administration

- Start NO at 10 ppm in <34 wk gestation or 20 ppm in older infants

- If no response after 30 min, increase to maximum of 20 ppm

- If still no response at 20 ppm, discontinue

- NO can be stopped abruptly without weaning if given for <4 hr

- Once responding, reduce dose gradually

- maintenance dose of 3-6 ppm usually adequate

Weaning

- If NO has been administered for ≥4 hr, wean gradually to prevent rebound

- Reduce by 1 ppm/hr until dosage reduced to 3 ppm

- Following this, more gradual weaning (i.e. 1 ppm/4 hr) necessary, until NO discontinued

- If a sustained and significant fall in SaO_2 occurs following reduction in dosage, increase dosage to previous level and continue to wean at half previous rate

- Once discontinued, wait a few hours before removing NO circuit from ventilator

MONITORING

- Use SaO_2 to monitor response

- Blood gases hrly

- Monitor methaemoglobin at least 12 hrly. If methaemoglobin levels >3% reduce NO and stop as soon as possible

- Monitor atmospheric NO_2 levels during treatment

- NO inhibits platelet function and can trigger bleeding if baby has bleeding problem or thrombocytopenia. Check FBC daily whilst baby is on NO

ENTERAL REQUIREMENTS

Refer to dietitian for nutritional advice and composition of supplements and formulas

Introduction

- To maintain optimal growth, it is essential to meet nutritional requirements of preterm infants

- Neonatal nutrition team will monitor, audit, educate, and advise to ensure vulnerable infants maintain appropriate growth

Daily recommendations

Daily recommendation (growing phase)	Preterm ELBW <1.0 kg	Preterm VLBW <1.5 kg	Term 0-3 month
Fluids mL/kg	160-220	135-190	150
Energy kcal/kg	130-150	110-130	115-100
Protein g/kg	3.8-4.2 4.4*	3.4-3.6 4.2*	2.1
Protein:energy ratio	3.3 g/100 kcal	2.8 g/100 kcal	
Sodium mmol/kg	3.0-5.0		2-3
Iron mg/kg	2.0-4.0 (not before 2 weeks)		1.7 mg/day
Calcium mmol/kg	2.5-5.5		13.1 mmol/day
Phosphorus mmol/kg	1.9-4.5		13.1 mmol/day
Vitamin A IU/ kg	700-1500 2000-3000/kg in chronic lung disease		1155/day
Vitamin D IU/ kg	150-400 400/day		340/day

* protein for catch-up growth (based on Tsang guidelines 2005)

MEETING DAILY REQUIREMENTS FOR PRE-TERM INFANTS

- Offer breast milk. If unavailable, use pre-term formula

- See **Vitamin and mineral preparations** for appropriate supplements and dosage for use with individual feeds

Pre-term formula

- Feed at 150-165 mL/kg/day
- average nutritional contents per 100 mL = 80 kcal/2.4 g protein

Breast milk

- Unfortified expressed breast milk (EBM) feed at >200 mL/kg/day

- EBM + Nutriprem breast milk fortifier (BMF) feed at 150-180 mL/kg/day

- fortifier can be added on day 14. Protein content of preterm breast milk falls from 1.8 g/100 mL to 1.3 g/100 mL by second week

- average nutritional contents of EBM (mature) per 100 mL = 70 kcal/1.3 g protein

- average nutritional content of fortified EBM (mature) per 100 mL = 86 kcal/2.1 g protein

When babies reach 1.8–2.0 kg and on discharge

Breast milk

- Encourage babies to breast feed
- Stop fortifier unless growth poor – refer to dietitian for assessment
- Continue with vitamins and iron

Formula milk

- Offer Nutriprem 2 (available on prescription ACBS) as feed of choice for preterm infants, and stop vitamins and iron
- Continue Nutriprem 2 until 6 months after expected date of delivery, then use formula milk until 12-18 months old
- If term milk given, continue vitamins and iron - see **Vitamin and mineral preparation** sections for dosage
- average nutritional content of Nutriprem 2 per 100 mL = 75 kcal/2.0 g protein
- average content of term formula per 100 mL = 67 kcal/1.4 g protein

Vitamin and mineral preparations

Multivitamins

Preterm infants on preterm formula or EBM plus Nutriprem BMF

- Abidec 0.3 mL orally daily
- start when oral feeds established 150 mL/kg
- stop when Nutriprem 2 given >150 mL/kg **but continue if term formula given**

or

- Healthy start vitamins – 5 drops orally daily

Preterm infants on breast milk only

- Abidec 0.6 mL orally daily
- start when oral feeds established 150 mL/kg
- reduce to 0.3 mL on discharge

or

- Healthy start vitamins – 10 drops orally daily - reduce to 5 drops on discharge

Vitamin K

- **Indications**
- all babies
- **Administration**
- see **Vitamin K** guideline

Folic acid

- **Indications**
- babies fed breast milk only
- Give 50 micrograms orally once daily
- start when oral feeding established – 150 mL/kg
- stop on discharge or when breast milk fortifier added

Phosphate

- Use phosphate supplements with unfortified EBM and Peptijunior/Pregestimil
- When on full feeds, give Joulies phosphate 0.5 mL 12 hrly, increasing to 0.7 or 1.0 mL 12 hrly to maintain serum phosphate >1.5 mmol/L (Joulies phosphate contains PO_4 1.35 mmol/mL and Na 0.87 mmol/mL)
- unless osteopenia of prematurity present, phosphate supplements are normally stopped at discharge or at 37 weeks
- Exclusively breastfed infants may require serum PO_4 check at 6 weeks post-term and may need phosphate supplements up to 3 months old if <1.49 mmol/L

Issue 02
Issued: October 2007
Expires: September 2009

Iron

Indications

- Birth weight <2 kg

Preparation

- Sodium feredetate (Sytron) liquid – containing elemental iron 5.5 mg/mL

Administration

- Sodium feredetate 1 mL daily to all infants <2 kg
- start at 6 weeks or when transfusions cease, whichever is later
- stop when Nutriprem 2 is started
- give 5.5 mg (1 mL) at discharge to all breastfed infants or those fed term formula

MONITORING GROWTH

- Critical in assessing nutritional needs of infant
- if not monitored **regularly**, optimum growth may not be achieved
- where monitoring not appropriate (e.g. very sick infant), ensure basic levels of nutrition – 120 kcal/kg and protein 3.4-3.8 g/kg/day

Plot weight/length/head circumference weekly on centile charts

Weight

- May reflect fluid balance rather than fat/lean body mass
- measure every 3 days and plot weekly on centile chart to assess growth
- An increase of 15-20 g/kg/day implies adequate weight gain **only** if reflected on centile charts

Length

- Essential in reflecting skeletal and organ growth
- In under-nutrition, length is spared over weight gain
- Some babies experience altered growth with stunting
- Early assessment of longitudinal growth can provide better indication of long term growth
- Aim to monitor all babies, especially those who are ELBW/IUGR/CLD/fed EBM
- Measure weekly and plot on centile chart

Head circumference

- Gives valuable information on cerebral growth in respect of cerebral injury and nutritional adequacy
- in moderate under-nutrition, head growth is spared in relation to length and weight
- Measure weekly and plot on centile chart

Monitor serum/urine concentrations weekly

- Phosphate (1.0-2.3 mmol/L)
- urinary TRP
- Sodium (135-145 mmol/L)
- Urea (1.9-6.2 mmol/L)
- Alkaline phosphatase
- FBC
- Hb
- reticulocytes

POOR GROWTH

Factors suggesting inadequate growth

- Failure to achieve optimum growth according to head/length/weight measurements plotted on centile charts
- Weight gain <15 g/kg/day
- Weight ± length falling across centile over 1-2 weeks

Review

- Before addition of supplements, check and correct/modify:
- fluid restriction
- inadequate human milk fortification
- sodium depletion
- anaemia
- sepsis
- corticosteroid treatment (can delay growth)
- respiratory/cardiac condition (resulting in increased energy requirement)
- use of diuretics
- malabsorption
- If volume cannot be increased, consider supplements

What to do after above factors checked

- Action will depend on which milk infant receiving
- Make changes **sequentially**, one at a time

If infant having low birth weight formula milk

- Increase fluid intake by 5 mL/kg increments to 180 mL/kg/day (provided medical condition allows)
- Once growth assessment checked, add Duocal in increments of 1 scoop (2.5 mL/6 kcal scoop)/100 mL /24 hr (maximum 3 scoops/100 mL)

- Review weight gain weekly before each increment increase
- Always consider increased volume before introducing supplements

If infant having breast milk

- Aim to **increase volume by 5 mL/kg increments to max 200 mL/kg** as tolerated (unfortified >220 mL/kg)
- Add Nutriprem BMF when taking full feeds 150 mL/kg but **not before day 14**
- full strength – 1 sachet (2.1 g)/50 mL
- if gastrointestinal symptoms present, use half strength – half sachet (1.1 g)/50 mL for 24 hr. If tolerating, increase to full strength

Documentation

- To ensure all staff aware, record all dietary modification in medical notes, including:
- number of 2.5 mL scoops and what is added – not just additives
- kcal/protein g/kg **or** per 100 mL after modification

If growth poor, refer to breast feeding specialist

MANAGING SPECIFIC CONDITIONS

Problems with initiating feeds

- Use EBM
- If EBM not available, prefer preterm formula
- if absorption poor, use Prenan – partially hydrolyzed whey protein or term formula
- if Prenan not tolerated, use Peptijunior or Pregestimil – hypoallergenic feeds made from extensively hydrolyzed whey/casein

Malabsorption ± post GI surgery

- Use Peptijunior or Pregestimil – both are hypoallergenic feeds made from extensively hydrolyzed whey/casein with MCT

Cholestasis

- Use Prenan, Peptijunior or Pregestimil – all have MCT, and Prenan meets nutritional needs of preterm infant

Galactosaemia

- If suspected, use infant soya formula milk

Cow's milk protein intolerance

- Use Peptijunior or Pregestimil – neither contains lactose or cow's milk protein

Note:

- Peptijunior and Pregestimil have low folic acid content and are formulated for term infants. If 200 mL/kg cannot be achieved, concentrate feed:
- normal dilution – 13% 1 scoop to 30 mL boiled water
- concentrated – 15% 1 scoop to 25 mL boiled water

Low albumin/low urea

- Contact dietitian for supervision
- Low albumin is a consequence of prematurity but a falling value may indicate inadequate protein
- Low urea <1.0 mmol/L – may indicate inadequate protein
- If <4 wk old, low urea may indicate liver unable to make urea, with consequent hyperaminoacidaemia/hyperammonia, especially in preterm infants with IUGR

- If infant stable and growing, low urea may reflect protein economy in rapidly growing infants
- plot length, weight and head circumference
- if falling away from centile or static, extra protein needed – contact dietitian

High blood glucose

- Contact dietitian to discuss replacing carbohydrate within feeds with fat
- Calogen is an emulsion of long chain fats 50:50 fat/water which can be added to feeds in 1 mL increments up to 2 mL/100 mL of milk (1 mL = 4.5 kcal)

Dexamethasone

- Can cause high blood glucose and high serum urea
- if infant poorly nourished, consider reducing blood glucose using medical means rather than by reducing nutrition

Indometacin

- May cause restriction of blood flow to GI tract
- avoid use of supplements while on this treatment

OBJECTIVE

- To put an effective plan in place to allow oxygen-dependent infants to be cared for safely at home

INDICATIONS FOR HOME OXYGEN THERAPY

- Chronic lung disease with ongoing demand for increased inspired O_2

Criteria

- Clinically stable on oxygen therapy via nasal cannulae for ≥2 weeks
- SaO_2 >92% (after 32 wks gestation and risk of retinopathy of prematurity passed) on <0.5 L/min oxygen
- a lower value may be appropriate in cyanotic congenital heart disease. Set threshold on an individual basis
- Ensure baby able to cope with short periods in air in case their nasal cannulae become dislodged – applies to those in <0.5 L/min
- Routine continuous oxygen monitoring discontinued including at feeding, awake and sleeping times apart from checks at 4 hrly intervals twice weekly before discharge
- Thermo-control well established
- Feeding orally 3-4 hrly and showing positive weight gain
- some babies may require tube feeding – if all other criteria are met, this should not hinder discharge
- Final decision on suitability for discharge lies with consultant

PREPARATION FOR DISCHARGE

Make arrangements with parents

- Discuss need for home oxygen with parents
- Obtain consent for home oxygen supply and for sharing information with oxygen supplier. This is obligatory before supplier can be contacted with patient details
- Arrange multi-disciplinary meeting one week before discharge with parents/carers, community nurse, health visitor and member of neonatal unit
- Arrange discharge plan. See **Discharge** guideline

Parent training

- Resuscitation techniques
- no smoking in the house or anywhere in baby's environment
- Recognition of baby's breathing pattern, colour and movements
- Use of oxygen equipment
- What to do in case of emergency
- contact numbers
- direct admission policy

Organise oxygen

- Prescribing physician to complete Home Oxygen Order Form (HOOF)
- fax completed form to appropriate supplier
- send copies of form to:
  - GP
  - appropriate PCT
  - clinical home oxygen lead for appropriate trust
  - Children's Home Oxygen Record national database (with parents' consent)
- file original in patient notes

Discharge checklist

- Discharge plan implemented (see **Discharge** guideline)
- Plan discharge for beginning of week to ensure staff available in event of problems
- Oxygen supply and equipment installed in the home
- Baby will go home on prescribed amount of oxygen; this may be altered on direction of medical or nursing staff, or in event of emergency
- GP and other relevant professionals (also fire and electricity companies – although oxygen supplier usually does this) informed of date and time of discharge
- Community team briefed to arrange home visit well in advance of discharge to ensure conditions suitable and equipment correctly installed
- Parents/carers trained to care for baby safely at home and have support contact numbers

AFTERCARE

- As oxygen dependant babies are at increased risk of contracting respiratory syncytial virus (RSV), give palivizumab and influenza vaccine (see **Immunisation** guideline)

> *Community team will advise when baby ready to be weaned off oxygen*

Issue 02
Issued: October 2007
Expires: September 2009

RECOGNITION AND ASSESSMENT

Symptoms and signs

Distinguish signs of pain and stress from signs of life-threatening conditions, such as hypoxia, seizures or CO_2 retention, which require other forms of management

A lack of behavioural responses (e.g. crying and movement) does not necessarily indicate a lack of pain

Behavioural

- Crying, whimpering
- Facial expressions:
- brow bulge
- eye squeeze
- deepening of nasolabial folds
- Active movement and attempts to withdraw from the painful stimulus:
- thrashing
- tremulousness
- limb withdrawal, flexion
- cycling movements
- arching
- Flexor reflexes; leg withdrawal
- Exaggerated reactivity
- Decreased sleep periods

Physiological

- Changes in heart rate and variability
- Respiratory rate and quality
- Fluctuations in blood pressure – up or down
- Decreased transcutaneous oxygen and carbon dioxide levels
- Oxygen desaturation
- Palmar sweat
- Pallor
- Flushing

Indications for pain management

- Before painful procedures:
- insertion of long lines
- intubation and IPPV
- LP
- insertion of chest drain
- venous sampling/access
- In response to behavioural changes
- To aid ventilation:
- respirations out of synchrony with the ventilator
- pulmonary hypertension
- In infants with raised ICP

NON-PHARMACOLOGICAL PAIN MANAGEMENT

- Non-nutritive sucking
- Swaddling
- Distraction
- Dummy
- Calming
- Tactile stimulation
- Rocking
- Expressed breast milk
- Skin-to-skin care

PRINCIPLES OF ANALGESIA

- Prophylactic or symptomatic
- Use stepwise approach with agents of increasing potency

ANALGESIA FOR NON-VENTILATED INFANTS

Sucrose

Activates opioid systems that provide natural analgesia and is recognised as an appropriate analgesia for newborn babies during some painful procedures

Contraindicated in unstable babies

Issue 02
Issued: October 2007
Expires: September 2009

Indications

- Heel pricks for blood sampling
- Cannulation and venous sampling
- Ventricular tap

Use

- Use sucrose in conjunction with other non pharmacological methods such as:
- dummy
- hands-on comforting
- swaddling
- performing procedure in a quiet environment
- Use sucrose solution (e.g. Sweet-Ease 24% or Hypostop 40%)
- preterm baby – 0.1-0.5 mL repeated as necessary
- term baby – 2 mL in repeated doses as necessary at 5 min intervals to a maximum of 3 doses per procedure
- Give first dose 2 min before procedure by one of following methods:
- dip cotton bud into solution and wipe around baby's mouth
- dip dummy into solution and give to baby
- via syringe

Topical pain relief

- Lidocaine (plain, not with adrenaline) 1% 0.3 mL/kg maximum per dose effective as a topical anaesthesia

Avoid EMLA cream – evidence of efficacy in neonate is inconsistent

Paracetamol

- Orally or rectally – absorbed more quickly if given via oral route
- oral dosage

Gestation	Loading dose	Maintenance	Max daily dose
>32 weeks	24 mg/kg	12 mg/kg 4 hrly	60 mg/kg
<32 weeks	24 mg/kg	12 mg/kg 8 hrly	30 mg/kg

- rectal dosage

Loading dose	Maintenance
36 mg/kg	24 mg/kg 8 hrly

- Whichever route is used, treatment is for maximum of 3 days. Total daily dose not to exceed 60 mg/kg

Oramorph

- Particularly useful for chronic pain relief and for terminal care

- Large doses such as 100 micrograms/kg 4 hrly can cause hypotension and respiratory depression

ANALGESIA FOR VENTILATED INFANTS

Either diamorphine or morphine may be used in addition to agents used for **Non-ventilated infants**

Diamorphine

- Loading dose 50 microgram/kg IV

- Maintenance 15 microgram/kg/hour IV

- Larger doses than this are no more effective but are associated with more adverse effects

- Effects can be reversed by naloxone 10 microgram/kg IV as a bolus

Morphine

- Loading dose 50 microgram/kg IV

- Maintenance 5 microgram/kg/hour IV

- Can cause hypotension, bradycardia and respiratory depression

- Half life between 1 and 6 hr – increases with decreasing gestational age

- Effects can be reversed by naloxone 10 microgram/kg IV as a bolus

SEDATION

Sedation has no analgesic effect. Always use in conjunction with appropriate analgesia

Chloral hydrate

- Can be useful in irritable fatigued child/cerebral irritation

- Has long half life and can accumulate, leading to hypotension and respiratory depression

- single dose treatment – 45 mg/kg (75 mg/kg for term infants) oral

- sustained sedation – 30 mg/kg 6 hrly oral

PAIN RELIEF DURING SPECIFIC PROCEDURES

Heel prick

- Dip a dummy in sucrose solution

- Breastfeeding during procedures – caution in poor feeders; try to avoid association between feeding and pain

- Control and swaddling to restrict physical movements (by parent or nurse)

Chest drain insertion

- Secure local anaesthesia using lidocaine ± systemic analgesia

RECOGNITION AND ASSESSMENT

Definition

- PDA is the continuation of blood flow through the duct following birth
- Persistent PDA is failure of functional closure of duct by 48 hr or of anatomical closure by 3 weeks

Factors associated with delayed closure

- Early gestation
- Lack of antenatal corticosteroid prophylaxis where indicated
- Surfactant-deficient lung disease
- Hypoxaemia
- Volume overload

Adverse effects of PDA

- Can become manifest in first 48 hr
- Significant right-to-left shunt and hypoxia until pulmonary pressure falls
- Reduced systemic blood flow leading to acidosis and hypotension
- Increased pulmonary blood flow leading to increased work of breathing
- Pulmonary haemorrhage
- Intraventricular haemorrhage and cerebral ischaemia (Steal)

Symptoms and signs

- Can be absent in a clinically significant duct for first 7 days of life
- Significant left-to-right shunt suggested by:
- active praecordium
- full pulses
- wide pulse pressure
- murmur
- hypotension
- hepatomegaly
- oedema
- Significant right-to-left shunt suggested by:
- hypoxia

Differential diagnosis

- Other cardiac pathology
- physiological left pulmonary branch stenosis
- ventricular septal defect
- atrial septal defect/patent foramen ovale
- Sepsis
- Right-sided cardiac pathology secondary to lung disease

INVESTIGATIONS

- Chest X-ray
- cardiomegaly
- pulmonary plethora
- Echocardiography
- not essential but advisable because duct-dependent cardiac lesion can be difficult to detect clinically
- important, if considering treatment with prostaglandin inhibitor, to assess cardiac anatomy and ductal status

MANAGEMENT

- Prostaglandin inhibitor to initiate ductal closure
- indometacin OR ibuprofen
- evidence to suggest that ibuprofen is not as effective as indometacin
- follow your unit's practice

IMMEDIATE TREATMENT

- Restrict fluid intake to ≤150 mL/kg/day
- Check suitability for indometacin or ibuprofen
- renal function
- urine output >1 mL/kg/hr
- platelet count >50 x 10^9/L
- feed tolerance

Issue 02
Issued: October 2007
Expires: September 2009

- Contraindications to indometacin or ibuprofen are:
- serum creatinine >130 µmol/L
- urine output <1 mL/kg/hr
- platelet count <100 x 10⁹/L

  platelet count $<100 \times 10^9$/L
- suspected necrotizing enterocolitis
- If not contraindicated, give loading dose of indometacin 100 microgram/kg IV over 20-30 min or ibuprofen 10 mg/kg IV administered in accordance with the **Neonatal Formulary**

SUBSEQUENT MANAGEMENT

- **If it is not possible to monitor the ductus sonographically,** give further doses of:
- Indometacin or ibuprofen according to the **Neonatal Formulary**
- **Check renal function and platelets before each dose**
- Feeds can be initiated and continued at a routine rate
- If PDA fails to close with medical therapy, discuss with consultant

Monitoring pharmacological treatment

- Check:
- urine output >1 mL/kg/day
- feed tolerance
- FBC – platelets >50 x 10⁹/L
- renal profile – an increase in urea and creatinine can be expected after administration of indometacin but urine output is of more clinical value. Discuss with senior colleague
- **Persistence or recurrence of the murmur does not necessarily indicate return of the PDA**
- Echocardiogram may demonstrate a physiological left branch pulmonary stenosis – this is common after ductal closure and not clinically significant

Surgical referral

- Consider surgical ligation if:
- pharmacological closure contraindicated or ineffective
- obvious cardiac compromise
- it is not possible to extubate the baby or there has been post-extubation failure
- there have been pulmonary haemorrhages or other symptoms suggestive of ductal steal

A second course of indometacin is unlikely to close the ductus

DISCHARGE POLICY FOR PERSISTENT PDA

- If duct does not close but baby can be extubated:
- monitor duct clinically
- Refer to cardiologist for further management if there is:
- evidence of cardiac failure
- failure to thrive
- persistent oxygen requirement
- If PDA still present echocardiographically or clinically by age 6 wks, refer to paediatric cardiology service

PERICARDIOCENTESIS • 1/1

INDICATION

Consider drainage of a pericardial effusion only if there is cardiovascular compromise

PERICARDIAL EFFUSION

Causes

- Neonatal hydrops
- Extravasation of TPN from migrated long lines
- Complication of central venous catheters

Clinical signs

- Tachycardia
- Poor perfusion
- Soft heart sounds
- Increasing cardiomegaly
- Decreasing oxygen saturation
- Arrhythmias
- Sudden collapse in baby with long line or UVC in situ

Investigations

- Chest X-ray – widened mediastinum and enlarged cardiac shadow
- Echocardiogram (if available)

EQUIPMENT

- Sterile gown and gloves
- Sterile drapes
- Dressing pack with swabs and plastic dish
- 22/24 gauge cannula
- 5-10 mL syringe with 3-way tap attached
- Aqueous chlorhexidine 0.05%

PROCEDURE

Preparation

- If skilled operator available, perform under ultrasound guidance
- In an emergency situation, the most experienced person present performs procedure without delay and without ultrasound guidance
- Ensure baby has adequate analgesia

Drainage

- Maintain strict aseptic technique throughout
- Clean skin around xiphisternum and allow to dry
- Attach needle to syringe and insert just below xiphisternum at 30° to skin and aiming for left shoulder
- Continuously aspirate syringe with gentle pressure as needle inserted. As needle enters pericardial space there will be a gush of blood or air
- Send aspirated fluid for microbiological and biochemical analysis
- Withdraw needle

AFTERCARE

- Cover entry site with clear dressing

RECOGNITION AND ASSESSMENT

Definition

- Peripheral venous haematocrit (Hct) >65%
- Symptoms rarely occur with a peripheral Hct of <70%
- Hct peaks at 2 hr after birth and then decreases with significant changes occurring by 6 hr

Clinical consequences

- Hyperviscosity
- Decreased blood flow and impaired tissue perfusion
- Microthrombus formation

Complications

- Cerebral micro-infarction and adverse neurodevelopmental outcome
- Renal vein thrombosis
- Necrotizing enterocolitis (NEC)

Causes

Intra-uterine erythropoiesis	Erythrocyte transfusion
● Placental insufficiency (SGA)	● Maternal-fetal
● Postmaturity	● Twin-to-twin transfusion
● Maternal diabetes	● Delayed cord clamping
● Maternal smoking	● Unattended delivery
● Chromosomal abnormalities – trisomy 21, 18, 13	
● Beckwith–Wiedemann syndrome	
● Congenital adrenal hyperplasia	
● Neonatal thryotoxicosis	
● Congenital hypothyroidism	

Symptoms and signs

- Commonly plethoric but asymptomatic

Cardiorespiratory

- Respiratory distress
- PPHN (persistent pulmonary hypertension of the newborn)
- Congestive cardiac failure

CNS

- Lethargy, hypotonia within 6 hr
- Difficult arousal, irritability
- Jittery
- Easily startled
- Seizures

GIT

- Poor feeding
- Vomiting
- NEC

Metabolic

- Hypoglycaemia
- Hypocalcaemia
- Jaundice

Issue 02
Issued: October 2007
Expires: September 2009

Haematological

- Thrombocytopenia

Renal

- Renal vein thrombosis
- Renal failure

INVESTIGATIONS

In all unwell infants and at-risk infants who look plethoric (as mentioned above)

- FBC/Hct
- If Hct >65%, repeat using a 21 gauge needle to check that venous blood flows freely, or obtain arterial Hct
- If polycythaemic, check blood glucose and calcium

IMMEDIATE TREATMENT

- Ensure infants at risk have liberal fluid intake – 90 mL/kg/24 hr
- Asymptomatic infants with Hct >70%:
- give increased fluids
- repeat venous Hct after 6 hr
- if still high, discuss with consultant (current evidence does not show any benefit in treating asymptomatic babies)
- Symptomatic babies with Hct >65% (e.g. fits and excessive jitteriness, with neurological signs and refractory hypoglycaemia) – will need dilutional exchange transfusion. Discuss with consultant
- Explain need for exchange and possible risks to parents before performing dilutional exchange transfusion using sodium chloride 0.9% (see **Exchange transfusion** guideline). Partial exchange transfusion slightly increases risk of NEC
- Volume to be exchanged = 20 mL/kg
- Perform exchange via UVC or via peripheral arterial and IV lines
- Take 5-10 mL aliquots and complete procedure over 15-20 min

SUBSEQUENT MANAGEMENT

- Babies who required dilutional exchange transfusion require long term neuro-developmental follow-up
- Otherwise, follow-up will be dependent on background problem

RECOGNITION AND ASSESSMENT

Definition

Clinical syndrome that can be primary (idiopathic) or secondary

Idiopathic

- Severe hypoxaemia (PaO_2 <5-6 kPa) in FiO_2 1.0
- No or mild lung disease (in primary/idiopathic PPHN)
- Right-to-left shunt (postductal PaO_2 1-2 kPa <preductal or a >5% difference in pre and post ductal saturations)
- Echocardiogram: normal heart, shunt at PFO and/or PDA

Secondary – may be associated with:

- Severe lung disease: meconium aspiration, surfactant deficiency
- Perinatal asphyxia
- Infection: Group B streptococcal pneumonia
- Structural abnormalities: pulmonary hypoplasia, congenital diaphragmatic hernia
- Maternal drugs: aspirin, non-steroidal anti-inflammatory drugs

CLINICAL FEATURES

Usually presents in first 12 hours of life

- Mimics cyanotic heart disease
- CVS: right parasternal heave, tricuspid regurgitant murmur, loud second heart sound, systemic hypotension
- In idiopathic PPHN respiratory signs mild
- In secondary PPHN – features of pre-existing disease

INVESTIGATIONS

- CXR: minimal changes in idiopathic PPHN
- ECG: often normal
- Echocardiogram: most useful to exclude cyanotic heart disease, assess pulmonary hypertension, delineate R ➤ L shunting, evaluate ventricular function
- Blood gases show primary hypoxaemia – PaO_2 <6 kPa – underlying disease will cause a mixed picture

MANAGEMENT

- Once PPHN suspected, inform and involve consultant neonatologist immediately
- Aims of management are to decrease pulmonary vascular resistance, using ventilation and vasodilators, and to increase systemic vascular resistance with volume expanders, and vasopressors

General measures

- Minimal handling – nurse in quiet environment
- Secure arterial and central venous access – see **Arterial lines** or **Umbilical arterial and venous access** guidelines
- Maintain normal temperature, biochemistry and fluid balance
- Keep Hb >12 g/dL
- Give antibiotics/surfactant where indicated – discuss with consultant
- Maintain systemic mean BP >40 mmHg – use inotropes early
- May need bolus fluids if perfusion poor – consider individual condition

Ventilation

- Paralyse and sedate – use adequate paralysis
- IPPV – aim for pH 7.35-7.45
- $PaCO_2$ 4.5-5.5 kPa (accept up to 6-7 kPa in parenchymal lung disease)
- best PaO_2 possible

- High frequency oscillatory ventilation (HFOV). See **High frequency oscillatory ventilation** guideline
- Monitor oxygenation index (O.I.)

$$O.I. = \frac{\text{mean airway pressure (cm } H_2O) \times FiO_2 \times 100}{\text{postductal PaO}_2 \text{ (mmHg)}}$$

Note - 1 kPa = 7.5 mmHg

Pulmonary vasodilatation

- Nitric oxide (NO) – selective pulmonary vasodilator: if OI >20 – see **Nitric oxide** guideline
- If NO not available, use magnesium sulphate – can cause systemic hypotension

If a term baby is not responding to NO and HFOV and the OI is approaching 35, discuss with ECMO centre

Criteria for ECMO (Extracorporeal membrane oxygenation)

- Severe but reversible cardiac or pulmonary disease
- unresponsive to optimal ventilation and pharmacological therapy
- no major ventilator-induced damage that might lead to chronic lung disease
- <10 days aggressive IPPV
- Estimated mortality risk greater than 80% (i.e. OI >40)
- No germinal matrix or intraventricular haemorrhage (GMH/IVH); low risk of spontaneous (or heparin-induced) GMH/IVH
- Birth weight >2 kg
- Gestation >35 weeks (with increasing experience, the ECMO centres do consider ECMO at slightly lower gestation and birthweight)
- Absence of prolonged asphyxia predicted to cause brain damage
- No chromosomal abnormality incompatible with quality of life

A baby accepted for transfer to ECMO centre will be retrieved by the ECMO team

- The ECMO centre will need:
- a cranial ultrasound scan
- maternal blood for group and cross-matching
- a referral letter
- copies of hospital notes/chest X-rays

PRE-DELIVERY PREPARATION

- Identify resuscitation team
- Counsel parents
- Prepare for resuscitation

Resuscitation team

- SpR or above responsible for early care of babies <28 weeks gestation, assisted by neonatal nurse trained to attend delivery of preterm babies. Discuss with consultant if <26 weeks

AT DELIVERY

Thermoregulation

- Resuscitation team ensures delivery room temperature 24°C
- Deliver babies <30 weeks gestation into a plastic bag without drying body
- dry head and cover with hat
- use transwarmer mattress if environmental temperature <24°C (do NOT put the baby directly onto the mattress)
- document admission temperature

See **Resuscitation** guideline

Early ventilatory management

- Aim for minimal mechanical ventilation and early extubation following caffeine loading

Early intravenous and intra-arterial access management

- Urgent arterial access is easier in first hour
- lines to be placed by a skilled practitioner to avoid delays
- do not waste time inserting peripheral venous line unless initial blood glucose <2.8 mmol/L

Prevention of sepsis

- Give antibiotics soon after admission after cultures taken
- give maintenance fluid (glucose 10% - see **Intravenous fluids** guideline) via UVC while awaiting x-ray

Monitor/record

- Time of first dose of surfactant
- Time of line insertion

Issue 02
Issued: October 2007
Expires: September 2009

Decision tree for ventilatory management at one hour

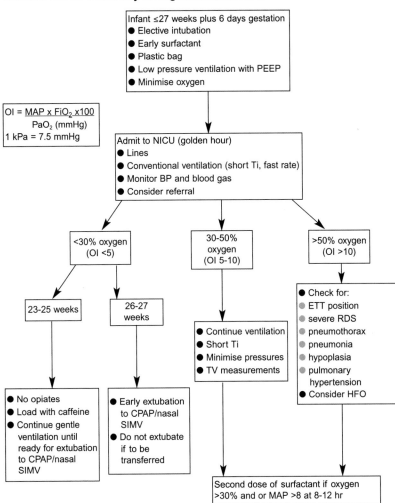

Infant ≤27 weeks plus 6 days gestation
- Elective intubation
- Early surfactant
- Plastic bag
- Low pressure ventilation with PEEP
- Minimise oxygen

$$OI = \frac{MAP \times FiO_2 \times 100}{PaO_2 \ (mmHg)}$$
1 kPa = 7.5 mmHg

Admit to NICU (golden hour)
- Lines
- Conventional ventilation (short Ti, fast rate)
- Monitor BP and blood gas
- Consider referral

<30% oxygen (OI <5)

30-50% oxygen (OI 5-10)

>50% oxygen (OI >10)

23-25 weeks

26-27 weeks

- Check for:
  - ETT position
  - severe RDS
  - pneumothorax
  - pneumonia
  - hypoplasia
  - pulmonary hypertension
- Consider HFO

- Continue ventilation
- Short Ti
- Minimise pressures
- TV measurements

- No opiates
- Load with caffeine
- Continue gentle ventilation until ready for extubation to CPAP/nasal SIMV

- Early extubation to CPAP/nasal SIMV
- Do not extubate if to be transferred

Second dose of surfactant if oxygen >30% and or MAP >8 at 8-12 hr

RECOGNITION AND ASSESSMENT

Definition

- Acute onset of bleeding from the endotracheal tube (ETT) associated with cardiorespiratory deterioration and changes on the chest X-ray
- Significant pulmonary haemorrhage is most likely to represent haemorrhagic pulmonary oedema. Differentiate from minor traumatic haemorrhage following endotracheal suction

Risk factors

- Preterm infants
- Respiratory Distress Syndrome (RDS)
- Large persistent ductus arteriosus (PDA)
- Excessive use of volume expansion (>20 mL/kg) in the first 24-48 hr in infants aged ≤28 weeks
- Coagulopathy
- Sepsis
- IUGR
- Use of synthetic rather than natural surfactant
- Grade 3 HIE (hypoxic ischaemic encephalopathy)

Symptoms and Signs

- Apnoeas, gasping respirations, desaturations
- Tachycardia >160/min, bradycardia, hypotension, shock, PDA, signs of heart failure
- Widespread crepitations, reduced air entry
- Pink/red frothy expectorate, or frank blood from oropharynx or ETT if intubated

Investigations

- Blood gas – expect hypoxia and hypercarbia with mixed acidosis
- FBC, clotting
- Chest X-ray – usually shows classic whiteout with only air bronchogram visible or may be less striking and resemble RDS

IMMEDIATE TREATMENT

- Basic resuscitation

Respiratory

- Intubate and ventilate
- Sedate and give muscle relaxant
- PEEP 6-8 cm, even higher PEEP of 10-12 cm of water may be required to control haemorrhage
- PIP to be guided by chest expansion and blood gases
- Long inspiratory times – 0.5 sec may be needed
- Endotracheal suction – generally to be avoided but may be necessary in extreme cases to reduce risk of ETT blockage
- Ensure adequate humidification
- Avoid chest physiotherapy
- Establish arterial access

Fluid Management

- If hypovolaemic – restore circulating volume with sodium chloride 0.9% 10 mL/kg or O–ve packed cells if crystalloid bolus already given over half and hour. Beware of overloading – added volume may be detrimental to LV failure
- If not hypovolaemic and evidence of left ventricular failure, give furosemide 1 mg/kg IV
- Correct acidosis – see **Neonatal Formulary**
- If PDA present, restrict fluids to 60-80 mL/kg/24hr in acute phase

Issue 02
Issued: October 2007
Expires: September 2009

● Further blood transfusion, vitamin K administration and FFP to be guided by haemoglobin concentration, PT and APTT – (see **Transfusion of red blood cells** guideline and **Coagulopathy** guideline)

Hypotension

● If still hypotensive after fluid resuscitation, treat hypotension with inotropes – See **Hypotension** guideline

Infection

● If infection suspected, request septic screen and start antibiotics

SUBSEQUENT MANAGEMENT

Once infant is stable

● Inform consultant on call

● Speak to parents

● Document event in case notes

● Consider single extra dose of natural surfactant in infants with severe hypoxaemia or OI >20

● If PDA suspected, arrange echocardiogram

● If PDA confirmed and haemodynamically significant, wait 24-48 hr after acute event until coagulopathy and acidosis corrected before treating PDA medically or by surgical ligation

RENAL ABNORMALITIES ON ANTENATAL SCAN • 1/2

ANTENATAL ASSESSMENT

Fetal diagnostic scans are undertaken in mid-trimester (18-20 wk) and may be repeated at 32-34 weeks

18-20 week scan

Possible renal abnormalities include:
- Upper tract dilation (pelviectasis):
- mild – renal pelvic dilation (RPD) [anterior-posterior (AP) diameter] 5–9 mm
- moderate – RPD 10–14 mm
- severe – RPD >15 mm
- Dilated bladder ± ureter
- Multi-cystic dysplastic kidney(s)
- Infantile polycystic kidney disease
- Renal agenesis ± oligohydramnios
- Abnormally positioned kidney

32–34 week scan

- Gauge severity of pelviectasis according to dimension:
- 7 mm abnormal
- 10 mm moderate
- >15 mm (high risk of obstruction)

Communication

- Provide mother with information leaflet about significance of these findings and proposed plan of management after birth

POSTNATAL MANAGEMENT

Indications for intervention

Urgent

- Lower tract obstruction in male posterior urethral valves (PUV)
- Bilateral RPD >10 mm

Non-urgent

- Bilateral mild pelviectasis (RPD <10 mm)
- Unilateral renal problems
- Infantile polycystic kidneys (provided renal function satisfactory)

Other conditions requiring renal evaluation

- Single renal artery in cord
- slightly increased risk of renal abnormality
- postnatal ultrasound scan only if antenatal scan missed or abnormal
- Ear abnormalities – ultrasound examination only if associated with:
- syndrome
- other malformations
- maternal/gestational diabetes
- family history of deafness

IMMEDIATE MANAGEMENT

For urgent indications

- Renal USS (<48 hr after birth if possible)
- Check voiding pattern
- Refer infants with PUV to paediatric urologist
- If indicated following post natal scan, micturating cysto-urethrogram (MCUG)
- Electrolytes at 1 week
- Discuss with consultant before discharge

For non-urgent indications

- Renal USS <28 days
- Review in clinic at 6 weeks of age

Antibiotic prophylaxis

- For all babies who may have obstructed or refluxing kidney, give trimethoprim 1–2 mg/kg as single night-time dose until meets criteria for stopping (see below)

Issue 02
Issued: October 2007
Expires: September 2009

SUBSEQUENT MANAGEMENT

Subsequent management depends on findings, especially of USS at 6-8 weeks clinic visit

Normal or mild isolated pelviectasis (<10 mm)

- Stop antibiotic prophylaxis
- Repeat scan after 6 months
- If 6 month scan normal or shows no change and there have been no UTIs, discharge

Moderate pelviectasis (10–15 mm) and/or ureteric dilation

- Presumed mild obstruction or reflux
- Prophylaxis until 1-yr-old
- MCUG if recurrent infection or parents not wishing to give prophylaxis
- Repeat scan every 6 months

Hydronephrosis (>15 mm)

- MAG3 scan after 6 weeks of age
- Repeat USS at 4 months of age
- Urology referral with results
- Antibiotic prophylaxis until problem resolved

Multi-cystic kidney

- DMSA to confirm nil function
- Repeat USS periodically to observe reabsorption of kidney (may take several years)
- Be aware of 20% risk of reflux in contralateral kidney – advise parents to be vigilant for UTI
- MCUG or prophylaxis for 1-2 years **ONLY** if dilated pelvis or ureter in good kidney
- Annual BP check until kidney resorbed
- Urology referral if cysts persistent, enlarging or hypertension

Outflow obstruction

- Urgent MCUG
- Prophylaxis until problem resolved
- Urology opinion
- Repeat electrolytes if initially abnormal

Ureterocoele

- MCUG
- MAG3 to check function and drainage from all poles
- Prophylaxis until problem resolved
- Urology referral

Renal parenchymal problem

- Bright kidneys
- Multiple cysts
- Nephrology opinion

DEFINITION

- Clinical syndrome resulting from abrupt reduction in GFR indicated by serum creatinine >132 µmol/L, often accompanied by oliguria (urine output <1 mL/kg/hr)

AETIOLOGY

It is essential to differentiate between the following four categories as their management differs

- **Pre-renal failure**
- Hypoperfusion in an otherwise normal kidney – caused by:
- hypovolaemia – dehydration, haemorrhage, third-space loss
- normovolaemic hypotension – asphyxia, CHD (especially postoperatively), sepsis, large PDA
- hypoxia – asphyxia

- **Intrinsic renal failure – acute damage to the renal parenchyma**
- acute tubular necrosis – resulting from hypoperfusion
- asphyxia
- nephrotoxins (e.g. gentamicin, penicillin, indometacin)
- infection/inflammation – acute pyelonephritis, sepsis
- vascular – renal vein or arterial thrombosis

- **Post-renal failure**
- obstruction to the flow of urine (e.g. posterior urethral valves)

- **Congenital chronic renal failure**
- multicystic dysplastic kidneys, polycystic kidneys

SYMPTOMS

- Oedema
- Oliguria
- Poor feeding
- Vomiting
- Seizures
- Breathlessness

SIGNS

Fluid overload
- Tachypnoeic
- Oedema
- Excessive weight gain
- Raised blood pressure
- Gallop rhythm
- Hepatomegaly

Fluid depleted
- Cold peripheries
- Delayed capillary refill
- Tachycardic
- Oliguric (<1 mL/kg/hr) or anuric

Cardiac arrhythmias
- Tall peaked T waves or VT on ECG

Renal abnormalities
- Palpable kidney/bladder

- Spinal abnormalities

INVESTIGATIONS

Monitor

- Weigh 12 hrly
- BP 12 hrly
- Cardiac monitor to detect arrhythmias
- Consider CVP monitoring

Urine

- Dipstick (proteinuria; sediment, such as blood, casts, tubular debris, indicate intrinsic ARF; WBC and nitrites suggest infection)
- Microscopy and culture
- Electrolytes, urea, creatinine, osmolality - daily

Blood

- U&E, creatinine 8 hrly
- Blood gas, pH 4-8 hrly
- Glucose 4 hrly

Issue 02
Issued: October 2007
Expires: September 2009

- Calcium, phosphate, magnesium, albumin 12 hrly
- Blood count (film and platelets) daily
- If bleeding, clotting studies

Typical biochemical changes in ARF

Increased urea, creatinine, K^+, PO_4^-

Reduced Na^+, $Ca2^+$, HCO_3^-, pH

Imaging

- Abdominal X-ray to determine UAC position
- confirm UAC tip does not sit at L1
- Renal ultrasound
- to exclude congenital causes, post-renal causes and renal vein thrombosis

---

Differentiation between pre-renal and intrinsic ARF (difficult using ultrasound)

- Use table below as guide but remember all indices are less reliable in preterm babies
- high fractional excretion of sodium (FE_{Na} – the most discriminatory index) does not necessarily indicate ARF

$$FE_{Na} = \frac{\text{excretion Na}}{\text{Filtration rate Na}} = \frac{U_{Na} \text{ (mmol/L)} \times P_{cr} \text{ (mmol/L)}}{U_{cr} \text{ (mmol/L)} \times P_{Na} \text{ (mmol/L)}}$$

Urinary indices that help to differentiate between pre-renal and intrinsic ARF

Test	Pre-renal	Intrinsic
FE_{Na}	Low (<1% term, <5% preterm)	High (>3% term, 6% preterm)
Urine urea	High	Low
U:P urea	High (>20)	Low (<10)
Urine creatinine	High	Low
U:P creatinine	High (>40)	Low (<40)
Urine osmolality	High (>500 mosmol/kg)	Low
U:P osmolality	High (>2)	Low (<1)
Urine sodium	Low (<10 mmol/L)	High (>20 mmol/L)

- If in doubt about extent of pre-renal component, and there is no evidence of fluid overload, consider IV fluid challenge – sodium chloride 0.9% 20 mL/kg

Issue 02
Issued: October 2007
Expires: September 2009

IMMEDIATE TREATMENT

Pre-renal

- Sodium chloride 0.9% 20 mL/kg IV
- if blood loss known or suspected, give packed red cells over 30-60 min
- If hypotensive in absence of fluid depletion, start inotrope infusion – dopamine 5 micrograms/kg/min or, if no central access (e.g. UVC), dobutamine 10 micrograms/kg/min
- If no response to fluid challenge (± inotrope), assume renal parenchymal damage and proceed to conservative treatment of intrinsic ARF

Post-renal

- Relieve obstruction by suprapubic or urethral catheter
- Contact urologist

INTRINSIC RENAL FAILURE MANAGEMENT

Supportive

- Stop all nephrotoxic drugs (e.g. aminoglycosides) if possible

Fluid balance

- Strictly monitor all intake and output
- Restrict fluid intake to minimal maintenance fluids
- Calculate maintenance fluid:
- maintenance fluid   =   insensible losses + urine output + GIT losses
- insensible losses
  <1500 g (at birth) = 50-80 mL/kg/day
  >1500 g (at birth) = 15-35 mL/kg/day
- for babies in well-humidified incubator or receiving humidified respiratory support, use lower figure
- Replace maintenance fluid as 10-20% electrolyte-free glucose
- ensure fluid volume in first stages less than ongoing losses, as most patients would be fluid overloaded at this point. Best guide of hydration is body weight

- Weigh twice daily
- stable weight indicates overhydration and need to reduce fluid intake further
- aim to achieve 1% loss of body weight daily

Hyperkalaemia

- See **Hyperkalaemia** guideline

Acidosis

- Monitor pH 8 hrly
- if pH <7.2, give sodium bicarbonate 1 mmol/kg IV

Hyperphosphataemia

- If >3 mmol/L add calcium carbonate (120 mg 6 hrly) to feeds and contact nephrologist

Hyponatraemia

- Most often caused by dilution from excessive fluid retention
- restrict fluid to amounts indicated above
- If severe (Na <120 mmol/L) and associated with neurological symptoms such as seizures:
- use hypertonic saline (sodium chloride 3%) 4 mL/kg over a minimum of 15 min. This dose can be repeated if baby is still fitting **after** assessing serum sodium concentration
- check Na immediately after completion of infusion

Hypocalcaemia

- Check ionised calcium rather than total calcium wherever feasible
- Do not give additional calcium until phosphate has fallen to near-normal
- Seek advice from paediatric nephrologist before starting alfacalcidol, then start at 20 nanograms/kg/day. However, because smallest measurable dose is 100 nanograms, if required dose is <100 nanograms, give it less than once a day. Increase dose of drug to keep ionised calcium in upper half of normal range

- If symptomatic, give 10% calcium gluconate 2 mL/kg IV over 10 min, then 2.5 mL/kg over 24 hr as maintenance therapy for 48 hr. Monitor for tissue extravasation

- if still hypocalcaemic after 48 hr, continue with alfacalcidol and start oral Calcium Sandoz 4 mL/kg/day in divided doses

- Once plasma calcium normal, stop Calcium Sandoz and wean alfacalcidol to 15-30 nanogram/kg/day maintenance dose

Nutrition

- Aim for 100 kcal/kg/d – often difficult because of severe fluid restriction

- Provide calories mainly as carbohydrate and fat

- If anuria prolonged, consider TPN and dialysis

Glucose

- Monitor blood glucose 4 hrly:

- hypoglycaemia is a common complication of fluid restriction

- If hypoglycaemic, increase concentration of glucose solution

- if >10% glucose required to maintain normoglycaemia, use central line

- In prolonged treatment, use TPN to prevent catabolism

- If nutrition inadequate

- discuss dialysis with nephrologist

DIALYSIS

Dialysis rarely required in neonatal acute renal failure but should be jointly discussed between neonatologist and paediatric nephrologist taking into consideration baby's other medical problems and potential for intact survival

Typical indications for dialysis

- Severe fluid overload ± pulmonary oedema
- Removal of fluid to make space for nutrition
- Severe hypertension
- Refractory hyperkalaemia (>8 mmol/L)
- Refractory severe metabolic acidosis (HCO_3 <12 mmol/L)
- Refractory changes in serum calcium and phosphate

CONGENITAL RENAL FAILURE

Treat as conservative intrinsic ARF and refer early to nephrologist

Issue 02
Issued: October 2007
Expires: September 2009

Check equipment daily, not at the time of resuscitation

Follow newborn resuscitation Guidelines, Resuscitation Council UK at all times

These are available on the Resuscitation Council Website at www.resus.org.uk

DRY AND COVER

- Ensure cord is securely clamped
- If ≥30 weeks, dry baby, **remove wet towels and cover baby with dry towels**
- If <30 weeks, do not dry but place in plastic bag, dry head only and put on hat

ASSESS

- Assess **colour, tone, breathing and heart rate**
- Reassess every 30 sec throughout resuscitation process
- If help required, request **immediately**

CHECK AIRWAY

For baby to breath effectively, airway must be open

- To open airway, place baby supine with head in **'neutral position'**
- If very floppy, consider chin support or jaw thrust

If baby not breathing adequately by 90 sec, assist breathing

IMMEDIATE TREATMENT

- Keep head in neutral position
- Use T-piece or self-inflating 'bag-valve system' and soft round face mask, extending from nasal bridge to chin
- Give 5 inflation breaths, sustaining inflation pressure (Table 1) for 2–3 sec for each breath

Table 1: Inflation pressure (avoid using higher inflation pressure)

| Term infant | 30 cm of water |
| Preterm infant | 20-25 cm of water |

No chest movement

Ask yourself:
- Is head in neutral position?
- Is a jaw thrust required?
- Do you need a second person to help with airway to perform a jaw thrust?
- Is there an obstruction and do you need to look with a laryngoscope and suck with a large-bore device?
- Consider the use of a Guedel airway placed under direct vision
- If no chest movement occurs after alternative airway procedures **above** have been tried (volume given is a function of time and pressure), a larger volume can be delivered if necessary by inflating for a longer time (3-4 sec)
- Is inflation time long enough?

Endotracheal intubation

Indications

- Severe asphyxia (e.g. terminal apnoea or fresh stillbirth)
- Stabilisation of airway
- Extreme prematurity

Slick insertion of tracheal tube requires skill and experience

If you cannot insert a tracheal tube within 30 sec, revert to mask ventilation

Subsequent management when chest moves

- Review every 30 sec. If no spontaneous breathing and cardiac output, see Table 2

Issue 02
Issued: October 2007
Expires: September 2009

Table 2: Outcome after 30 sec of inflation breaths

Heart rate	Breathing	Action
Increases	Not started breathing	Provide 30–40 breaths per min. Where available, use PEEP at 3-4 cm water with the T-piece system
Not increase <60	Obvious chest movement	Start chest compressions. See below

Chest compression

● Use if heart rate is slow (<60 beats/min)

Chest compression should start only after inflation of lungs

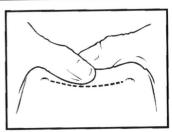

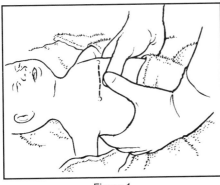

Figure 1

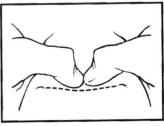

Figure 2

Pictures taken from NLS manual and Resuscitation Council (UK) and reproduced with their permission

Ideal hold - figure1/figure 2

● Circle chest with both hands so that thumbs of both hands can press on the sternum just below an imaginary line joining the nipples with fingers over the baby's spine

Alternative hold (less effective)

● Compress lower sternum with fingers whilst supporting baby's back. The alternative hand position for cardiac compressions can be used when access to the umbilicus for UVC catheterisation is required as hands around the chest may be awkward

Action

● Compress chest quickly and firmly to reduce the antero-posterior diameter of the chest by about one-third, followed by full re-expansion to allow ventricles to refill

● remember to relax grip during IPPV

Coordinate compression and ventilation to avoid competition.

Aim for 3:1 ratio of compressions to ventilations, and 90 compressions and 30 breaths (120 'events') per min

Issue 02
Issued: October 2007
Expires: September 2009

Blood

- If there is evidence of fetal haemorrhage, consider giving O NEGATIVE emergency blood

Consider use of drugs

- Always ask about drugs taken recently by, or given to mother
- Consider drugs only if there is an undetectable or a slow heartbeat despite effective lung inflation and effective chest compression
- Umbilical venous catheter (UVC) is preferred venous access

Adrenaline 1:10,000

- 10 microgram/kg (0.1 mL/kg) IV
- If this dose is not effective, consider giving 30 microgram/kg (0.3 mL/kg)

Sodium bicarbonate 4.2%

- 1-2 mmol/kg (2-4 mL/kg) IV (**NEVER** give via ET tube)

Glucose 10%

- 2.5 mL/kg IV

Sodium chloride 0.9%

- 10 mL/kg IV

Naloxone

- Consider only after ventilation by mask or endotracheal tube has been established with chest movement seen and heart beat >100 beats/min
- If mother has been given pethidine within 2-4 hr of delivery, give 'adult strength' naloxone (200 microgram/mL) IM or 0.5 mL 'adult' naloxone
- small 'premature' baby 0.25 mL
- all other babies 0.5 mL

Do not give naloxone to babies born to mothers who abuse narcotics

WHEN TO STOP

- If no sign of life present after 15 min of full resuscitation, outlook is poor with few survivors – majority will have cerebral palsy and learning difficulties
- If no sustained spontaneous breathing after 30 min, majority also have poor prognosis

Continue resuscitation until a senior paediatrician advises stopping

DOCUMENTATION

Make accurate written record of facts (not opinions) as soon as possible after the event

Record

- When you were called, by whom and why
- Condition of baby on arrival
- What you did and when you did it
- Timing and detail of any response by baby
- Date and time of writing your entry
- A legible signature

COMMUNICATION

- Inform parents what has happened (the facts)

Issue 02
Issued: October 2007
Expires: September 2009

INDICATIONS

● All babies either ≤1500 g birth weight or ≤31 completed weeks gestation

PROCEDURE

When to screen

● Infants ≤25 weeks gestation at 7 weeks postnatal age, then every 2 weeks until 36 weeks post conceptual age

● Infants 26-32 weeks gestational age, 7 weeks postnatally and at 36 weeks post conceptual age, whichever is earliest

● Infants >32 weeks gestational age but birth weight <1500 g are seen when 36 weeks post conceptual age

● Any other infant where there is concern about eyes

How to screen

● Arrange screening with ophthalmologist

Preparation for screening

● Give cyclopentolate 0.5% and phenylephrine 2.5% 1 drop into each eye 30-60 min before examination

● if in any doubt whether the drop has gone into the eye, give another drop immediately (the pupil must be fully dilated)

AFTER CARE

● Eye examination results and recommendations for further screening must be included in transfer letter

Seizures occur in 1-3% of term newborn infants and in a greater proportion of preterm infants. They can be subtle, clonic, myoclonic or tonic

RECOGNITION AND ASSESSMENT

Physical signs

- In addition to obvious convulsive movements, look for:
- apnoea
- eye fluttering and deviation
- staring
- sucking, chewing, tongue thrusting
- changes in blood pressure and heart rate
- limb cycling/pedalling
- Perform a detailed examination and neurological assessment

Infants who have been given paralysing drugs may display only autonomic features, such as changes in blood pressure and heart rate, with or without changes in oxygen saturation

Differential diagnosis

- Jitteriness – tremulous, jerky, stimulus-provoked and ceasing with passive flexion
- Benign sleep myoclonus – focal or generalised, occurring only during sleep; EEG normal; resolves by 2 months of age

Investigations

First line

- Pulse oximetry
- Blood gas analysis
- FBC, coagulation
- Plasma glucose
- LFT
- CRP
- Serum electrolytes, including Ca^{++} and Mg^{++}, PO_{4-}
- Infection screen, including CSF
- Metabolic screen (plasma ammonia, lactate and amino acids, urine amino and organic acids)
- Cranial USS – if inconclusive or suggestive of haemorrhage, request further imaging

Second line

If seizures persist or difficult to control and first line investigations normal

- EEG
- MR scan (investigation of choice); CT head if MR scan unavailable or haemorrhage suspected
- Drug screen - maternal consent necessary
- If other signs:
- congenital infection screen (TORCH)
- VLCFAs, biotinidase levels
- Wood's light
- Ophthalmology review

TREATMENT

- Ensure ABC satisfactory

Causes

- Treat any underlying cause (e.g. hypoxia, hypoglycaemia, electrolyte abnormalities, infection)
- hypoglycaemia: give glucose 10% 5 mL/kg IV bolus, followed by maintenance infusion
- hypocalcaemia (total Ca <1.7 mmol/L or ionised Ca <0.64 mmol/L): give calcium gluconate 10% 2 mL/kg IV over 5-10 min with ECG monitoring (beware of tissue damage if extravasation: ensure cannula is working well)
- hypomagnesaemia (<0.68 mmol/L): give magnesium sulphate 50% 0.2 mL/kg IM (also use for refractory hypocalcaemic fit)

Prolonged fits

If fits continue for >3 min, recur more then 3 times/hr or are associated with hypoxia:

- Give phenobarbital 20 mg/kg by IV bolus over 20 min
- if no response, give further 10 mg/kg by IV bolus up to twice
- If response good, consider maintenance phenobarbital 4 mg/kg/day 24 hr after loading dose
- if loading dose in excess of 20 mg/kg required, defer maintenance dose for 3-4 days

If no response to phenobarbital after 40 mg/kg:

- Give phenytoin 20 mg/kg by IV infusion over at least 20 min (maximum 1 mg/kg/min) with ECG monitoring
- Give maintenance phenytoin 2 mg/kg by IV infusion every 8 hr

If no response to either phenobarbital or phenytoin:

- Give clonazepam 100 microgram/kg by IV bolus over 5-10 min, once every 24 hr for 2-3 days
- if treatment necessary for more than a few days, eventual withdrawal of clonazepam must be gradual over 3-6 weeks, tapering dosage to avoid risk of withdrawal seizures

If no response to any of above:

- Consider thiopental

Breakthrough fits

If occasional breakthrough fits occur during maintenance treatment using any of the above agents:

- Consider paraldehyde 0.4 mL/kg PR mixed with equal volume of sodium chloride 0.9%/olive oil, or midazolam (see **Neonatal Formulary**)

Intractable fits

For intractable fits with no apparent cause:

- Pyridoxine 100 mg IV over at least 5 min, but beware of neurological and respiratory depression following use in true pyridoxine-dependent seizures
- Lidocaine 4 mg/kg (0.4 mL/kg of 1% adrenaline-free lidocaine) over 1 hr IV (see **Neonatal Formulary**)

SUBSEQUENT MANAGEMENT

- Once free of seizures for 5 days, if no need for continued maintenance, stop anticonvulsants
- withdraw most recently added drug first
- except for clonazepam, dosage need not be tapered

Recurrence

- Consider continued maintenance treatment with phenobarbital if seizures recur during or after withdrawal in infants with following conditions:
- underlying CNS malformation
- following severe HIE
- meningitis
- initial difficulty controlling fits
- persisting clinical or EEG abnormalities

DISCHARGE POLICY

- Arrange hearing test
- Outpatient follow-up at 6 weeks
- Long term follow-up for developmental assessment and monitoring of head growth
- No contraindication to vaccinations unless fits secondary to a progressive neurological disorder
- Arrange MR brain scan if not already done, and no cause identified on initial investigations

SKIN BIOPSY FOR INBORN ERRORS OF METABOLISM • 1/2

INDICATIONS

- Diagnosis of inherited metabolic disorders
- check with your laboratory for local arrangements

Skin biopsy is often collected for histological analysis. Contact your local histopathology department for advice on sample handling

EQUIPMENT

- Forceps – fine non-bend watchmaker's or dissecting
- Cotton wool balls and gallipots
- Dressing towel
- Size 15 scalpel blade and no. 3 handle
- 25 gauge needle (orange top)
- 23 gauge needle (blue top)
- 21 gauge needle (green top) for drawing up lidocaine
- 2 mL syringe
- Chlorhexidine gluconate 0.05%
- Lidocaine 1%
- Bottles of culture medium obtained from clinical chemistry, virology or cytogenetics – according to local practice
- Sterile gloves
- Steristrips
- Dressings:
- 1 small transparent dressing (e.g. Tegaderm)
- gauze swabs
- elasticated cotton or other bandage

SAMPLE REQUIREMENTS

- At least 1 mm^2 of skin – ideally 2 mm x 2 mm from preferred site (e.g. inner side of forearm or posterior aspect just above elbow)

- choose site carefully as even a small scar on coloured skin will be very obvious
- if post-mortem, take skin from over scapula as this leaves less obvious damage (see **taking post-mortem specimens**)

PROCEDURE

Transport

- Once sample taken, send to the Inherited Metabolic Diseases Laboratory as soon as possible
- if unable to arrange transport immediately, store sample at +4°C for maximum of 12 hr before despatch
- **do not freeze sample**

Consent

- Explain procedure and reassure parents
- Obtain and record consent

Technique

Maintain strict asepsis using 'no touch' technique

- Sterilise site with chlorhexidine gluconate 0.05% and dry off with a gauze swab
- Inject lidocaine 1% – a little intradermally and the remainder subcutaneously to anaesthetise an area 1.5 x 1 cm
- Wait 5 min to ensure site anaesthetised
- Cleanse again using chlorhexidine gluconate 0.05%, wipe off and dry using sterile cotton wool or gauze swabs

Issue 02
Issued: October 2007
Expires: September 2009

Method A

- Using fine watchmaker's forceps, grip a fold of skin between blades so that a length of skin 3 mm x 2 mm protrudes

- slice off in one stroke by running scalpel blade along upper edge of forceps blades

- if skin too thick or oedematous to grip, proceed to method B

- place skin in culture medium (lid of bottle removed by assistant for shortest possible time)

- Complete request form with:

- clinical details

- date and time of sampling

Method B

- Pierce skin with 23 or 21 gauge needle and lift to produce 'tenting'

- Cut off tip of tent to produce piece of skin approximately 2 mm with a round 'O' shape

- place into culture medium bottle immediately

- Complete request form with:

- clinical details

- date and time of sampling

Dressing wound

- Although it may bleed freely, wound is usually partial thickness and should not require stitching

- Apply pressure to stanch bleeding

- apply Steristrips and sterile dressing – bandage if necessary

- Remove bandage after a few hours, but leave dressing for several days

- Reassure parents that scar, when visible, is seen as a fine line

POST-MORTEM SPECIMENS

- In accordance with the Human Tissue Act, post-mortem samples must be taken only on licensed premises (or satellites thereof) - Check locally

> *Specimens taken after death present a high risk of infection and possible failure of culture. Follow strict asepsis technique*

- Take two biopsies from over scapula (as this leaves less obvious damage), as soon as possible after death, ideally before 48 hr have elapsed

- Send sample to inherited metabolic disease laboratory immediately, or store at +4° C before dispatch for maximum of 12 hr – **do not freeze**

- Include clinical details, date and time of sampling, and date and time of death on request form

SURFACTANT REPLACEMENT THERAPY
• 1/2

Together with antenatal corticosteroid administration, surfactant replacement therapy is the most important therapeutic advance in neonatal care in the last decade. Early administration of selective surfactant decreases risk of acute pulmonary injury, neonatal mortality, and chronic lung disease. Multiple doses result in greater improvements in oxygenation and ventilatory requirements, a decreased risk of pneumothorax, and a trend toward improved survival

INDICATIONS

Infants born ≤26 weeks gestation

● Give surfactant as prophylaxis as soon as possible following delivery, and certainly within 30 min of life

Infants born at 27 and 28^{+6} weeks gestation after an incomplete course of antenatal corticosteroids

● Give surfactant as prophylaxis

Infants born at 27 and 28^{+6} weeks gestation after a complete course of antenatal corticosteroids

● If intubation required at birth for respiratory distress or poor respiratory effort, give prophylactic surfactant

Infants born at 29 and 30 weeks gestation

● If continued intubation for respiratory distress, give early (within 2 hr of birth)

All other infants requiring intubation and needing FiO$_2$ >0.3 for respiratory distress syndrome

● Give rescue surfactant

Others (after senior discussion)

● Ventilated babies with meconium aspiration syndrome

● Term babies with pneumonia and stiff lungs

CONTRAINDICATIONS

● Discuss use in infants with massive pulmonary haemorrhage with neonatal consultant

EQUIPMENT

● Natural surfactant, either beractant (Survanta®) 100 mg/kg (4 mL/kg) or poractant alfa (Curosurf®)

● dosage of poractant alfa is unit specific (100 mg/kg or 200 mg/kg) – check locally

● Sterile gloves

● 5F feeding tube cut to length of endotracheal tube with sterile scissors OR Trachcare max catheter

● Suction

● Experienced personnel to administer directly or supervise

● An assistant

Issue 02
Issued: October 2007
Expires: September 2009

PROCEDURE

Preparation

- Calculate dose of surfactant required and warm to room temperature
- Ensure correct endotracheal tube (ET) position
- check ET length at lips
- listen and look for bilateral air entry and chest movement
- if in doubt, ensure ET in trachea using laryngoscope and adjust to ensure bilateral equal air entry
- chest X-ray not necessary before first dose
- Refer to manufacturer's guidelines and **Neonatal Formulary**
- Invert surfactant vial gently several times, without shaking, to re-suspend the material
- Draw up required dose and connect to cut 5F feeding tube

Instillation

- Assistant clears trachea of any mucus and saves secretions to send for culture and sensitivity
- With baby supine, quickly instil prescribed dose down tracheal tube; give 2-4 boluses of beractant, 1-2 boluses of poractant alfa
- Wait for recovery of air entry/chest movement and oxygenation between boluses

Post-instillation care

- Do not suction ET for 8 hr (suction is contraindicated in RDS for 48 hr)
- Be ready to adjust ventilator/oxygen settings in response to changes in chest movement, tidal volume and oxygen saturation
- Take an arterial/capillary blood gas within 30 min

SUBSEQUENT MANAGEMENT

- If baby remains ventilated at FiO_2 >0.3, give further dose of beractant 12 hr after first dose (6-12 hr if using poractant alfa), or earlier if lung disease severe with a minimum dosing interval of 6 hrs
- 3rd and 4th doses may be given only at request of on-take/on-call consultant

DOCUMENTATION

- For every dose given, document in case notes:
- indication for surfactant use
- time of administration
- dose given
- condition of baby pre-administration
- response to surfactant
- reasons why second dose not given, if applicable
- reason(s) for giving 3rd/4th doses

MATERNAL VDRL OR RPR POSITIVE

- Confirm maternal treponemal test (e.g. TPPA, TPHA, EIA or FTA-ABS)
- Check maternal HIV and Hepatitis B status
- Take blood from infant for VDRL or RPR and anti-treponemal EIA IgM (not cord blood)
- Examine infant thoroughly for evidence of congenital syphilis, looking for:
- non-immune hydrops
- jaundice
- hepatosplenomegaly
- rhinitis
- rash
- pseudoparalysis of an extremity
- Identify infants with probable or possible disease, or probably not infected-see **below**

INFANTS WITH PROBABLE OR POSSIBLE DISEASE

Probable disease

- Abnormal physical examination consistent with congenital syphilis
- VDRL/RPR titre the same or >4 x maternal titre

Possible disease

- Normal physical examination AND
- VDRL/RPR titre the same or <4 x maternal titre AND
- One or more of the following:
- mother not treated, inadequately treated, or has no documentation of having been treated
- mother treated with erythromycin or other non-penicillin regimen
- mother treated ≤4 weeks before delivery; or

- mother has early syphilis and has a nontreponemal titre that has either not decreased fourfold or has increased fourfold (e.g. re-infection suspected)

INVESTIGATIONS

- FBC, differential, and platelet count
- If clinically indicated:
- chest X-ray
- liver function tests
- cranial ultrasound
- ophthalmologic examination
- auditory brainstem response
- CSF VDRL, cell count and protein
- do not use cord blood for serological testing on neonate

TREATMENT

Benzylpenicillin **30 mg/kg 12 hrly IV for first 7 days; then 8 hrly for a further 3 days**

INFANTS PROBABLY NOT INFECTED

Normal physical examination AND VDRL/RPR titre the same or <4 x maternal titre BUT not meeting criteria above for possible disease

TREATMENT

- Procaine penicillin 100 mg/kg IM single dose or, if unavailable, Benzathine penicillin 50,000 units/kg IM single dose
- No LP, long bone x-ray or follow up necessary as routine unless otherwise clinically indicated if treatment given

FOLLOW UP OF ALL INFANTS

- Serological testing (nontreponemal) every 3 months until test is non-reactive or titre has decreased fourfold
- If titres stable or increase after 6-12 months, consider further evaluation (e.g. CSF) and treatment

Issue 02
Issued: October 2007
Expires: September 2009

DEFINITION

- Platelet count <150 x 10⁹/L. Mild (platelet count 100-150 x 10⁹/L) and moderate (50-100 x 10⁹/L) thrombocytopenia occur frequently in preterm infants who are ill, and in those born to women with pregnancy-induced hypertension (PIH)

- Severe thrombocytopenia (<50 x 10⁹/L) is uncommon, particularly in otherwise healthy appearing term infants (0.12-0.24%) and should raise possibility of neonatal allo-immune thrombocytopenia (NAIT; see below)

CAUSES

	WELL		ILL
	Term	**Preterm**	
Common	● NAIT ● IUGR ● Maternal diabetes ● Maternal ITP ● Trisomies (13, 18, 21)	● IUGR ● Congenital infections (TORCH)	● Infection ● NEC ● Disseminated intravascular coagulation ● Perinatal asphyxia ● Congenital infections (TORCH) ● Thrombosis (renal, aortic) ● Congenital leukaemia
Rare	● Thrombocytopenia absent radii (TAR) syndrome ● Congenital amegakaryocytic thrombocytopenia (CAMT)		

Severe thrombocytopenia in an otherwise healthy term newborn infant is NAIT until proved otherwise

INVESTIGATIONS

When, who and how?

- Evaluation of early-onset (<72 hr after birth) thrombocytopenia (see flowchart)
  - in preterm infants with early-onset mild to moderate thrombocytopenia in whom there is good evidence of placental insufficiency, further investigations are not warranted unless platelet count does not recover within 10-14 days
  - in preterm infants without placental insufficiency, investigate first for sepsis
  - in term infants, investigate for sepsis and NAIT (see below)

Evaluation of late onset thrombocytopenia

- Thrombocytopenia presenting in neonate after first 3 days of life – presume underlying sepsis or necrotising enterocolitis (NEC) until proved otherwise

  - these infants are at significant risk of haemorrhage, though the benefit of platelet transfusion is not clear-cut

Flowchart

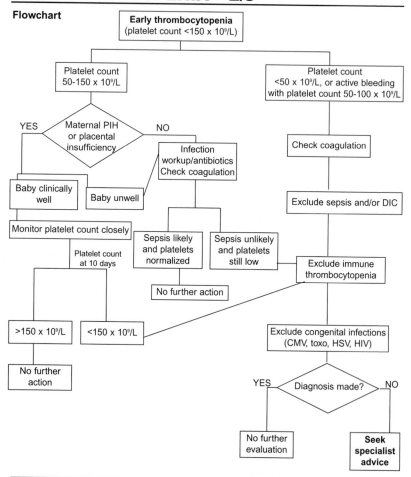

Early thrombocytopenia
(platelet count <150 x 10⁹/L)

Platelet count
50-150 x 10⁹/L

Platelet count
<50 x 10⁹/L, or active bleeding
with platelet count 50-100 x 10⁹/L

YES — Maternal PIH or placental insufficiency — NO

Infection workup/antibiotics
Check coagulation

Check coagulation

Baby clinically well

Baby unwell

Exclude sepsis and/or DIC

Monitor platelet count closely

Sepsis likely and platelets normalized

Sepsis unlikely and platelets still low

Exclude immune thrombocytopenia

Platelet count at 10 days

No further action

>150 x 10⁹/L

<150 x 10⁹/L

Exclude congenital infections
(CMV, toxo, HSV, HIV)

No further action

YES — Diagnosis made? — NO

No further evaluation

Seek specialist advice

MANAGEMENT

General

Avoid

- Heel prick – use venepuncture
- Invasive procedures
- Intramuscular injections
- Lumbar puncture
- If any of above are unavoidable:
- discuss with consultant on call

- consider use of platelet transfusion before undertaking unavoidable invasive procedures
- give particular attention to haemostasis

Platelet transfusion

- This is the only available immediate and specific therapy for thrombocytopenia but carries a very high risk of transfusion-related infections and transfusion reactions

- The guidance overleaf is based on expert opinions and consensus statements

Type of platelets

- NAIT – HPA compatible platelets wherever possible
- All others – blood group compatible cytomegalovirus (CMV)-negative
- Irradiation of platelets is not routinely required but should be considered for infants with definite or suspected immunodeficiency or those who have undergone intrauterine transfusions

Platelet count (x 10⁹/L)	Non-bleeding neonate	Bleeding	NAIT (proven/suspected)
<30	● Consider transfusion in all cases	● Transfuse	● Transfuse (with Human Platelet Antigen [HPA] compatible platelets)

30-49	● Do not transfuse if clinically stable
	
	● Consider transfusion if:
	
	  < 1kg and <1 week old
	
	  clinically unstable (e.g. fluctuating blood pressure or perfusion)
	
	  previous major bleeding
	
	  (e.g. grade 3-4 IVH or pulmonary haemorrhage)
	
	  current minor bleeding (e.g. petechiae, puncture site oozing or bloodstained ET secretions)
	
	  concurrent coagulopathy
	
	  requires surgery or exchange transfusion
		● Transfuse	● Transfuse if any bleeding (with HPA compatible platelets)

50-99	● Do not transfuse	● Transfuse	● Transfuse if any **major** bleeding (with HPA compatible platelets)
>99	● Do not transfuse	● Do not transfuse	● Do not transfuse

Volume of platelets

- 10 mL/kg (should raise platelet count by >50 x 10⁹/L). Babies with suspected NAIT will require higher dose – 20 mL/kg

ADMINISTRATION OF PLATELETS

Never administer platelets through an arterial line or UVC

- Use platelets as soon as they arrive on ward (ensure IV access before requesting platelets from blood bank)
- Keep platelets at room temperature
- To minimise loss, draw contents of pack into 50 mL syringe through a special platelet or fresh blood transfusion set with a 170-200 µm filter and infuse, using a narrow bore extension set linked to IV line, primed with sodium chloride 0.9%
- Transfuse platelets over 30-60 min, mixing syringe from time to time to avoid platelets settling down

- There is no need for routine use of diuretic after platelet transfusion
- Check platelet count 1 hr after transfusion

NEONATAL ALLO-IMMUNE THROMBOCYTOPENIA (NAIT)

- This is analogous to rhesus haemolytic disease and is caused by transplacental passage of maternal alloantibodies directed against fetal platelet antigens inherited from father but absent in mother. Majority caused by antibodies against platelet antigens, HPA-1a (80%) and HPA-5b (10-15%). NAIT can affect first pregnancy, has a 10% risk of severe intracranial haemorrhage, and 20% of survivors exhibit significant neurodevelopmental sequelae

Recognition

- For known HPA-1a antigen-negative women, complete a neonatal alert form
- Petechiae, purpura, excessive bleeding and severe thrombocytopenia in an otherwise healthy term newborn infant indicate NAIT until proved otherwise
- NAIT can also present with:
- fetal intracranial haemorrhage or unexplained hydrocephalus
- postnatal intracranial haemorrhage in term infant

If NAIT suspected, involve consultant neonatologist immediately

Assessment

- Check baby's platelet count daily until >100 x 10^9/L
- Check mother's platelet count (may already be in maternal notes)
- Obtain blood from mother, baby and father for platelet typing and antibodies – liaise with haematology department

about appropriate samples
- Arrange cranial ultrasound scan

Treatment

- In 30% of cases, maternal antibody may not be found and can be detected later
- treat babies with suspected NAIT empirically with antigen-negative platelets
- Transfuse baby with suspected NAIT with accredited HPA-1 antigen-negative platelets if:
- bleeding or
- platelet count <30 x 10^9/L
- National Blood Transfusion Service has a pool of suitable donors, and platelets are available at short notice from blood bank
- if accredited HPA-1a negative platelets not available, administer random donor platelets

Inform blood bank and consultant haematologist as soon as NAIT is suspected.

Do not delay transfusion for investigations

- If thrombocytopenia severe (<50 x 10^9/L), or haemorrhage persists despite transfusion of antigen-negative platelets, administer Intravenous Human Immunoglobulin (IVIG) – 1g/kg/day for two consecutive days
- Aim to keep platelet count >30 x 10^9/L for first week of life, or as long as is active bleeding
- Report newly diagnosed babies with NAIT to fetal medicine consultants for counselling for future pregnancies

NEONATAL AUTO-IMMUNE THROMBOCYTOPENIA

Clinical features

- Caused by transplacental passage of autoantibodies in women with ITP or SLE, and affecting about 10% of babies born to such women
- Severity is generally related to severity of maternal disease
- Risk of intracranial haemorrhage in baby is <1%

Management

- Report all women with thrombocytopenia and those splenectomised through Neonatal Alert System, and instigate plan of management
- Send cord blood for platelet count
- Check baby's platelet count 24 hr later, irrespective of cord blood result
- If baby thrombocytopenic, check platelet count daily for first 3-4 days or until >100 x 10^9/L
- If platelet count <30 x 10^9/L, whether bleeding or not, treat with IVIG (dose as in NAIT)
- Discharge baby when platelet count >100 x 10^9/L
- For babies requiring IVIG, recheck platelet count 2 weeks later. A few may require another course of IVIG at this time because of persistence of maternal antibodies

Issue 02
Issued: October 2007
Expires: September 2009

DEFINITION

Parenteral nutrition (PN) is the intravenous infusion of some or all nutrients for tissue maintenance, metabolic requirements and growth promotion in neonates unable to tolerate full enteral feeds

Seek advice from TPN pharmacist

INDICATIONS FOR PN

- Temporary supply of nutrients <2 weeks:
- decreased enteral intake
- functional gut immaturity
- necrotising enterocolitis (10-14 days)
- extremely low in birth weight, <1,000 grams
- temporary feeding intolerance
- medical instability
- meconium ileus

- Prolonged non-use of the gastrointestinal (GI) tract >2 weeks:
- necrotising enterocolitis (14 days maximal)
- surgical GI disorders – gastroschisis, large omphalocoele
- short bowel syndrome

PRESCRIBING PARENTERAL NUTRITION

Peripheral vs central PN (long line/UVC)

Peripheral PN

- Limited by glucose concentration (usually no more than 10-12%)
- Indicated if full enteral feeds likely to be introduced relatively soon
- some post-surgical infants
- larger premature infants tolerating enteral feeds relatively quickly
- short episodes of feeding intolerance or suspected NEC

Central TPN

- Requires placement of a central catheter (see **Long line** guideline) with tip in either the superior vena cava or the inferior vena cava

TPN prescription

- Most units have specific PN bags that are used to allow nutrients to be increased over 4 days. These may be added to (but nothing may be removed) by discussing with TPN pharmacist
- Modify PN infusion according to requirements and tolerance of each infant and taper as enteral feeding becomes established

Daily requirements

<2.5 kg	Day 1	Day 2	Day 3	Day 4	Comment
Amino acid (g/kg/day)	1	2	3	3 (3.5*)	
Carbohydrate (g/kg/day)	6-15 (based on maintenance)	↑ by 2 each day			If possible, calculate Day 1 glucose from maintenance infusion
Fat (g/kg/day)	1	2	3	3.5 (4*)	*If acceptable not routine

*for neonates <1.5 kg

2.5 - 5 kg	Day 1	Day 2	Day 3	Day 4	Comment
Amino acid (g/kg/day)	1	2	2.5	2.5	
Carbohydrate (g/kg/day)	6-14 (based on maintenance)	↑ by 2 each day	14	14	If possible, calculate Day 1 glucose from maintenance infusion
Fat (g/kg/day)	1	2	3	3.5	

	<2.5 kg	2.5 - 5 kg
Na (mmol/kg/day)	3 (range 2-4)	3 (range 2-4)
K (mmol/kg/day)	2.5	2.5
Ca (mmol/kg/day)	1	1
PO$_4$ (mmol/kg/day)	1.5	1
Mg (mmol/kg/day)	0.2	0.2
Peditrace (mL/kg/day)	0.5 (day 1), 1 (day 2 onwards)	0.5 (day 1) 1 (day 2 onwards)
Solvito N (mL/kg/day)	1	1
Vitilipid (infant)	4 mL/kg/day	10 mL daily (total)

Glucose – maximum concentration:

- Peripheral PN 10-12%
- Central PN up to 20-25% (may rise occasionally)

Fat

- Fat >4 g/kg/day only in very preterm with normal TG, not septic, not on phototherapy
- fat should provide ideally 35-40% of non-protein nitrogen (NPN) calories

Nitrogen

- For effective nitrogen utilisation 150-200 kcal NPN for every gram of nitrogen
- as rough guideline, maintain P:NPN ratio approx. 3.5 g/100 kcal

Volume and calories

- Remember to account for volume, and electrolyte and glucose content of other infusions (e.g. UAC/UVC fluid, inotropes, drugs)
- Healthy preterm requires 50 kcal/kg/day for basal energy expenditure (not growth) and 1-1.5 g protein to preserve endogenous protein stores
- 60 kcal/kg/day will meet energy requirements during sepsis
- 90 kcal/kg/day and 2.7-3.5 g protein will support growth and positive nitrogen balance

NUTRITIONAL SOURCES

Fluids

- Maintenance up to 150 mL/kg/day (see **Intravenous fluid** guideline for fluid requirement) – maximal fluid volume vary with individual management

Glucose
(provides 3.4 kcal/g)

- Initiated at the endogenous hepatic glucose production and utilisation rate of 4–6 mg/kg/min; [8–10 mg/kg/min in extremely low birth weight (ELBW) infants]. The osmolality of glucose limits its concentration

Protein (provides 4 kcal/g)

- At least 1 g/kg/d in preterm and 2 g/kg/d in ELBW decrease catabolism
- 3-3.5 grams protein/kg/d and adequate non-protein energy meets requirements for anabolism

Fat (provides 2.0 kcal/mL)

- To minimise essential fatty acid deficiency, hyperlipidaemia, bilirubin displacement, and respiratory compromise, lipid infusion rates ≤0.15 g/kg/h are recommended to span over 24 hr
- in neonates, the maximal removal capacity of plasma lipids was shown to be 0.3 g/kg/hr
- delivery of 3 g/kg/d of a 20% lipid emulsion equates to an infusion rate of 0.125 g/kg/hr

Energy

- Carbohydrate (glucose) and fat (lipid emulsions) provide the necessary energy to meet the demands and, when provided in adequate amounts, spare protein (amino acids) to support cell maturation, remodelling, growth, activity of enzymes and transport proteins for all body organs
- PN requirement for growth 90-115 kcal/kg/day

Electrolytes

- Sodium, potassium, and chloride dependent on obligatory losses, abnormal losses and amounts necessary for growth, and can be adjusted daily

- Infants who receive electrolytes solely as chloride salts may develop hyperchloraemic metabolic acidosis (may need to add acetate to PN)

Vitamins

- Vitamin and mineral requirements are best estimates based on limited data

Increased energy needs

- Infection
- Chronic lung disease
- Healing, growth
- Babies who have experienced IUGR

Decreased energy needs

- Sedation
- Mechanical ventilation

SPECIAL NEEDS

Hyperglycaemia

- If hyperglycaemia severe or persistent, start insulin infusion – Actrapid 0.01–0.05 units/kg/hr

Osteopenia

- If infant at risk of, or has established, osteopenia, give higher than usual intakes of calcium and phosphorus
- consult dietitian and/or pharmacist regarding prescribing information
- permissible concentrations depend on amino acid and glucose concentrations in the TPN solution

Metabolic acidosis

- For management of metabolic acidosis, add acetate as Na or K salt
- choice of salt(s) will depend on serum electrolytes

MONITORING

Daily	fluid input
	fluid output
	energy intake
	protein
	NPN calories
Daily	urine glucose
	BM
	blood glucose (if urine glucose positive)
Thrice weekly	urine electrolytes
	weight
Weekly	length
	head circumference
Twice weekly*	FBC
	Na
	K
	glucose
	urea
	creatinine
	albumin
	bone
	bilirubin **
	blood gas (arterial or venous)
Weekly	serum TG**
	magnesium
	zinc**
	head circumference
	length

*Initially daily and decrease frequency once stable
**In prolonged TPN more than 2 weeks

COMPLICATIONS

- Catheter related: (see Long lines guideline)
- Peripheral catheters – extravasations and skin sloughs
- Electrolyte and acid-base disturbances

Metabolic

- Hyper/hypoglycaemia, osmotic diuresis
- Metabolic bone disease – mineral abnormalities (Ca/PO_4/Mg)
- Hyperlipidaemia and hypercholesterolaemia
- Conjugated hyperbilirubinaemia

PN-associated cholestatic hepatitis

- Infants having prolonged TPN (>10-14 days) can develop cholestasis, probably owing to TPN toxicity combined with reduced oral feeding, and often transient – usually manifest as rising serum bilirubin (with increased direct component) and mildly elevated transaminases – leads to deficiencies of fatty acids and trace minerals
- even small enteral feeds will limit or prevent this problem
- consider reduction of fat or infusion hours
- add trace minerals
- consider other causes direct hyperbilirubinaemia (TPN-induced cholestasis is diagnosis of exclusion)

WEANING PN

- When advancing enteral feedings, reduce rate of PN administration to achieve desired total fluid volume
- Assess nutrient intake from both PN and enteral feed in relation to overall nutrition goals

TRANSFUSIONS OF RED BLOOD CELLS
• 1/2

INDICATIONS

- For acute blood loss with shock:
- transfuse to re-establish adequate blood volume and haemoglobin of 13 g/dL
- For top-up blood transfusion, **consider** red cell transfusion for the following:

Infant	Hb (g/dL)
Ventilated infant	12
Infant in supplemental oxygen/CPAP	10
Severe congenital heart disease	12
Apnoeas (while on caffeine citrate; >9 episodes in 12 hr, or ≥2 episodes in 24 hr needing face mask ventilation)	8
Poor weight gain (<10 g/kg/d over 4 days despite nutritional intake of 120 kcal/kg/d), and no other cause (e.g. hyponatremia, recent use of corticosteroids or diuretics)	8
Circulatory strain (Heart rate >180/min, or respiratory rate >80/min for 24 hr in the absence of a medically treatable cause other than anaemia)	8
Asymptomatic infant (Retic count <4%)	7

PRE-TRANSFUSION

Crossmatch

- Crossmatch against maternal serum
- For first transfusion, send samples of baby's and mother's blood
- naturally occurring anti-A and anti-B do not develop before 6 months of age and neonates very rarely form red cell antibodies before this age – all antibodies are therefore passively derived

Direct Coombs testing

- The laboratory will perform Direct Coombs test (DCT) on maternal serum for any atypical antibodies
- If maternal DCT negative, blood issued will be cross-matched **once** against maternal serum. No further blood samples are necessary for repeat top-up transfusions
- If maternal DCT positive, cross-matching of donor red blood cells against maternal serum is required **every time**

Multiple transfusions

- In babies <29 weeks who will need multiple transfusions, use paediatric satellite packs from one donor (if available) to reduce multiple donor exposure

Communication

- If clinical condition permits before transfusion, inform parents that baby will receive a blood transfusion

TRANSFUSIONS OF RED BLOOD CELLS
• 2/2

When to use irradiated blood

Blood for **routine** top-up transfusions does not need to be irradiated except for infants:

- Who have received intra-uterine transfusion
- With suspected or proven immunodeficiency
- Receiving blood from a first or second degree relative, or an HLA-selected donor

When to use CMV-free blood

- As CMV seronegativity cannot be guaranteed in untested blood, **use only CMV-seronegative blood for neonatal transfusions**
- Blood products in use in the UK are leuco-depleted to <5 x 10^6 leucocytes/unit at point of manufacture

Special situations

Infants with necrotising enterocolitis (NEC)

Neuraminidase-producing organisms such as clostridia in the occasional infant with NEC can strip sialic acid residues from red cell sialoglycoproteins, exposing the T-crypto-antigen. This can result in T-cell activation and haemolysis

- Transfuse infants with NEC using red cells in SAG-M as it is relatively plasma-free
- Any unexpected haemolysis associated with transfusion in a baby with NEC should be investigated for T-cell activation in consultation with local haematology department and with close involvement of consultant neonatologist

Exchange transfusion

- See **Exchange transfusion** guideline

TRANSFUSION

Volume of transfusion

- Ignore pre-transfusion Hb when estimating volume required
- give 20-25 mL/kg of red cell transfusion irrespective of pre-transfusion Hb

A paediatric pack contains approximately 50 mL blood. Use one pack if possible

Rate of administration

- Administer blood at 5 mL/kg/hr (over 4 hr for a 20 mL/kg transfusion)
- Increase rate in presence of active haemorrhage
- Decrease rate if there is a risk of cardiac failure
- Clearly document reason for top-up transfusion and, if it was because of symptoms, response to transfusion

Use of furosemide

- Routine use of furosemide is **NOT** recommended
- It may be used after a blood transfusion for infants:
- with chronic lung disease
- in heart failure
- If required, administer furosemide after (not during) transfusion

DEFINITION

Transfer of critically ill newborns from hospital of birth to a tertiary care facility for ongoing intensive care or surgical/cardiac assessment, or back from tertiary care facility to hospital of birth

INDICATION

- Preterm babies requiring intensive care not available at base unit
- Babies requiring:
- surgical care or review
- cardiology review or care
- drive-through surgical procedures
- diagnostic procedures (e.g. CT scan, MR scan, barium meal)
- return transfer for ongoing care

RETRIEVAL PROCESS

Communication

Referring centre

- Make decision to transfer with parents' agreement
- Locate NICU/PICU bed or contact cot locator bureau for cot

> *In the event of possible unavailability of a level 3 cot, referring consultant and consultant in level 3 unit must discuss to determine whether another infant not requiring intensive care could be moved to a level 2 unit to facilitate the transfer of the baby requiring intensive care within the region*

- Provide clinical details to Newborn Transport Service (NTS)/receiving centre/surgeon

- If baby deteriorates further, inform NTS/receiving unit
- Document advice given/received
- Prepare copy of baby's notes, X-rays and transfer letter
- Obtain parental consent for transfer
- Obtain sample of mother's blood (if required)

Receiving centre

- Ensure consultant and NICU/PICU co-ordinator agree to accept referral
- Transport team to give details of management before departing for receiving centre

Newborn Transport Service (NTS)

- Ensure consultant agrees for NTS to carry out transfer
- Inform NTS of transfer
- Give clinical details, interventions and medications
- NTS will organise ambulance and response time
- NTS will ensure appropriate staff and equipment available for transfer

Parents

- Update with plan of care
- Ensure parents aware that transport is in baby's best interests and warrants the upheaval and added risks
- Give unit information and contact number and map
- Photographs of baby
- Determine method of feeding
- Show baby to parents before departure
- Ensure mother transferred nearer to baby as soon as possible
- Ensure baby transferred back as soon as possible

Issue 02
Issued: October 2007
Expires: September 2009

STABILISATION BEFORE ARRIVAL OF NTS OR BEFORE TRANSFERRING

Preparation for transport begins as soon as decision made to transfer baby

- Ensure X-rays are sent with baby
- Ensure all tubes and lines very securely taped
- Change underwater seal drains to Heimlich flutter valve
- Ensure there are TWO reliable IV access sites
- Prepare extra fluid boluses for gastroschisis and septic babies

Monitoring

- Monitor temperature throughout stabilisation process and transit
- Document temperature before and after stabilisation, on arrival back at retrieval unit and throughout transport process
- Check blood glucose
- Monitoring for transit see below

SPECIAL CONDITIONS

Always discuss baby's clinical condition with surgical team to finalise management plan before and during transport

Necrotizing enterocolitis

- Largest possible naso-/orogastric tube on free drainage
- Nil by mouth
- IV fluids
- Check clotting and consider administration of FFP/extra vitamin K
- Antibiotics:
  - benzylpenicillin, gentamicin and metronidazole (see **NEC** guideline)

- If UAC in situ, do not remove
- AP and lateral shoot-through X-rays if indicated
- If hypotensive or acidotic, ventilate

Oesophageal atresia/tracheo-oesophageal fistula

- Largest possible naso- or orogastric tube
- On continuous drainage and aspirated at least every 10 min to keep pouch empty
- Suction mouth with standard suction catheter if required
- Nurse prone with head tilted

Abdominal distension or suspected bowel obstruction

- Large naso- or orogastric tubes 8 or 10 FG
- On free drainage and aspirated regularly
- Document amount and type of aspirate
  - if aspirate >20 mL/kg, replace with sodium chloride 0.9%
- IV fluids, and correction of shock
- AP (and, if perforation, lateral shoot-through) X-rays
- Do not instrument anus
- Nurse in supine position
- Ventilate if hypoxic or significant distension

Congenital diaphragmatic hernia

- Do not use bag and mask ventilation
- Intubate and ventilate
  - compliant lung ventilation to avoid barotrauma or pneumothorax (no hyperventilation)
  - ventilate in 100% oxygen regardless of saturations

- largest possible naso- or orogastric tube on free drainage
- Aspirate regularly at least every 10 min to decompress stomach
- Keep baby well sedated and paralysed if fighting ventilator
- Surfactant not usually indicated (see **Surfactant** guideline)
- Keep head tilted upwards where possible (never allow head down position)
- Observe for pneumothorax (unaffected side)

Pneumothorax/ pneumomediastinum

- Pneumothorax not under tension does not require drainage
- Keep saturations high
- Tension pneumothorax requires drainage
- If pneumomediastinum present, place infant in ambient oxygen concentration of 100% to enhance absorption of gas collection

Choanal atresia

- Provide oropharyngeal airway
- Avoid feeding for at least 2 hr before transfer
- Observe breathing pattern during transfer

Pierre Robin micrognathia

- If respiratory distress, insert oropharyngeal or nasopharyngeal airway
- Discuss endotracheal intubation with referring or receiving consultant before any attempt is made; expect to seek help from an experienced anaesthetist
- Airway patency can be improved by nursing and transferring in prone position

Neural tube defects meningocele, encephalocele

- If sac ruptured, apply sterile dressing
- Nurse in prone position to prevent pressure on lesion
- Cover back with cling film to prevent stool contamination
- IV antibiotics: amoxicillin and gentamicin

PACKAGING, MOVING AND OTHER ISSUES

Minimise handling on transit

- Move baby into transport incubator
- ensure smooth transfer and minimise heat loss
- Identify staff responsible for:
- transferring baby from incubator to transport incubator
- infusion lines
- opening and closing incubator doors
- Inform receiving unit of baby's condition and predicted time of arrival
- Mother may accompany only if baby stable and at discretion of NTS or transport team

DURING TRANSIT

- In ambulance:
- secure transport incubator
- mains or battery supply
- oxygen and air supply
- Minimise handling – if any handling required, stop ambulance in a safe place
- Avoid hypothermia by minimising interference – see **Hypothermia** guideline

Issue 02
Issued: October 2007
Expires: September 2009

Monitor

- Apex, respiration, blood pressure and temperature continuously
- Record readings every 15 min and note type and volume of infusions
- If central access used, ensure umbilical stump visible and observe for any bleeding
- Monitor peripheral IV site(s) for any leakage and patency
- Ensure any peripheral arterial line site visible

AT RECEIVING UNIT

- When moving baby from transport incubator to incubator, identify staff responsible for:
- transferring baby from transport incubator to incubator
- infusion lines
- opening and closing incubator doors
- Hand over care to medical and nursing staff
- Photocopy all transport and referring documents and give to receiving team – DO NOT leave the receiving unit until this has been done as you are asking them to be responsible for the ongoing care and part of the transport of the baby
- Give the receiving team X-rays/disk
- When baby settled, check and document blood gases, BP, temperature and blood glucose
- Inform referring centre and parents of safe arrival of baby
- Complete documentation and provide receiving unit with photocopy before you depart

Do not leave a baby at a unit without all necessary documentation – it is not acceptable to fax the information to them at a later hour or date

ON RETURN TO BASE

- Stock up equipment bag
- Check transport incubator
- Replace oxygen and air cylinder if needed
- Complete documentation

EQUIPMENT FOR TRANSFER

Check all equipment daily and prepare before use

- Transport incubator
- Ventilator
- Gas cylinders
- CPAP
- Incubator oxygen
- Suction
- Humidification device
- Thermoregulation equipment, including mattresses

Monitoring facilities

- Heart rate
- Respiratory rate
- Saturations
- Invasive blood pressure
- Temperature toe and core
- Glucose monitor
- Infusion pumps – 6 for ICU and 3 for SCBU babies

Emergency drugs

- Sodium bicarbonate 4.2% (or 8.4% diluted 1:1)
- Adrenaline
- Glucose
- Sodium chloride 0.9%

Equipment bag

- **Intubation**
- laryngoscope
- endotracheal tubes (ETT) 2.5 mm to 4 mm
- introducers
- hats and ties/clips for ETT
- scissors

- **Cannulation**
- selection of cannulae (Jelco 24 g, Insytes with or without wings 24 g, Neoflons 24 g)
- strapping
- dressing packs
- sterets
- cleaning lotion

- **Umbilical catheterisation** (see **UVC** and **UAC** guidelines)
- arterial catheters
- venous catheters
- forceps
- probes
- sutures
- cord ties
- zinc oxide tape
- non-alcohol containing cleaning lotion

- **Thoracocentesis**
- 21 g green butterfly (can use blue to aspirate air easily and reduce pain)
- small bottle of sterile water

- selection of chest drains (size 8 ch to 12 ch)
- dressing packs
- scalpel
- Spencer-Wells forceps
- clamps
- syringe and needles
- local anaesthetic – lidocaine 1%
- Steristrips
- Tegaderm
- flutter valves

- Camera
- Documentation
- Parent information leaflet

Do not attempt to carry out this procedure unless you have been trained to do so and have demonstrated your competence

INDICATIONS

- Frequent blood gas analysis:
- ventilated infants
- non-ventilated infant requiring >40% O_2 at 4-6 hr of age
- Continuous monitoring of arterial blood pressure
- Exchange transfusion

CONTRAINDICATIONS

- Umbilical sepsis
- Necrotizing enterocolitis (NEC)
- Evidence of vascular compromise in legs or buttocks

EQUIPMENT

- Umbilical artery catheterisation pack
- Sterile mask, gown and gloves
- Sterile drape
- Infusion pump
- Sodium chloride 0.9% infusion containing heparin 1 unit/mL
- Umbilical tape

PROCEDURE

Non-sterile preparation

- Monitor infant's SaO_2 during procedure
- Estimate length of catheter to be inserted:
- measure from shoulder tip to umbilicus
- use graph in pack to determine catheter placement
- prefer high catheter position – tip above diaphragm (T6-T9 vertebral bodies) but below T6 **OR**
- in absence of graph use formula (weight in kg x 3) + 9 cm

- whichever calculation used, add length of cord stump to give final length
- Inspect legs and buttocks for discolouration
- Tie an umbilical tape loosely around base of cord

Sterile preparation

- Scrub up, mask and gown
- Use sterile technique
- Clean cord stump and surrounding skin with non-alcoholic antiseptic solution
- Attach 3-way tap to catheter and flush all parts with sodium chloride 0.9%. Leave syringe attached
- Put sterile towels into incubator
- Place all equipment to be used on sterile towel covering a sterile trolley
- Drape umbilical stump with sterile towels

Insertion of arterial catheter

- Cut cord cleanly leaving a 2-3 cm stump
- remember to measure length of cord stump and add to calculated placement to give final advancement distance
- Clamp across cord with artery forceps
- Apply gentle upward traction
- Cut along underside of forceps with a scalpel blade
- Identify vessels
- single thin walled vein
- two small thick-walled arteries that can protrude from the cut surface
- Support cord with artery forceps placed near to chosen artery
- Dilate lumen using either dilator or fine forceps
- Insert catheter with 3-way tap closed to catheter – if resistance felt, apply gentle steady pressure for 30-60 sec
- Advance catheter to the calculated distance
- Open 3-way tap to check for easy withdrawal of blood and for pulsation of blood in the catheter

If catheter will not advance beyond 4-5 cm and blood cannot be withdrawn, it is likely that a false passage has been created. Remove catheter and seek advice from a more experienced senior person

Securing catheter

- If an Umbilical Vein Catheter (UVC) is also to be inserted, site both catheters before securing either. Secure each catheter separately to allow independent removal

- To secure catheter:

  - place purse string suture around UAC

  - knot suture round catheter three or four times

  - sandwich catheter and two ends of suture between zinc oxide tape as close to cord as possible without touching cord. It is not necessary to stitch suture to zinc oxide tape

  - if catheter requires adjustment, open zinc oxide tape, pull back catheter to desired length and retape

- Connect catheter to infusion

- Confirm position of catheter by X-ray – unlike a UVC, a UAC will go down before it goes up

  - a high position tip (above diaphragm but below T6) is preferred

  - if catheter below diaphragm resite at L3-L4 (low position)

  - if catheter position too high, withdraw to appropriate length

Avoid L1, the origin of the renal arteries.

Never attempt to advance a catheter after it has been secured; either withdraw it to the low position or remove it and insert a new one

DOCUMENTATION

- Record details of procedure in patient notes, including catheter position on X-ray and whether any adjustments were made

AFTERCARE

- Nurse baby supine whilst an UAC is in situ

- Monitor circulation in lower limbs and buttocks whilst catheter is in situ

- Leave cord stump exposed to air

- Infuse sodium chloride 0.9% (or 0.45% if sodium is high) 0.5 mL/hr containing 0.5-1 unit of heparin/mL

- Do not infuse any other solution through UAC. Glucose, sodium chloride (at rate faster than 0.5 mL/hr) or drugs may be administered through UAC in exceptional situations, on the authority of a consultant

COMPLICATIONS

- Bleeding due to accidental disconnection

- Vasospasm – if blanching of the lower limb occurs and does not resolve within 30 min, remove catheter

- Embolization from blood clot or air in the infusion system

- Thrombosis involving:

  - femoral artery, resulting in limb ischaemia

  - renal artery, resulting in haematuria, renal failure and hypertension

  - mesenteric artery, resulting in necrotizing enterocolitis

- Infection – prophylactic antibiotics are not required

Do not attempt to carry out this procedure unless you have been trained to do so and have demonstrated your competence

INDICATIONS

- Catheter no longer required, no longer patent, infected or complications (e.g. NEC, white toes)

EQUIPMENT

- Alcohol swab
- Sterile stitch cutter
- Sterile blade
- Umbilical tape

PROCEDURE

- Scrub up, gown and mask
- Clean cord stump with non-alcohol antiseptic (cord stump may need to be soaked with a damp gauze swab to loosen any umbilical tissue adherent to catheter)
- Ensure that an umbilical tape is loosely secured around the base of umbilicus
- Turn infusion pump off and clamp infusion line
- Withdraw catheter slowly over 2-3 min taking particular care with last 2-3 cm
- If bleeding noted, tighten umbilical tape
- Do not cover umbilicus with large absorbent pad – a small piece of cotton gauze should suffice
- Inspect catheter after removal – if any part missing, contact consultant immediately
- Send catheter tip for culture and sensitivity

AFTERCARE

- Nurse baby supine for next 4 hr following removal, and observe for bleeding

COMPLICATIONS

- Bleeding
- Catheter tip inadvertently left in blood vessel

Do not attempt to carry out this procedure unless you have been trained to do so and have demonstrated your competence

INDICATIONS

- Infants <1000 g
- Larger sick infants (a double lumen catheter may be indicated if infant requires significant support)
- Exchange transfusion
- Central venous pressure monitoring
- Administration of hypertonic solutions [e.g. 12.5% glucose, or vasopressors (e.g. dopamine)]

CONTRAINDICATIONS

- Umbilical sepsis
- Necrotizing enterocolitis (NEC)
- Exomphalos

EQUIPMENT

- Umbilical vein catheterisation pack
- Sterile mask, gown and gloves
- Sterile drape
- Infusion pump
- Sodium chloride 0.9% infusion containing heparin 1 unit/mL
- Umbilical tape

PROCEDURE

Non-sterile preparation

- Monitor SaO_2 during procedure
- Estimate length of catheter to be inserted:
- measure from shoulder tip to umbilicus
- high catheter placement preferred – tip above diaphragm but not in heart
- use graph in pack to determine catheter placement

OR

- in the absence of graph use formula (weight in kg x 1.5) + 5.5 cm

- Whichever calculation is used, remember to add length of cord stump to give final distance catheter needs to be advanced
- Tie umbilical tape loosely around base of cord

Sterile preparation

- Scrub up, mask and gown
- Use sterile technique
- Clean cord stump and surrounding skin with non-alcohol antiseptic solution
- Attach 3-way tap to catheter and flush all parts with sodium chloride 0.9%. Leave syringe attached
- Put sterile towels into incubator
- Place all equipment to be used on sterile towel covering sterile trolley
- Drape umbilical stump with sterile towels
- Place sterile sheet with a hole in the centre over the cord. Pull the cord through the hole

Cut cord

- Clamp across cord with artery forceps at 3 cm
- Apply gentle upward traction
- Cut along underside of forceps with a scalpel blade
- Cut cord cleanly to leave 2-3 cm stump

Remember to measure length of cord stump and add to calculated placement distance to give final length catheter needs to be advanced

Insert catheter

- Identify the vessels:
- single thin walled vein
- two small thick-walled arteries that can protrude from cut surface
- Support cord with artery forceps placed near to vein
- Dilate lumen using either a dilator or fine forceps

- Insert catheter with 3-way tap closed to catheter – if resistance felt, apply gentle steady pressure for 30-60 sec
- Advance catheter to desired distance – open 3-way tap to check for easy withdrawal of blood

If catheter will not advance beyond 4-5 cm and blood cannot be withdrawn, it is likely that a false passage has been created. Remove catheter and seek advice from a more experienced senior person

Securing catheter

- If an Umbilical Artery Catheter (UAC) is also be inserted, site both catheters before securing either – secure each catheter separately to allow independent removal
- To secure catheter:
  - place purse string suture around UVC
  - knot suture round catheter three or four times
  - sandwich catheter and two ends of suture between zinc oxide tape as close to cord as possible without touching it – it is not necessary to stitch suture to zinc oxide tape
  - if catheter requires adjustment, open zinc oxide tape, pull back catheter to desired length and retape
- Connect catheter to infusion
- Confirm position of catheter in IVC by X-ray
- If catheter found to be in right atrium, withdraw it to avoid risks of cardiac tamponade or cardiac arrhythmia
  - if catheter is in liver, withdraw it so that it lies in IVC, or remove it and insert replacement

DOCUMENTATION

- Record in notes details of procedure, including catheter position on X-ray and whether any adjustments were made

AFTERCARE

- Monitor circulation in lower limbs and buttocks whilst catheter is in situ
- Leave cord stump exposed to air
- The catheter may remain in place for up to 7-10 days

COMPLICATIONS

- Air embolism
- Bleeding resulting from accidental disconnection
- Refractory hypoglycaemia due to malpositioning of catheter
- Infection – prophylactic antibiotics are not required
- Cardiac tamponade – suspect in presence of:
  - tachycardia
  - poor perfusion
  - soft heart sounds
  - increasing cardiomegaly
  - decreasing oxygen saturation
  - arrhythmias
- Confirm diagnosis by:
  - chest X ray – widened mediastinum and enlarged cardiac shadow
  - echocardiogram (if available)
- Consider drainage if there is cardiovascular compromise (see **Pericardiocentesis** guideline)

Issue 02
Issued: October 2007
Expires: September 2009

> *Do not attempt to carry out this procedure unless you have been trained to do so and have demonstrated your competence*

INDICATIONS

- Catheter no longer needed
- Concerns regarding sepsis
- Catheter in place for >10 days

EQUIPMENT

- Sterile stitch cutter
- Sterile blade

PROCEDURE

- Wash hands and put on gloves
- Clean cord stump with non-alcohol antiseptic
- Turn infusion pump off and clamp infusion line
- Ensure umbilical tape secured loosely around base of umbilicus
- Withdraw catheter slowly
- If any bleeding noted, tighten umbilical tape
- Send catheter tip for culture and sensitivity
- If infection suspected, remove

AFTERCARE

- Nurse baby supine for 4 hr following removal and observe for bleeding

COMPLICATIONS

- Bleeding
- It is also possible to lose tip of umbilical venous catheter

Issue 02
Issued: October 2007
Expires: September 2009

RECOGNITION AND ASSESSMENT

Definition

- If mother develops chickenpox rash (not zoster) during 3 weeks before delivery, there is a 25% chance of baby developing the illness
- This risk is greater for babies exposed to secondary maternal viraemia, who do not have a chance to receive transplacental maternal antibodies (e.g. babies born within 5 days of appearance of maternal rash)
- Premature babies <1 kg, <28 weeks are considered high risk

SYMPTOMS AND SIGNS

Fetal varicella

Congenital varicella syndrome – following maternal chickenpox usually in the first 20 weeks of pregnancy

- Limb atrophy
- Scaring of extremities
- Cortical atrophy
- Chorioretinitis and cataracts

Neonatal varicella

- Mild: vesicular rash
- Severe: pneumonitis, pulmonary necrosis, fulminant hepatitis
- mortality 30% without varicella zoster immunoglobulin (VZIG)

INVESTIGATIONS

Maternal

- If no history of chickenpox, check maternal VZ IgG at time of contact
- urgent assays can be done within 48 hr

Neonatal

- VZ IgM for evidence of fetal varicella infection

IMMEDIATE TREATMENT

Varicella zoster immunoglobulin (VZIG)

- VZIG is usually obtained from Microbiology

Neonate born to mother who develops chickenpox rash (but not zoster) within 7 days before birth, or 7 days after birth

- Give VZIG 250 mg (2 mL) IM (not IV) as soon as possible after delivery (must be within 72 hr)
- VZIG can be given without antibody testing of infant
- VZIG is of no benefit once neonatal chickenpox has developed
- VZIG is not needed for neonates born after 7 days of appearance of maternal chickenpox, or where mother has zoster, as these neonates should have transplacental antibodies
- VZIG can be given for up to 10 days after initial exposure
- If VZIG not available, give IVIG (less effective)

Postnatal exposure to chickenpox - see flow diagram

- Significant exposure: household, face-to-face for 5 min, in same room for >15 min
- a case of chickenpox or disseminated zoster is infectious between 48 hours before onset of rash until crusting of lesions

● VZIG is also given in the following cases of postnatal exposure to chickenpox:

◉ varicella antibody-negative infants (this can be determined by testing mother for varicella antibodies) exposed to chickenpox or herpes zoster from any other contact other than mother, in first 7 days of life (see flow chart)

◉ VZ antibody-negative infants of any age, exposed to chickenpox or herpes zoster while still requiring intensive or prolonged special care nursing

◉ for infants in these two exposure groups who were weighing <1 kg at birth, or were <28 weeks gestation at birth, or are more than 60 days old, or who have had repeated blood sampling with replacement by packed cell infusions

Aciclovir

Indications:

● Infants with postnatal exposure for whom VZIG was indicated (as above) but did not receive VZIG within 24 hr of exposure

● Chickenpox in infant currently treated with corticosteroids or who was born prematurely or is immunocompromised

● If rash develops within 5 days of birth, give aciclovir 10 mg/kg IV (over 1 hr) 8 hrly, diluted to 5 mg/mL

◉ increase dose to 20 mg/kg if severely systemically symptomatic

◉ treat for at least 7 days, up to 14 days if severe

SUBSEQUENT MANAGEMENT

● On postnatal wards, unless infant requires neonatal intensive care support:

◉ isolate mother and baby together in separate room until 5 days after onset of rash and all lesions crusted over

◉ if infant already exposed, breastfeeding can continue but explain to mother the risk of transmission

● Exposed staff with no history of chickenpox, VZ vaccination or of unknown VZ IgG status should have VZ IgG measured by Occupational Health

◉ if VZ IgG negative, immunise with varicella vaccine

◉ remove from clinical duties during days 7-21 following exposure

◉ offer VZIG if in high risk group for complications (immunocompromised)

Decision pathway for VZV contact

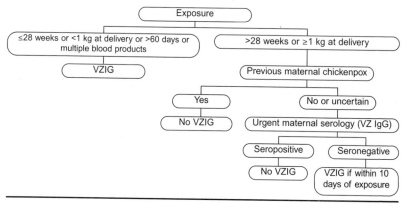

MONITORING TREATMENT

● Aciclovir

◉ ensure good hydration

◉ stop once clinical improvement occurs or when all lesions crusted

DISCHARGE POLICY

Maternal infection

● After neonate has had VZIG, discharge

● Monitor neonate for signs of infection, especially if onset of maternal chickenpox occurred 4 days before to 2 days after delivery

● Advise GP and midwife to recommend admission to isolation cubicle if rash develops

Fetal infection

● **Diagnosed with positive VZ IgM**

● Ophthalmic examination

● Cranial ultrasound

● Developmental follow up

INDICATIONS

● Blood sampling in a patient without indwelling arterial line, or when sampling from arterial line inappropriate

CONTRAINDICATIONS

● Active bleeding

EQUIPMENT

● Cleaning solution
● Appropriately labelled blood bottles and request cards
● Non-sterile latex gloves
● 23 gauge (green) butterfly needle
● 2 mL syringe
● **Do not use EMLA cream and alcohol swabs in neonates**

PROCEDURE

Preparation

● Wash hands and wear gloves
● Identify a suitable vein – it should be clearly visible but, unlike in adults, neonatal veins are rarely palpable
○ arms: forearm or back of hand
○ legs: long saphenous vein or feet
● **Avoid sampling from potential drip or long line veins whenever possible**

Insertion and sampling

● Apply hand pressure around limb to distend the vein
● Place thumb on skin slightly distal to proposed puncture site. Hold butterfly at a 10-20° angle and puncture skin
● Advance needle towards vein. Resistance may diminish slightly as needle enters vein and blood will be seen in the tubing

● Gently aspirate required volume of blood. This is easier using a small (2 mL) syringe. If large volumes of blood are needed it may be easier to change syringes halfway rather than use a bigger syringe

● When sampling complete, place cotton wool over insertion point and withdraw needle. Maintain pressure on site until bleeding ceases

● Transfer samples to appropriate bottles taking care to mix but not shake the blood

DIFFICULT VENEPUNCTURE

● Do not break the hub off a green needle: use a commercial version, or cut butterfly tubing close to the needle and allow blood to drip into bottle directly from needle

● If small quantities of blood required (<1 mL), use heel prick, but remember that squeezing can cause haemolysis and elevate serum potassium

Check ventilator prior to use

MODES OF VENTILATION

The mode used is determined by patient characteristics and unit policy and is a consultant-led decision

Intermittent mandatory ventilation (IMV)/ intermittent positive pressure ventilation (IPPV)

Description

● Pressure-limited time-cycled with a conventional rate (generally up to 60 breaths/min but can go up to 150 breaths/min)

Use

● Start in this mode for transport or if infant is receiving muscle relaxants
● Change to synchronous modes of ventilation or Volume Guarantee (VG) – see **below**

Synchronous intermittent mandatory ventilation (SIMV)

Description

● Set a mandatory rate
● Set trigger to most sensitive threshold
● Ventilation is weaned on back-up rate and pressures
● Breaths above back-up rate are unsupported and work of breathing is increased

Use

● Can be used for all stages of ventilation

Synchronous intermittent positive pressure ventilation (SIPPV)

Description

● The ventilator recognises baby's effort to breathe and supports each breath
● After each breath there is a refractory period of 0.2 sec when ventilator will not generate next breath
● In apnoea, ventilator delivers back-up rate set by clinician
● If breathing rate too high, it increases minute ventilation and this can lead to hypocapnia
● Ventilation is weaned on pressure

Use

● Weaning ventilation

Volume guarantee (VG) or targeted tidal volume (TTV)

Description

● A pressure-controlled mode of ventilation, which will deliver a set volume
● Set a volume between 4-6 mL/kg – depending on compliance and resistance
● pressure adjusts automatically to maintain this volume
● set alarm limits for minute ventilation
● Ventilator automatically adjusts inspiratory pressure to achieve a set tidal volume despite changes in compliance, resistance or respiratory drive
● Ventilator will use only the pressures it needs to achieve volume set
● Tidal volume is measured on each breath and compared to target set and pressure is adjusted breath by breath until it reaches target

- The pressure limits set on the ventilator are the maximum

- if pressure limits are not wide enough, there is an alarm saying 'VT low'

- The pressure limits set on the ventilator are above the desired pressure; however, the actual pressure delivered is only that required to achieve desired volume

Use

- Not routinely used but may be considered by a consultant for difficult to ventilate babies

Pressure support ventilation (PSV)

Description

- The ventilator supports each breath to the patient

- The inspiratory pressure support determines the amount of work of breathing supplied by the ventilator

- The time on inspiration is automatically adjusted to the baby's desired inspiratory time (IT)

- Similar to SIPPV, every breath is supported. However in that mode, SIPPV has a fixed IT

- The IT is variable and ventilator determines when to switch off the inspiratory phase and that is determined by the flow

- When the deceleration of flow reaches 15% of peak inspiratory pressure the ventilator automatically switches to exhalation

- This mode allows for big sighs or short rapid breaths and the set IT acts as the maximum

- The ventilator is able to measure and adapt for any leak providing it is less than 60% of the volume

Use

- PSV can be used in combination with VG

COMPLICATIONS OF MECHANICAL VENTILATION

Mechanical problems

- ETT blocked
- ETT displaced (e.g. in right main bronchus or oesophagus)
- Circuit losing pressure

Patient problems

- Infection
- Lung inflammation
- Air leaks (pneumothorax, pulmonary interstitial air)
- Asynchrony
- Chronic lung disease

SEDATION AND MUSCLE RELAXANTS

Indications

- Sedation may be required to achieve adequate oxygenation and ventilation – it is good practice to sedate babies who are intubated and ventilated unless there is a specific reason not to do so

- Muscle relaxants may be necessary to manage babies with severe RDS or larger babies with severe meconium aspiration syndrome and/or persistent pulmonary hypertension or congenital diaphragmatic hernia

Notes on use

- When starting muscle relaxants, it may be necessary to increase ventilator pressure to compensate for loss of baby's own respiratory efforts

- Do not use muscle relaxants in the absence of sedation

- After starting muscle relaxants, baby is likely to need significantly more cardiorespiratory support

Discuss muscle relaxants with consultant

These principles provide a rational basis for changing ventilation settings guided by blood gas results and the baby's condition

OBJECTIVES

● Appropriate oxygenation, determined by the inspired oxygen concentration (FiO_2) and mean airway pressure (MAP)

● Appropriate ventilation (CO_2 removal), influenced by the amount of gas able to be moved in and out of the lungs (minute ventilation)

There are several modes of conventional ventilation, see **Ventilation (Modes)** guideline

CHANGING THE SETTINGS

Think about what you are trying to achieve

Change Oxygenation (PaO_2)	● Alter the FiO_2 (turn the knob!) ● Alter the mean airway pressure (MAP)
Change Ventilation ($PaCO_2$)	● Change the tidal volume by changing the pressure ● Change the rate of breathing

Target blood gas values

● Set ventilator settings to achieve target oxygen saturations as per unit policy
● Set ventilation settings that determine $PaCO_2$ with the following guidelines in mind:

pH	$PaCO_2$	Base Excess	Rationale
7.25 to 7.35	5.5 to 8.0 kPa	0 to −4	These targets avoid over ventilation and preserve metabolic function. A base excess more negative than −4 despite target values for pH and $PaCO_2$ indicates metabolic acidosis which may be a sign of impaired tissue oxygenation. Action is definitely required if base excess is more negative than −10

Exceptions to this guideline include infants with:

● Severe chronic lung disease where high $PaCO_2$ levels with a lower pH may be tolerated in order to further minimise ongoing lung injury
● Pulmonary hypertension where, after discussion with consultant, decision may be made to maintain baby in an alkalotic state (pH >7.45) with bicarbonate/THAM

PREPARATION

Before touching the ventilator:

Look at the blood gas result

- Do you believe it?
- Does it fit with baby's clinical condition?
- Does it fit with expected course for baby (e.g. improving compliance after surfactant for RDS)?

If it differs greatly from what you expected, what is the explanation?

- If arterial gas, was there an air bubble in the specimen?
- If capillary gas, is perfusion impaired or did baby bleed easily?
- If venous gas, disregard all information apart from electrolytes and glucose

Look at baby

- Is chest moving?
- What is air-entry like?
- Is baby struggling on ventilator?
- Is baby very tachypnoeic or apnoeic?
- Is chest movement symmetrical and trachea central?
- Does one side of chest transilluminate more brightly than the other?

Look at the ventilator

- Is it cycling?
- Are you using the ventilator settings you thought you were?
- What tidal volume (VT) is baby getting?
- Is there a significant leak?
- Are the inspiratory time and pressures appropriate?

Look at nursing flow chart

- How stable has baby been over past few hours or days?
- Are there lots of secretions?
- How is baby handling?

Issue 02
Issued: October 2007
Expires: September 2009

Changing ventilation settings

Problem	Possible solutions	Comment
Low Oxygenation Low PaO$_2$ or Saturations (SaO$_2$)	Increase FiO$_2$	*The easiest solution* ● Babies whose oxygen requirements are changing significantly require clinical reassessment ● If FiO$_2$ increases by >10%, transilluminate chest and consider a chest X-ray
	Increase Mean Airway Pressure (MAP)	● Increase PIP (this may also affect PaCO$_2$) ● Increase inspiratory time (this may just hold lungs fully inflated at a high pressure). Ensure inspiratory time is shorter than expiratory time (maximum Ti usually 0.4 sec) ● If you suspect pulmonary haemorrhage, increase PEEP
High Oxygenation High PaO$_2$ or Saturations (SaO$_2$)	**Decrease FiO$_2$**	*The easiest solution* (unless baby already in room air – if in room air, high saturations or PaO$_2$ generally acceptable)
	Decrease MAP	● Decrease PIP (may adversely affect PaCO$_2$) ● If PEEP is >5, you may drop this down (if reason for high PEEP e.g. pulmonary haemorrhage, has resolved) ● Decrease inspiratory time if too long

Overventilation Low PaCO$_2$	**Decrease tidal volume** **Do this first if baby has good chest movement and/or high tidal volumes**	● Decrease difference between PIP and PEEP (usually by decreasing the PIP by 1–2 units)
		There are no rules by how much to drop PIP
		  observe chest movement and delivered tidal volume on ventilator
		  dropping PIP by 2 mbar (or more if significantly over ventilated) is usually sufficient, but observe tidal volume
		  if baby on Volume Guarantee, reduce set tidal volume

	Decrease frequency	● Drop ventilation rate
		  if gas slightly alkalotic, drop by 5
		  if very alkalotic, drop by 10 or more
		Note for modes where every breath is assisted (e.g. PTV, SIMPV), it is **futile** to reduce rate if baby is breathing above back up rate.
		Wean the pressure (or Tidal Volume) instead

| Under ventilation Low pH with a High PaCO$_2$ | Increase tidal volume **Do this first if baby has no chest movement and/or low tidal volumes** | • Increase PIP until chest movement is achieved but look at tidal volume too
• In general do not increase PIP too much as tidal volume may increase significantly; but give enough pressure to achieve chest movement
• If necessary to increase PIP significantly to achieve same tidal volume you were giving previously, compliance is decreasing:
  ask why?
  look at baby, listen to air entry
  consider X-ray, particularly if FiO$_2$ increasing
• If baby on Volume Guarantee, increase set Tidal Volume. But you may also have to increase PIP |
| | Increase frequency | • Increase ventilatory rate
  if slightly high PaCO$_2$ increase by 5
  if PaCO$_2$ very high, consider increasing by 10 or more. For fast rates, expiratory time must be longer than inspiratory time
  baby log will indicate if you get it the wrong way around. Decrease inspiratory time accordingly
  if >70 breaths/min necessary, discuss with consultant and consider HFOV as a ventilation mode |

Balance is important

• Balance ventilator settings, e.g. if baby in 100% oxygen but with low pressure settings, it may be preferable to reduce FiO$_2$ but increase pressures

• If baby on high pressure settings but a low rate, a faster rate and lower pressures may be necessary

DOCUMENTATION

• Inform bedside nurse what changes you have made

• Document your changes

Issue 02
Issued: October 2007
Expires: September 2009

MONITORING

When to perform next blood gas

How abnormal is last gas?	● If outside normal target range, repeat soon (e.g. 15-30 min) to ascertain whether changes have had desired effect
How stable is the baby?	● Discuss with senior colleague
	● If baby stable and you have not changed ventilation much, it is not necessary to check it immediately after the change. Some babies who are chronically ventilated may need a gas only once a day
	● Monitor new tidal volume to check for effects of change
	● if baby really unstable, consider carrying out regular gases
	● if surfactant has been given, check gas within 30-60 min to see effect of a change in compliance on gas exchange
How confident are you?	● If you are new to ventilation, you may need reassurance with a gas soon after you make your change
	● Avoid too many tests. To reassure yourself, discuss with senior colleague
	● Blood letting is the most common reason for transfusions in first two weeks of life
When the nurses tell you	● If concerned, they will inform you (and you should listen!)

Remember SaO$_2$ and transcutaneous CO$_2$ monitoring are useful for monitoring trends and can give guidance on timing of blood gas analysis

INDICATIONS

Prophylaxis

- Neonates are relatively deficient in Vitamin K (phytomenadione) and those who do not receive supplements are at risk of bleeding (Vitamin K deficient bleeding, formerly known as haemorrhagic disease of the newborn)

All babies should be offered Vitamin K prophylaxis

Therapy

- Vitamin K can also be used to treat any baby with active bleeding that might be due to Vitamin K deficiency after blood has been taken for clotting studies

- a prolonged prothrombin time (INR ≥3.5) that falls within 1 hr of treatment, with a normal platelet count and fibrinogen levels, confirms diagnosis

ADMINISTRATION

Prophylaxis

- A single dose of Vitamin K (Konakion MM Paediatric) 1 mg IM is the most clinically and cost-effective mode of administration

- If parents decline IM route, offer oral Vitamin K as second line option (safety fears of parenteral Vitamin K appear to be unfounded)

- Give in accordance with manufacturer's instructions in order to ensure clinical efficacy

- Babies who are exclusively breast fed will require additional doses after discharge from hospital

IM use

- Do not dilute or mix with other parenteral injections

Oral use

- Break open ampoule and withdraw 0.2 mL (2 mg) into oral dispenser provided. Drop contents directly into infant's mouth by pressing plunger

Although the product is licensed for IV use, this route does not provide the prolonged protection afforded by IM doses, and subsequent doses are often unintentionally omitted

Prophylaxis dosage

	Konakion MM Paediatric
Healthy neonates of ≥36 weeks	First line ● 1 mg IM at birth or soon after Second line ● 2 mg orally at birth ● Plus 2 mg orally at 4–7 days ● Plus 2 mg orally at 1 month if exclusively breast fed
Term neonates at special risk ● Instrumental delivery, caesarean section ● maternal treatment with enzyme-inducing anticonvulsants (carbamazepine, phenobarbital, phenytoin), rifampicin or warfarin ● requiring admission to NICU	1 mg IM at birth or soon after **Do not** offer oral Vitamin K
Preterm infants <36 weeks but ≥2500 g	1 mg IM at birth or soon after
Preterm infants of <36 weeks and <2500 g	0.4 mg/kg (equals 0.04 mL/kg) IM shortly after birth Do not exceed this parenteral dose The frequency of further doses should depend on coagulation status

Therapy dosage

● 1 mg/kg IV initially
● Further doses as required depending on clinical picture and coagulation status
● may need to be accompanied by a more immediately effective treatment such as transfusion of fresh frozen plasma

IV use

● Do not dilute or mix with other parenteral injections but may be injected directly into the lower part of an infusion set

A

Abstinence Syndrome	10
Aciclovir	41, 210, 211
Activated Partial Thromboplastin Time (APTT)	39, 131, 169
Actrapid	194
Admission to neonatal unit (NNU)	13
Alcohol	28, 137
Ambiguous genitalia	61, 121
Analgesia	33, 124, 156, 161
Anaphylaxis	114
Antenatal ultrasound abnormalities	15
Apgar score	63, 109
Apnoea and bradycardia	16
Arterial line insertion	18
Arterial line sampling	20
Atelectasis	46, 48
AZT	92

B

Bag and mask ventilation	124, 125, 199
BCG immunisation	22
Beractant	184, 185
Blood Gas analysis	20, 180, 203, 219
Blood Group Incompatibilities	24
Blood Sampling from Arterial Lines	20
Blood Transfusion	196
Blue baby	54, 100
Brachial plexus injury	26
Breastfeeding preterm infant	27
Breast milk handling and storage	29

C

Caesarean section	79, 86, 128, 211
Calcium resonium	96
Calcium gluconate	96, 111, 120, 122
Cannulation	31
Cardiac arrhythmias	67, 172, 207
Cardiac failure	83, 101, 160, 162
Cardiac murmurs	32
Cardiology referral	100, 101, 160, 198
Cephalhaematoma	64, 126
Chest drain Insertion	33
Chickenpox	209-211
Chlamydia	41, 42
Chloral Hydrate	11, 158
Chloramphenicol	41
Chlorhexidine	33, 133, 161, 182
Chlorpromazine	11
Chronic lung disease	35
Cleft Lip/palate	15, 64
Clonazepam	111, 181
Clostridia	197
CMV	37
Coagulopathy	39
Congenital spherocytosis	126
Conjunctivitis	41

Consent	43
Convulsions	10, 11, 97, 110
Coombs positive infants	24, 196
CPAP and Bubble CPAP	46
Cranial ultrasound scans	51
Curosurf	184
Cyanotic congenital heart disease (blue baby)	54

D

Death and extremely ill babies	57
Dexamethasone	35, 44, 45, 153
Dialysis	96, 140, 175
Diamorphine	146, 158
Diaphragmatic hernia	46, 54, 164, 199
Direct Coombs	24, 126, 196
Discharge	59
Disorders of sexual development	61
Domperidone	77
Drug Withdrawal	11

E

EBM	149-152
ECMO	165
Eczema	22
Endocrine deficiency	99
Erythromycin	41, 77, 186
Examination of the newborn	63
Exchange transfusion	67
Extravasation injuries	70
Extreme prematurity	72

F

Fresh Frozen Plasma (FFP)	39, 102, 221
Fluid Restriction	97, 111, 152, 175
Follow up of infants discharged from NNU	74

G

Gastro-oesophageal reflux (GOR)	76
Gastroschisis	78
Glycosuria	94, 122
Gonococcus	41
Gram-negative organisms	135
Gram stain	41
Group B streptococcus	79

H

HBsAg	28, 86, 87, 93
HCV	88
Hearing screening	81
Heart failure	83
Heart murmur	32
Heel prick	157, 188, 212
Hepatitis B	86
Hepatitis C	88
Hepatosplenomegaly	37, 126, 186
HFOV	89

Issue 02
Issued: October 2007
Expires: September 2009

HIV 92
Hydronephrosis 171
Hydrolysate 77
Hyperglycaemia 94
Hyper-insulinism 99
Hyperkalaemia 95
Hyperoxia 100, 110
Hypoglycaemia 97
Hyponatraemia 120, 174
Hypoplastic left heart syndrome (HLHS) 100
Hypostop 157
Hypotension 102
Hypothermia 104
Hypothyroidism 106
Hypoxic-ischaemic
  encephalopathy (HIE) 109

I

Immunisations 113
Infection 116
Intubation 124
Isoniazid 22, 27
IUT 24
IV fluid therapy 119

J

Jaundice 126

K

Kleihauer test 24, 25, 67
Konakion 220, 221

L

Labour Ward Calls 128
Liver dysfunction in preterm infants 129
Liver disease 114, 126
Long lines 133
Lumbar puncture 13, 79, 188

M

Maternal diabetes 128, 129, 162, 187
Maxijul 98
Meconium aspiration syndrome 184, 214
Meconium staining 128
Meningococcus C 113
Metabolic disorders 136
Myasthenia Gravis 128

N

Nasogastric tube insertion 141
Necrotizing enterocolitis 145
Nitric oxide 148
Nutrition 149

O

Ophthalmology 37, 41, 59, 180
Oramorph 158
Oxygen on discharge 154

P

Pain and Stress 156
Palivizumab 36, 60, 114, 155
Paracetamol 157
Paraldehyde 181
Patent ductus arteriosus (PDA) 159
Pelviectasis 170, 171
Pericardiocentesis 161
Pericardial tamponade 135
Persistent fetal circulation 104
Persistent pulmonary hypertension
  (PPHN) 164
Phenobarbital 11, 111, 181, 221
Phenytoin 111, 181, 221
Phytomenadione 39, 220
PKU 28
Polycystic kidneys 170, 172
Polycythaemia 162
Poractant 184, 185
Preterm care 166
Prothrombin Time (PT) 39, 220
Pulmonary haemorrhage 168

R

Radioisotope 27
Renal abnormalities on ultrasound scan 170
Renal failure 172
Respiratory distress syndrome 109, 119,
  168, 184
Resuscitation 176
Rhesus disease 24, 128
Retinopathy of prematurity (ROP) 179

S

Salbutamol 95
Seizures 180
Skin biopsy 182
Staphylococcus 41, 134, 135
Stenosis 83, 106, 147, 159
Streptococcus 41, 79, 118
Steroids 22, 113, 145
Sucrose 156-158
Surfactant replacement therapy 184
Survanta 184
Syphilis 186
Systemic lupus erythematosus 128

T

Tachycardia 24, 32, 55, 83
TB 22, 23, 27
Tetanus pertussis 113
Thrombocytopenia 187
Thromboembolism 19, 20
Total parenteral nutrition (TPN) 192
Transfusion of red blood cells 196
Transillumination 18, 91
Transport and referral 198

Trimethoprim	118, 170
Tuberculin	22, 27

U

Umbilical arterial catheterisation	**203**
Umbilical arterial catheter removal	**205**
Umbilical venous catheterisation	**206**
Umbilical venous catheter removal	**208**

V

Vaccination (BCG)	22, 59, 93
Vaccination (Hep B)	86
Varicella	**209**
Vasospasm	19, 204
VDRL	186
Venepuncture	**212**
Ventilation modes	**213**
Ventilation basic principles	**215**
Vitamin K	**220**
VZV	28, 210

W

Warfarin	221

Z

Zidovudine	92, 93

UNIVERSITY OF WOLVERHAMPTON
LEARNING & INFORMATION SERVICES

Issue 02
Issued: October 2007
Expires: September 2009

NOTES

NOTES

Issue 02
Issued: October 2007
Expires: September 2009